MY YEAR 2001:
KEEPING HISTORY A SECRET

D1157180

SELECTED BOOKS BY THE AUTHOR

POETRY

Dinner on the Lawn (1979, 1982)
Some Distance (1982)
River to Rivet: A Manifesto (1984)
Maxims from My Mother's Milk/Hymns to Him: A Dialogue (1985)
Along Without: A Fiction for Film in Poetry (1993)
After (1998)
Bow Down (2002)
First Words (2004)
Dark (2012)

PROSE

Letters from Hanusse (2000)
My Year 2001: Keeping History a Secret (2016)
My Year 2002: Love, Death, and Transfiguration (2015)
My Year 2003: Voice Without a Voice (2013)
My Year 2004: Under Our Skin (2008)
My Year 2005: Terrifying Times (2006)
My Year 2006: Serving (2009)
My Year 2007: To the Dogs (2015)
My Year 2008: In the Gap (2015)
My Year 2009: Facing the Heat (2016)
Reading Films: My International Cinema (2012)

My Year 2001:
Keeping History a Secret

READINGS
EVENTS
MEMORIES

by
Douglas Messerli

GREEN INTEGER
KØBENHAVN & LOS ANGELES
2016

GREEN INTEGER
Edited by Per Bregne
København / Los Angeles
www.greeninteger.com / (323) 857-1115

Distributed in the US by Consortium Book Sales & Distribution
/ Perseus Books, www.cbsd.com / (800) 283-3572
Distributed in England & throughout Europe by Turnaround
Publisher Services, Unit 3, Olympia Trading Estate
Coburg Road, Wood Green, London N22 6TZ
www.turnaround-uk.com / 44 (0)20 88293009

First Green Integer Edition 2016
Copyright ©2016 by Douglas Messerli
Essays in this volume have previously appeared in *American Book
Review, American Cultural Treasures, EXPLORING* fictions, *Green
Integer Blog, Hyperallergic Weekend,* L=A=N=G=U=A=G=E, *The*
L=A=N=G=U=A=G=E *Book, Los Angeles Times Book Review, The
New Review of Literature, N*th *Position* [England], *The PIP (Project for
Innovative Poetry) Blog, Ribot, Sagetrieb, The Washington Post Book
World, Washington Review, World Cinema Review* (formerly *International
Cinema Review*), and in the books *A Still Moment: Essays on the Art of
Eudora Welty* (Metuchen, New Jersey: Scarecrow Press, 1978) and *Reading
Films: My International Cinema* (Los Angeles: Green Integer, 2012).
Back cover copy ©2016 by Green Integer

Design: Per Bregne
Typography: Pablo Capra
Cover photographs: (clockwise, from top left):
Javier Marías, Susan Howe, Eudora Welty and William Carlos Williams

LIBRARY OF CONGRESS IN PUBLICATION DATA
Douglas Messerli [1947]
My Year 2001: Keeping History a Secret
ISBN: 978-1-55713-428-8
p. cm – Green Integer 256
I. Title II. Series

Green Integer books are published for Douglas Messerli
Printed in Canada

Table of Contents

Secrets : An Introduction

SINCE I DETERMINED from the beginning of this series of cultural memoirs to have very few secrets from the reader, it is important to explain that all volumes *before* 2003, the year in which I began these works, are constructions—what some might even describe as fictions. The events depicted in them are all real, and my readings and participation in these events represent true experiences. Yet, as the reader will surely note, many of the pieces were written after 2001. Although most of the books and incidents in this volume were published and occurred in that year, my experiences of them and my writings about them came after the fact. One might describe the three volumes between 2000 and 2002 to be, in part, a re-creation of what I might have read, seen, and participated in had I begun writing these books earlier on.

It is not insignificant, however, that many of the big events of 2001 are re-experienced "after the fact," with the vision of hindsight hanging over them. For what I now realize, looking back, is that during 2001 there was a concerted attempt by government officials and the society as a whole, leading up to that year and including it, to keep history a secret: to obfuscate, confuse, and to actually lie about realities that I could not have known had I been writing in the moment. Lawrence Wright's powerful book of 2006, *The Looming Tower*, revealed, for example, how this purposeful obfuscation and withholding of information contributed to the events of 9/11. My own recollection of that fateful day, moreover, is evidence, in hindsight, of how disorienting those events were within the moment.

The historical nature of this volume also allowed me to go back and read or see works by major figures who died in 2001—the filmmakers Hiroshi Teshigahara and Budd Boetticher, fiction writer W. G. Sebald, and my poet-friend Robert Crosson—whose works I had not truly assimilated at the time. Looking back on this year, I also had an opportunity to see and read works such as Tom Cairns' 2001 filming of Leonard Bernstein's *Trouble in Tahiti*, Per Olov Enquist's *The Royal Physician's Visit,* and Orhan Pamuk's *My Name Is Red*—all of which I had missed during that year.

I added to these pieces from other years that seemed appropriate to the theme of 2001, two films by G. W. Pabst, an essay I had written long before on William Carlos Williams, a longer essay on Eudora

Welty's *The Golden Apples*, a review of early collections of poetry by Susan Howe (which already contained this volume's title), and other pieces such as those on Larry Eigner, Andrzej Wajda, Allen Ginsberg, Max Ophuls, and Joseph Roth, along with short memories of my years in Washington, D.C., the latter representing events and figures that, perhaps, are a bit dangerous to reveal even now.

There were, as well, a few works which were actually written in 2001, such as the review of Juan Goytisolo's *The Garden of Secrets*, my essay on Don DeLillo's *The Body Artist*, a short discussion of the film *Monster's Ball,* and pieces on other films I saw during the year such as *Laura* and *Out of the Past*, along with a review of a novel by Yoel Hoffmann and a commentary on the fiction writers Ascher/Straus. It was not until I was working on the American avant-garde poet Bob Brown, in 2014, that I realized how appropriate his writing was to this volume.

Such a mix, many of these essays anthologized after the fact, may make this volume seem even more disjunctive than usual, appearing to some readers, I am sure, as a kind of random assortment of writings. I have always warned against the reader seeking too coherent of a structure within these *My Year* books. A careful reading, however, may reveal to some just how significantly we have as a people, both nationally and internationally, accidently and intentionally sought to keep numerous realities at bay, realities that we recognize as terrifying and possibly destructive. Some of this "history" must necessarily be attenuated if imagination is to survive; but a consistent resistance to reality will ultimately burst out as a destructive force if we hide the past too carefully—which, in some respects, is why I was willing to restore that past even in a form in which it was not precisely lived.

I thank the many editors and friends who read and commented on these works. They include David and Eleanor Antin, Sheila Ascher, Thérèse Bachand, Guy Bennett, Charles Bernstein, Tina Darragh, Rosemary DeRosa, Rebecca Goodman, Allen Ginsberg, Juan Goytisolo, Edith Heal, Burton Hatlen, Susan Howe, Zbigniew Kaminski, Tom La Farge, Sidney Lawrence, Eric Lorberer, William McPherson, Deborah Meadows, Martin Nakell, Marjorie Perloff, Joe Ross, Jerome Rothenberg, Craig Saper, Frank Schork, Milos Sovak, Val Stevenson, Dennis Straus, Carroll F. Terrell, Paul Vangelisti, Wendy Walker, Steve Wasserman, and my companion Howard Fox. Pablo Capra again proofread and edited many of my blunders and brought this book into print.

A World Detached

WILLIAM CARLOS WILLIAMS **POEMS** (RUTHERFORD, NEW JERSEY: PRIVATELY PRINTED, 1909)

EZRA POUND **THE SPIRIT OF ROMANCE: AN ATTEMPT TO DEFINE SOMEWHAT THE CHARM OF THE PRE-RENAISSANCE LITERATURE OF LATIN EUROPE** (LONDON, J. M. DENT, 1910)

WILLIAM CARLOS WILLIAMS **THE TEMPERS** (LONDON: ELKIN MATHEWS, 1913)

WILLIAM CARLOS WILLIAMS **KORA IN HELL: IMPROVISATIONS** (BOSTON: FOUR SEAS, 1920)

WILLIAM CARLOS WILLIAMS **SOUR GRAPES** (BOSTON: FOUR SEAS, 1921)

WILLIAM CARLOS WILLIAMS **SPRING AND ALL** (PARIS: CONTACT EDITIONS, 1923)

WILLIAM CARLOS WILLIAMS **THE AUTOBIOGRAPHY** (NEW YORK: RANDOM HOUSE, 1951)

EZRA POUND **SELECTED LETTERS 1907-1941**, EDITED BY D. D. PAIGE (NEW YORK: NEW DIRECTIONS, 1950)

WILLIAM CARLOS WILLIAMS **THE SELECTED LETTERS**, EDITED BY JOHN C. THIRWALL (NEW YORK: MCDOWELL, OBOLENSKY, 1957)

WILLIAMS CARLOS WILLIAMS IN CONVERSATION
WITH EDITH HEAL **I WANTED TO WRITE A POEM** (BOS-
TON: BEACON PRESS, 1958)

WILLIAM CARLOS WILLIAMS **THE SELECTED
PROSE: 1909-1965** (NEW YORK: NEW DIRECTIONS, 1973)

WILLIAM CARLOS WILIAMS **THE EMBODIMENT OF
KNOWLEDGE**, EDITED WITH AN INTRODUCTION BY
RON LOEWINSOHN (NEW YORK: NEW DIRECTIONS, 1974)

AMONG CRITICS AND SCHOLARS of American poetry, it has long been generally acknowledged, if less
generally discussed, that Ezra Pound was the dominat-
ing influence upon the early poetics of William Carlos
Williams. The irascible "missionary"—an epithet to
which Pound himself admitted (see *The Selected Letters of Ezra Pound: 1907-1941*, in which Pound writes
to George Santayana: "I plead the missionary sperrit:
GUILTY!!")—began what amounted to a personal *ji-
had* to convert Williams to his viewpoints. This effort
began as early as their first encounters in the University
of Pennsylvania dormitories and would last throughout Williams' life. It is as if upon taking up his violin
to antiphonally respond to the piano music of Morrison Robb Van Cleve—which led, a short while later,
to his being introduced to Pound—Williams interned
himself to a mentor more zealous and jealous than
any university don or religious guru could have been.

The relationship with Pound, unquestionably, was "a painful experience"—as Williams describes what it was like to listen to Pound read from the poems of *A Lume Spento* (Williams, *The Autobiography*). "...He bore with me for sixty years," Pound confessed via cable upon hearing of Williams' death.

It is easy to envision Williams, in this context, as a grandly patient assimilator, quietly enduring Pound's harangues to sort out those truths applicable to his own poetry and life—a picture Williams himself encourages throughout his writings by stressing his uncertainty about his own critical comments and by emphasizing his early stance as observer and listener. "I paid attention very assiduously to what I was told," he writes in his 1948 "autobiography" *I Wanted to Write a Poem*; "I often reacted violently, but I weighed what had been told me thoroughly."

There is little doubt that Williams did seriously pay "attention to what he was told," particularly by Pound. The radical differences between Williams' *Poems* of 1909—of which Pound writes, "Your book would not attract even passing attention here" [*here* being London]—and *The Tempers* of 1913 reveal the enormous influence of Pound's and the Imagists' manifestoes, the origins of which Pound outlined in his famous letter to Williams of 1908. One need only compare a poem such as the 1909 poem "The Uses of Poetry":

> I've fond anticipation of a day
> O'erfilled with pure diversion presently,
> For I must read a lady poesy
> The while we glide by many a leafy bay,
>
> Hid deep in rushes, where at random play
> The glossy black winged May-flies, or whence flee
> Hush-throated nestlings in alarm,
> Whom we have idly frightened with our boat's
>   long sway.

with "Contemporania" of 1913:

> I go back and forth now
> And the little leaves follow me
> Talking of the great rain,
> Of branches broken,
> And the farmer's curses!
>
> But I go back and forth
> In this corner of a garden

And the green shoots follow me
Praising the great rain.

to perceive that the "mushy technique" of Williams' earlier work (Pound's phrase used to describe the poetry of the Symbolists) had given way in a few short years to a "direct treatment of the thing" and "rhythm composed in the sequence of the metrical phrase, not in the sequence of the metronome" (statements from the Imagist manifesto published in *Poetry* in 1913). Williams' critical observations in *Five Philosophical Essays*, written during this period, often parallel Pound's ideas as expressed in the first decade or so of their acquaintance. Arguments Williams makes for economy in living, for example—

> Insofar as life is to see, it is: "Do not waste space." Thus we see that life is to confine our energy and for us to expand our view. Which, again, shows that a perfection is the object of our activity, any perfection which alone at once contains a universal expansion concentrated into a minimum of elements constituting it, for in a perfection is no waste.

—unavoidably remind one of Pound's and the Imagists' insistence upon using "absolutely no word" in poetry "that does not contribute to the presentation." While Pound aspires to a poetry free from didacticism ("The poet grinds the axe for no dogma," from "The Wisdom of Poetry," 1912), Williams attacks dead words "which are symbols of symbols, twice removed from vitality" [*The Embodiment of Knowledge*], contending that man's only actions can be "to prance to cheer and to point, all of which are but one thing: praise." And like Pound, Williams links these ideas of art and poetry with his concept of beauty:

> We shall have the most beautiful before us; singing and architecture and painting and poetry, not as the dirty Cinderella of worship as it is now but as the thing itself [*EoK*, p. 181].

Certainly, several of these ideas were current among poets and painters in these years from 1902 to 1913, and some of Williams' concepts have roots that go back farther than his first encounter with "sweet Ezra" (Williams' endearment for Pound expressed in *The Autobiography*), but one cannot dismiss the impact of Pound upon Williams' critical writings of this period, and, particularly, upon what was to become the rallying-cry of Williams' poetics: "Nothing is good save the new" [*Kora in Hell*]. Observations such as those Williams makes in his *Philosophical Essays*—

But shall we not find this freedom appearing under other names? ...It is universal change, it is the new, it is that no two trees are alike, it is the thrill of surprise, mystery, the unaccountable against the accountable.... It is change, then, against the unchanged... [*EoK*, p. 171]

—and in his chastisement of Harriet Monroe in 1913—

Now life is above all things else at any moment subversive to life as it was the moment before—always new, irregular. Verse to be alive must have infused into it something of the same order, some tincture of disestablishment, something in the nature of an impalpable revolution, an ethereal reversal, let me say. I am speaking of modern verse. [*Selected Letters*, pp. 23-24]

—clearly re-echo Pound's statements expressed in *The Spirit of Romance* in 1910:

Art is a fluid moving above or over the minds of men.

...

Let us consider the body as pure mechanism. Our kinship to the ox we have constantly thrust upon us; but beneath this is our kinship to the vital universe, to the tree and the living rock, and, because this is less obvious—and possibly more interesting—we forget it.

We have about us the universe of fluid force, and below us the germinal universe of the wood alive, of stone alive....

Indeed, Pound's continual exhortation for a poetry that functions as a "liberating force" ["The Wisdom of Poetry"], for a poetry through which the poet can create experience anew, was quickly to become the major issue of Williams' aesthetics. Not surprisingly, Williams acknowledges in *I Wanted to Write a Poem* that "Before meeting Ezra Pound is like B.C. and A.D."

Yet, on the very next page of that 1958 text, Williams states what seems to be a contradiction: "I was a listener. I always kept myself free from anything Pound said" [p. 6]. One may, at first, simply shrug off such a comment—which appears to be a disavowal of Pound's influence—as part of Williams' endeavor to establish a poetic identity separate from that of his mentor-friend's, an endeavor that began with his quoting of Pound's letter in the 1920 introduction to *Kora in Hell* and with his criticism of Pound in "Yours, O Youth" a few months later. But, by the late 1950s, when Williams surely had sufficiently accomplished that dissociation, it seems somewhat insincere of him to admit to the impact of Pound upon his life while denying the influence of what Pound said—irrational almost, unless in his use of the word "free," Williams means something other than a disregard of or a disconnection from Pound's early poetics. If we explore this issue a bit further, perhaps we can better comprehend why in 1958 Williams takes this position.

Several of Williams' concepts of freedom—that it is inextricably connected with universal change, which opposes it to the "unchanged," "The old," and the "permanent"—have already been mentioned. In his early essay, "Constancy and Freedom," Williams further explores how those notions of freedom seem diametrically opposed to the values of "persistency, solidity, permanency," opposed even to the constancy necessary for friendships and love [*EoK*, p. 170]. He goes to great lengths to demonstrate that such an opposition between the two does not really exist—at least in the abstract. The knowledge of our limitations and possibilities is the "ultimate freedom," Williams argues, and it is only in knowledge that a human can be truly free. For knowledge or truth seeks to distinguish natural laws—laws to which we are subject by ignorance; and, in that distinction, it points to our human limitations, one of the most obvious of which is our inability to explore all possibilities equally. Because of time and energy, human beings cannot seek for truth in all its forms through all vocations; recognizing the law of economy, knowledge teaches humankind the need for constancy, which, when enacted, leads to the revelation of similar abstract truths in each vocation. Thus, in theory, there can be no opposition between constancy and freedom, since they result in the same knowledge. It is only ignorance, Williams claims, that leads us to see these two forces as a duality. As Williams restates time and again in his later work, however, humankind, as the embodiment of that knowledge, wanders through "the forests of ignorance" [*EoK*, p. 64], unable to resolve the duality and to live with the paradox.

Without giving undue emphasis to Edith Heal's records of Williams' statements or the philosophical musings of an adolescent poet, I suggest that it is in the context of this paradox or tension between freedom and continuity in which we must consider Williams' accounts of Pound and his relationships with his fellow poets in general. Although Williams apparently comprehended that his poetic development was dependent, in part, upon a contiguity and continuity of personal friendships with poets—was dependent, if you will, upon *contact*—his aggrandizement of freedom led him throughout his life to argue not only against the past and for renewal, but to actively work against his own past, his friends, and their influence—to detach himself from all that might preclude growth and divergence. Ezra Pound, for Williams, was just such a force.

Certainly, there were more aggravating opponents in Williams' career. In 1920 he took on Wallace Stevens in *Kora in Hell*, addressing him as "dear fat Stevens," and likening him (in a description borrowed from Skipworth Cannell) to "a Pennsylvania Dutchman who has suddenly become aware of his habits and taken to 'society' in self-defense." And in the same work, Williams begins what was to become a lifelong campaign against T. S. Eliot [*KiH*, p. 24]—the whipping boy of Pound and Wyndham Lewis as well—that can be summed up in his 1958 reflections:

> I had a violent feeling that Eliot had betrayed what I believed in. He was looking backward; I was looking forward. He was a conformist, with wit, learning I did not possess. He knew French, Latin, Arabic, god knows what. I was interested in that. But I felt he had rejected America and I refused to be rejected and so my reaction was violent [*IWTWAP*, p. 30].

But the fact that he also sounds off in the Prologue about his friends Hilda Doolittle and Pound should indicate that Williams' gripes were not simply an evincing of "sour grapes" (the words Williams chose to title the book of poetry he published in the following year), that he was not just lashing back at his fellow poets for their criticism of his poetry, but was responding to specific attitudes that belied their criticisms: viewpoints which he felt demanded a constancy—consistency of viewpoint (Stevens), uniformity of language (H. D.), and continuation of the Tradition (Eliot)—which translated in his thinking to arrestment and death. For Williams, reaction was directly bound to his ideas on personal freedom, a phenomenon which he most clearly reveals in his response to the letter from H.D.:

> There is nothing in a literature but change and change is mockery. I'll write whatever I damn please, whenever I damn please and as I damn please and it'll be good if the authentic spirit of change is on it [*KiH*, p. 13].

Predictably, his reactions to Pound are related to these very issues of change and freedom. For Pound, according to Williams' logic, had committed two major sins: like Eliot, he overvalued the Tradition and he had abandoned his country to write. To Williams these were inseparable issues; his lifelong commitment to primary knowledge over authoritarian knowledge, to the modern over the Tradition, and to the present over the past were grounded in his belief that such values were peculiarly American; that American culture had made a necessary and irreparable "break" with the classical valuation of education over knowledge [*EoK*, p. 146]. The American artist, accordingly, cannot go to Paris to study art, Williams avers, because there he can learn only French art; as an American, the artist can come to his own art only through *contact* with his culture and country. "France is France," he wrote Harriet Monroe in 1913, "We are not France" [*SL*, pp. 25-26]. Or, as he put it in *Contact* 4:

> Nothing will be forwarded, as it is persistently coughed at us for our children to believe, by a conscious regard for traditions which have arrived at their perfection by force of the stimuli of special circumstances foreign to us, the same which gave them birth and dynamise them to-day ["Sample Critical Statement/Comment," *Contact* 4, p. 18].

By essay's end, Pound and Eliot are linked to those whom Williams is soon to call the "Traditionalists of Plagiarism," those who would tell him to read Laforgue rather than "believe in [his] bayonets" [see Williams' "The Writers of the American Revolution," *Selected Essays*]. A few years later, Williams proclaims, "Ezra Pound is already looking backward" [*A Novelette* in *Imaginations*, p. 54].

This reaction against Pound, however, was not limited to such literal accusations, but found more artful expression in *Spring and All*, the document central to Williams' early critical theory. For in the first half of his pivotal work—a work which I read as a more-or-less coherent manifesto rather than as a potpourri of poetry and prose—Williams chooses the most common of poetic subjects: night, spring, and flowers, not to mention trees, wind, clouds, rain, and war—the very subjects, in fact, which Pound ridiculed in his letter to Williams of 1908:

> Why write what I can translate out of Renaissance Latin or crib from the sainted dead?
>
> Here are a list of facts on which I and 9,000,000 other poets have spieled endlessly:
>
> 1. Spring is a pleasant season. The flower, etc. etc. sprout, bloom etc. etc.
> 2. Young man's fancy. Lightly, heavily gaily etc. etc.
> 3. Love, a delightsome tickling. Indefinable etc.
> 4. Trees, hills etc. are by a provident nature arranged diversely, in diverse places.
> 5. Winds, clouds, rains, etc. flop thru and over 'em.
> 6. Men love women....
>
> ...
>
> 7 Men fight battles, etc. etc.
> 8. Men go on voyages.

It seems extraordinarily unlikely, after having accused Pound of being too reliant upon the Tradition, that Williams should accidentally have taken up the subjects which Pound argues are better copied than re-employed by modern poets. Rather, it is apparent that in *Spring and All* Williams confronts Pound on his own turf, so to speak. For what Williams seems previously to have been unable to convey to Pound—let alone to Stevens, Eliot, and the American reader—is that his pursuit of the NEW—his focus on change as freedom—does not demand a break with reality, the commonplace, or nature. To the contrary, as Williams comes to perceive in *Spring and All*, spring, love, flowers, trees, winds, clouds, war, and rain are subjects worthy of a lifelong investigation. "Thank you, I know well that I am plagiarizing," he exclaims in the midst of his commentary in Chapter XIII, as if addressing his 1908 correspondent. However, as Williams is soon to explain, what *he* means by plagiarism is something different from what Pound argues. The confusion arose, Williams suggests, at least as far back as Samuel Butler, who observed that "There are two who can invent some extraordinary thing to one who can properly employ that which has been made use of before" [*S&A*, p. 97]. The Traditionalists of Plagiarism have seized upon this statement, Williams argues, to proclaim the value of past traditions in literature, which has resulted, he hints, in poets like Eliot and Pound looking backwards and in a constant reference to the poets of the past, their metrics, their rhetorical devices, their themes. Williams, on the other hand, would retain the same subjects as past poets, but would endow them, through the *imagination* (the key word of *Spring and All*), with new life, a life detached from that of the everyday world because it emanates not from nature itself, or from an illusionary presentation of nature, but from an emotionally-charged consciousness reflecting its existence from moment to moment *in* nature. Pound, Williams implies, has got it all wrong; the plagiarism does not lie in using the same subjects, but in cribbing from "the sainted dead" (something Pound would do in poetry throughout his life). While Pound argues in his 1908 letter for a manipulation of past *methods* ("Sometimes I use rules of Spanish, Anglo-Saxon and Greek metrics that are not common in the English of Milton's and Miss Austen's day," [*SL*, p. 4]) and against the use of timeworn subjects, Williams contends in *Spring and All* that the *subjects* of the past can be revitalized, but its methods are unusable because they do not permit the expression of the modern poet's imagination. As a subject for poetry, "The rose is obsolete," he tentatively admits (and his conjunction is the pivot of the poem), "but each petal ends in / an edge"..."so that to engage in roses / becomes a geometry..." as polymorphic as the individual personality [S&A, p. 107-108].

This distinction between his own thinking and Pound's is an important one, for it recapitulates the same duality that Williams attempted to tackle in his early essay on "Constancy and Freedom." Obviously, Williams understood that Pound was an ally in his struggle for a new poetry, for a freedom of poetic expression; in his attachment to the methods of the Tradition, however, Pound could not but have appeared to Williams as opting for constancy over freedom, to be electing the European tradition over the American landscape and the predisposition of its artists to remain separate, detached, even isolate. "My whole life," Williams summarizes in *Spring and All*, "has been spent (so far) in seeking to place a value upon experience that would satisfy my sense of inclusiveness without redundancy—*completeness...with the liberty of choice*" [italics mine, S&A, p. 116].

Williams comprehended that, as a modern American poet, as a representative of the new American poetics—in short, as a leonine abstraction—Pound stood for causes similar to his own. Wrote Williams in 1919, two years before his attack on Pound in *Contact*:

I find matter for serious attention in Ezra

Pound's discordant shrieking....

It is the NEW! not one more youthful singer,
one more lovely poem. The NEW, the everlasting
NEW, the everlasting defiance. Ezra has the smell
of it. Any man can slip into the mud. Any man can
go to school ["Belly Music," *Others* 5 (July 1919),
28].

From this perspective, in his vision of Pound as a pioneer of American poetics, there was no question of
influence. "Ain't it enuf that you so deeply influenced
my formative years without your wanting to influence
also my later ones?" he asked Pound in a letter of 1954.
But as a fellow poet, as a living, breathing, speaking,
shrieking being, Pound, like so many others, was someone from whom Williams felt he had to free himself,
was someone against whom he had to fight to live in
"A world detached from the necessity of recording it,
sufficient to itself, removed from him...with which he
has bitter and delicious relations and from which he is
independent—moving at will from one thing to another—as he pleases, unbound, complete" [*S&A,* p. 121].

PHILADELPHIA, 1983
Reprinted from *Sagetrieb*, III, no. 2 (Fall 1984).
Presented as a talk on August 24, 1983 at the University of Maine,
  William Carlos Williams Centennial Conference.

I mention Edith Heal in the essay above. Heal, born in 1903, had been a neighbor of Williams, and in 1958 published a book, I Wanted to Write a Poem: The Autobiography of the Works of a Poet, *in which she and Williams discussed each book of his career and many individual poems. Simply because of its inclusiveness, along with the often insightful musings of Williams himself, the book has become a classic in the studies of William Carlos Williams.*

At the 1983 conference on Williams in Orono, Maine, I met Heal, and we became fast friends. Soon after, she sent me a manuscript of a new novel she had written, along with an earlier published novel, The Shadow Boxers. *She also had written, evidently, an earlier book on fashion and a manual on popularity and success for teenagers.*

Her new fiction, about the difficulties of psychological patients when their doctors go on vacation in August, was well-written, if not exactly a profound work. And I decided to publish it on Sun & Moon Press. We met for dinner at the Algonquin in New York some time later, where we had a wonderful discussion during which she discerned—expressing it in the terminology of her generation—that I was not the "marrying kind." I have always enjoyed the company of older women and men, for it often reveals to me how things in language and culture change so quickly. And I thoroughly enjoyed the evening.

In 1984 I published the book, which I had retitled August Break (I believe the original title was something like When the Psychiatrists Go on Vacation), to fairly good reviews. Perhaps we sold out of the book; scanning my vast library, I, evidently, have no copy of it.

LOS ANGELES, MAY 17, 2009

Complexity Out of Simplicity

MICHEL SEUPHOR **THE EPHEMERAL IS ETERNAL**,
ADAPTED BY DONN B. MURPHY AND JUDITH ZILCZER,
SETS BY PIET MONDRIAN / PERFORMED AT THE HIRSH-
HORN MUSEUM AND SCULPTURE GARDEN, WASHING-
TON, D.C., JUNE 25-27, 1982

WITH SETS BY Piet Mondrian and a script by Mondrian biographer Michel Seuphor, the first American
production of *The Ephemeral Is Eternal*, billed as a
"Dada play," could not help but intrigue museum-goers
and devotees of drama alike. In the context of the De
Stijl show at the Hirshhorn Museum and Sculpture
Garden, this production inherently raised the question why Mondrian, the genius of order, harmony, and
color, the artist who declared himself as dedicated to
communicating "the imminent order of nature," would
have agreed to participate in an event connected with
the Dadaists, who by 1926, the year in which this play
was written, had long since established an international

33

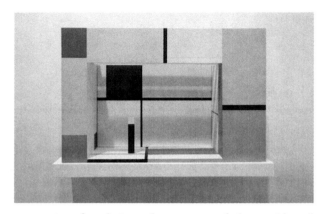

reputation for their embracement of the accidental and the absurd. How one answers that question and what this production reveals concerning Mondrian's attitudes towards Dadaism depend, I suggest, on how much one is able to separate text from context, critical perspective from expectation.

For in many respects the play shares the Dadaist love of illogic and its relish of the gestures of shouting, screaming, and babbling. A conductor, dressed in white tails, undershorts, and bowler hat, leads his chosen chorus in groans and songs of gibberish; an actress, attended by Turkish and Japanese peddlers, soliloquizes nonsense in the style of Sarah Bernhardt; three robotized Black dancers glissade across the stage; and throughout, the play is filled with self-referential commentary, statements directed to the audience, and irrelevant intrusions that one has come to associate with Dadaist theater and its influence upon and assimilation into postmodern performance art. As with much of the most interesting of contemporary performance, *The Ephemeral Is Eternal* seems to be less a play—a dramatic statement frozen within dialogic plot—than it is a theater of process, an event occurring in real time and space.

Yet, for all this, there is a certain tension at work in these "theatrical demonstrations"—as the subtitle describes the piece—that pulls one away from experienc-  ing it as such. For all of its sense of happenstance, its seemingly clever inanities, and its automatic word associations, there is a stiltedness about the free-for-all that works against spontaneity, against accident and chance. There is always a tendency to dismiss such feelings by historicizing the work, by imagining that it was more shocking, more revelatory, more...whatever in its day than it is in our self-conscious and overly-literate age. Such historiographic apologies are generally dangerous, but in this case such a notion not only reveals a cultural myopia, but obscures the focus of the play. In its opposition between what it seems and what it is, *The Ephemeral Is Eternal*, I argue, is not only a fascinating work, but actually is a formalist, anti-Dadaist work of art.

The play begins, in fact, with a metaphor that suggests the play will be a dialectic between the two: a woman enters from stage left and draws in pantomine a series of rounded figures—a circle, an ellipse, a disk; a male figure follows her, erasing her figures and replacing them with angular ones—a rectangle, a triangle, a square. Momentarily, these acts may appear as mere Dadaist gestures; but one soon perceives that for Seuphor the erasure has served less as a meaningless game between the old art and the new than as a dialogue between the irrational and the rational, between the ideal and the concrete—all polarities which in Seuphor's day were summed up in the female/male dichotomy. Later, during the soliloquy of a melodramatic actress, an off-stage voice shouts: "No women on stage!"; and soon thereafter the actress, dressed in green (a color detested by the members of De Stijl), is banned from the play. Throughout this piece, in fact, the sentimental, the mystical, the circle, the feminine are opposed to the tree, the horizon, the straight line, the male, the art of Mondrian.

For Seuphor, I suggest, this was less a sexist statement than it was a comment on the societal linkage of art to the feminine mystique. Like the De Stijl artists, the Futurists (Ezra Pound and Wyndham Lewis), and dozens of other visual and literary artists of the day, Seuphor clearly felt that society had connected art for too long with prettiness, sublimity, gentility—to all those things by which it defined woman. It was not woman Seuphor hated, but society's notion of art as it related to its sexual stereotypes. What he and others desired was a tougher art, a sparer, leaner notion of the creative act, an artistic sensibility expressed in his play by a vaudeville-like ballet between two males, dressed black and white. With only a handkerchief for a prop, these two enact various human emotions—joy, frivolity, sexual arousal, anger, hate, pain, and forgiveness—by transforming the cloth into various shapes and patterns. It is this ability to shape and reshape nature with a single motif, with one simple focus, one realizes, that is at the heart of Mondrian's art and his sets for the play. And it is that complexity out of simplicity, it becomes clear, for which Seuphor is arguing.

The Dadaist humor, the echolalia, pratfalls, and buffoonery are merely tools to point up the clarity and completeness of formal abstraction. Ultimately, *The Ephemeral Is Eternal* stands as a sort of formalist manifesto in Dadaist drag, a manifesto that uses a rival in an attempt to destroy an absolute enemy. To blow up the old art—the production ends with the detonation of a model of the theater itself—it uses the shock-value, the absurdity of Dadaism; but underneath lies a plea for order, for harmony, for an art that stands against the ephemeral in its eternality. Mondrian, one can surmise, comprehended that in participating in this Dada-like spectacle he was remaining true to his cause.

WASHINGTON, D.C., JUNE 29, 1982
Reprinted from *Washington Review*, VIII (October-November 1982).
Reprinted from *Green Integer Review* (May 2009).

Two Pabst Operas

Bread or Knife

G. W. PABST AND LADISLAUS VAJDA (WRITERS),
BASED ON PLAYS BY FRANK WEDEKIND, G. W. PABST
(DIRECTOR) **DIE BÜCHSE DER PANDORA (PANDORA'S
BOX)** / 1929

LOOSELY BASED ON Frank Wedekind's two plays
Erdgeist (1895) and *Die Büchse der Pandora* (1904),
Pandora's Box, directed by Austrian G. W. Pabst, is per-
haps one of the greatest films of the Weimar Republic.

Watching the movie the other day, I could easily
see why composer Alban Berg was also attracted to the
Wedekind plays as the source to his opera, *Lulu*. For
Pabst's film, despite its silence, is basically a visual opera, as it counts down the numerous acts in Lulu's fall.

In the first act, Lulu, formerly living as a woman of
the streets, is currently having an affair with the respectable newspaper publisher Dr. Ludwig Schön; and as we

encounter her, she is beautifully caged in Schön's lovely apartment. But her former pimp Schigolch—whom she first describes as a former patron and later as her father—visits her in this paradisiacal world, insisting that he has better plans for her, suggesting that, through his friend Rodrigo Quest, she perform on the stage, making her great beauty known to the world.

Schön returns home, and she is forced to hide Schigolch on the balcony. The publisher is clearly distressed, proclaiming that he is to be married and must give up his mistress. She attempts to both distract him and allay any such decision, but he soon discovers Schigolch, and becomes even more determined to end his affair. Lulu insists, foretelling events of the plot, "You'll have to kill me to get rid me."

Meanwhile, Schön's son, Alwa—secretly in love with Lulu himself—is planning to produce a musical, and discusses the costumes with his designer, Countess Anna Geschwitz. As Lulu enters the room, she takes up one of the designs and insists that Geschwitz design such a dress for her as well. Alwa becomes determined to cast her in his show, and his father agrees to finance her, realizing it may be a perfect way to get her off his hands.

The long scene of the performance, filmed from backstage, as cast, workers, sets, and props jostle and push against the visiting Schön and his intended wife,

Charlotte, is one of the most brilliant scenes of the movie. Like a Boulevard farce, the entire world seems to be in constant motion—until Lulu, seeing Charlotte with her former lover, refuses to go on. The dance begins without her, as one by one the director, Alwa, the choreographer and others attempt to change her mind and make her realize her responsibility, all to no avail. Finally Schön himself is asked to help. Perceiving her intractability, he takes her into a small room to force her into agreement. She remains resistant until he finally takes her in his arms to kiss her, the very moment Charlotte, having been searching the stage area for him, opens the door. Schön has now been trapped into a marriage with Lulu, a woman he has warned his son "to beware of." "Now I'll marry Lulu. It will be the death of me."

At the wedding ceremony in the Schön house, we encounter the publisher's wealthy friends along with Lulu's derelict "father," Schigolch, others of his friends, and the Countess, who clearly is a lesbian who has equally been charmed by Lulu, and with whom the beauty dances the first dance.

While family friends stand about the living room, drinks in hand, Schigolch and the entire kitchen staff appear to be drunk. Schigolch determines to cover Lulu's wedding bed with roses. Alwa, meanwhile, takes his father aside, announcing that he is leaving "for a long time."

As Lulu goes off to bed, beckoning Schön to join her, she discovers Schigolch and attempts to send him away; he refuses, pulling her down onto his lap. Schön enters, outraged again at Schigolch's appearance in his house, and orders him out, the party guests witnessing the event in shock. Taking up a gun, Schön reenters the bedroom, insisting that Lulu commit suicide so that he can get her out of his life. Forcing her to embrace the gun, he attempts to make her shoot, but when the gun goes off, it enters his own body. As Alwa returns for one goodbye to Lulu, his father falls to the floor, blood dripping from his mouth.

In the courtroom scene following, the prosecution describes Lulu as Pandora: in Greek mythology "the first woman," who opened a jar the gods had given her, releasing all the evils of the world before she closed it, leaving behind only "Hope." Attempting to use her allure to free herself from the charges, Lulu is a strange mix of a mysterious woman in funeral attire and an alluring call girl. But, as Louise Brooks plays Lulu, it is her eyes that seem to subjugate all men, while here she is  forced for propriety's sake to hide them behind her veil. The jury finds her guilty of manslaughter. Schigolch and his friends, however, swarm into the courtroom, surrounding Lulu and sweeping her up into escape.

Lulu has no place to go but to Schön's. Strangely, she seems incapable of understanding her possible fate, and she quickly glances at the newest fashion magazines, imagining herself dressed like the models. Alwa enters, convincing her of the dangers, and takes her away by train, out of the country. As they prepare to leave the train, however, she is spotted by the Marquis Casti-Piani, who threatens Alwa with the police unless he pays. Alwa has no choice.

Casti-Piani suggests they join him, for their protection, on a gambling boat. Once there, Alwa begins to gamble heavily, losing any money they may have previously had. Rodrigo Quest, in search of money himself, demands Lulu pay him. Casti-Piani attempts to sell her to an Egyptian. As Lulu declares: "MONEY! All they want is money!"

Desperate, Lulu pleads for money from the Countess so that her lover can continue gambling, as Schigolch shows him how to play "when you're sure to win." Caught cheating, Alwa, along with Lulu and Schigolch, escapes.

As the film comes to a close, we witness them in complete destitution in their London hovel. Alwa, half frozen, lies in bed, while Lulu attempts to cut a loaf of stale bread. Even a knife won't break it open, and the taste is unbearable. Only the seemingly unflappable Schigolch seems likely to survive; he has somehow been able to come up with a bottle of liquor. As Alwa declares, "It's strange how you can get booze on credit but not bread."

Without food or warmth, Lulu begins to make up her face. She has clearly been forced to return to the streets. Her only commodity in the male-driven world she inhabits is her body.

On the street she discovers a handsome-looking man, and pulls him toward her, just as Alwa and Schigolch abandon the room, the latter declaring that he could enjoy just one more plum pudding before he dies.

The girl's pick-up reports that he has no money,

but Lulu offers her-
self to him despite
that fact, luring him
up the staircase to her
room. In a brilliant
shot from behind, we
witness Lulu draw-
ing him up the steps

as he holds a knife behind his back. Her alluring look
and kindness force him to drop the knife. The audience
now divines that he is the renowned Jack the Ripper, of
whom a street poster has warned.

Below, on the street, we see Alwa in anguish (is
his suffering for his own failure to provide for her and
for the fact that she is having sex with another man?).
Schigolch sits in a nearby pub, his pudding before him.

As the murderer enters Lulu's room, he spots the
knife that would not cut the bread, and as Lulu pulls
him to the bed, he takes it up. Holding a piece of mis-
tletoe over her head, he raises the knife, which, we are
certain, will easily cut through human flesh.

Alwa walks off, apparently determined to leave his
lover.

One might see this clearly theatrical and melodramatic work as simply another Naturalistic film with a
Theodore Dreiser-like story about a doomed woman,
were it not for the stunning acting of Louise Brooks.

45

Her face, with its large eyes, long nose, and delicate lips—all enwrapped in her deeply black bangs—seems in constant motion in every frame of the film, shifting from a look of girlish wonderment, to vampire-like flirtation and impish delight. Brooks' Lulu, moreover, is less of a siren than a charming plaything, an innocent who nonetheless understands the force she has over others, and uses it to her advantage. Her body, as I suggest above, is the only thing that permits her survival, and yet it is also what destroys her in the end. As Pabst presents her, Lulu is sexuality itself, a container of energy that has no other end than to burn itself up. In the choice between sustenance (bread) and phallic excitement (the knife), Lulu inevitably chooses the latter. But then, she has had no other choice; to put it somewhat coarsely, she has been taught that to eat she has to fuck.

LOS ANGELES, AUGUST 10, 2009
Reprinted from *Reading Films: My International Cinema* (2012).

46

Able to Forget

BÉLA BALÁZS, LÉO LANIA, AND LADISLAUS VAJDA
(WRITERS), BASED ON A MUSICAL DRAMA BY BERTOLT
BRECHT AND KURT WEILL, KURT WEILL (MUSIC), G. W.
PABST (DIRECTOR) **DIE DREIGROSCHENOPER** (**THE
THREEPENNY OPERA**) / 1931

> Only that man survives
> Who's able to forget.
> —Kurt Weill

G. W. PABST'S expressionistic production of Brecht's
and Weill's *Threepenny Opera* has many failings, and
perhaps for the director's excising of most of that work's
original songs, he deserved to be sued, as he was, by its
creators; however, they lost the suit. Although the film
contains a fair amount of dialogue and reproduces several of Weill's noted songs, for the most part Pabst uses
the tropes of silent filmmaking, shooting many of his
scenes in the melodramatic overstatement of a time before the "talkies." He basically presents the songs, more-

over, as dramatic commentary by the musical narrator.

Nonetheless, Pabst's carefully framed sequences do capture the overall sense of the Brecht-Weill original, and the excellent performances by Carola Neher (as Polly), Rudolf Forster (as Mackie Messer) and Lotte Lenya (in her signature role of Jenny) redeem his rhetorical approach. In a sense, of course, the theatrical conventions used by Pabst recreate some of the *Verfremdungseffekt* (the alienating effects) of Brecht's original.

For the first half of the musical, we go along with the suave manners of the anti-hero as the narrator sings of Mackie's seemingly coinciden-  tal (and apparently unproveable) involvement in a series of robberies, murders, and sexual escapades. His clumsy wooing of Polly as he sweeps her into an underground bar, where he intimidatingly stares down two men, a Laurel and Hardy-like pair who we later discover are his own henchmen, in order to take over their table, demonstrates his true temperament. The important thing in these scenes is that Polly appears to be a complete innocent about to become prey to Mackie's machinations.

The hilarious preparations for the suddenly announced wedding between the two, including the arrest, soon after, of one of the gang members while carrying a wedding present of a stolen grandfather clock, ultimately reveal Mackie's close friendship with the Chief of Police, Tiger-Brown.

No sooner has the viewer recovered from that revelation than the script lets us know that the innocent-seeming Polly is the daughter of "the poorest of the poor," the wealthy Beggar King. Suddenly Polly is wise to all of Mackie's doings, asking outright, "Is all of this stolen, Mackie?"

Polly's powerful explanation of why she has married Mackie is one of the high points of Pabst's production:

> You must be cold and heartless as you know
> Or else all sort of things happen
> You must say *no*.

But because Mackie has not offered any of the nice things a young lady in her position might expect, because he has been so crude and clumsy in his attempts at romance, she admits she had no choice this time 'round but to say *yes*: "You can't be cold and heartless now!"

Discovering that his daughter has run away with

Mackie, the Beggar King Peachum demands that Tiger-Brown bring him to justice, and when the Police Chief wavers, he threatens to interfere with the Queen's coronation by organizing a staged protest by the beggars, who marching toward the Queen will be somewhat impervious from violent threats—after all, what will it say of the Royal family if the police heartlessly shoot down these poverty-stricken citizens as they attempt to "pay homage" to the Queen?

Hearing of her father's intentions, Polly convinces Mackie that he must escape. And he, in turn, hands over the operation of his underworld activities to his wife. Returning to his prostitute friends, Mackie is betrayed by Jennie and, after several attempts at escape, is arrested. One of the best moments of this film is Mackie's sudden appearance upon the brothel's rooftop minutes before we observe his arms and hands maneuvering along the building's drainpipe.

While Peachum plans his protest, Polly takes the gang's ill-gotten money and purchases a bank. Dressed now as bankers at a board meeting, Polly and the former gang members clearly demonstrate Brecht's the-

orem that there is little difference between robbing a bank and controlling others' money.

When Peachum's wife announces that Polly and Mackie will be attending the coronation, sitting in the stands near where  the Beggar King's minions will attempt to interrupt the event, Peachum runs off to stop the march. Pabst's brilliant presentation of their slow robot-like forward advance makes clear that Peachum has unleashed a monster in riling up the masses! The Queen's absolute terror in facing her people, moreover, explains everything, particularly the survival of those who can forget. In Pabst's handling nearly all the action takes place while the screen goes dark, reiterating Weill's observation: "Some men live in darkness, while others stand in light."

At film's end, Peachum also willfully forgets, joining forces with his banker-daughter and Mack the Knife. Together they will rule the world, the wealthy and the poor alike.

LOS ANGELES, AUGUST 6, 2009
Both essays reprinted from *N^th Position* [England] (May 2009).
Reprinted from *Reading Films: My International Cinema* (2012).

I have published two of my 1977-78 essays on Eudora Welty in later volumes of My Year *(see* My Year 2002 *and* 2006*). Upon the announcement of her death this year on July 23, I determined to reprint the essay below on my favorite of her works,* The Golden Apples.

Metronome and Music: The Encounter Between History and Myth in Welty's The Golden Apples

EUDORA WELTY **THE GOLDEN APPLES** (NEW YORK: HARCOURT, BRACE, 1949)

ACCORDING TO EUDORA WELTY, *The Golden Apples* (1949) is a book of short stories; nonetheless, as Thomas L. McHaney recently noted in his essay "Eudora Welty and the Multitudinous Golden Apples" (*Mississippi Quarterly*, XXVI [Fall 1973]), "it...manages to create a complex unified impression in the manner of the novel." Certainly, an appreciation of the structural and thematic density of the whole is lost if the work is considered merely in its parts. As McHaney has shown, the book as a whole functions almost as a musical composition, structured according to various and diverse mythological analogues. To a lesser degree, several other critics have also explored some of these mythological patterns (see Harry Morris, Ruth M. Vande Kieft, and F. D. Carson), but thus far no one except McHaney

has recognized the vast importance of these analogues to the structure and the philosophical matter of the work, and even McHaney has failed to note that Welty's concern for myth, as sweeping as it is, is but half of her conception in this fiction. For *The Golden Apples* is also deeply grounded in Welty's concept of time, and centers, specifically, upon what she considers not merely the *problem* of time, but the *order* of time. Knowing that time may be seen as occurring either in a linear or a cyclical pattern, that time may be experienced as either history* or as myth, Welty has structured the individual stories and, consequently, the whole book around the encounter between these two perceptions of the order of time.

On one hand, *The Golden Apples* is a history. It is a series of stories ordered chronologically which concerns the small Mississippi town of Morgana from a period before World War I until post-World War II, a span of about 40 years**. Within this time-span Welty's characters move in linear time; they are born, they mature, and some of them die. Indeed, a great part of the power of the work as a whole derives from this historical framework. As one watches characters such as the MacLain twins, Cassie Morrison, Virgie Rainey, Nina Carmichael, and Jinny Love Stark grow from childhood to maturity, one cannot but come to love and judge them, to feel linked to them in the same way they and the townspeople do to one another. In Morgana, as in any small town, because of this shared experience in linear time, the individual's life is inextricably connected with, is even defined by, the lives of the others in the community. But this fact can also bring about a destructive set of circumstances in which individual lives become community property and individual acts lose meaning or, because they are seen as a threat to the homogeneity of the community, are outrightly opposed.

Welty establishes this idea immediately in "Shower of Gold" by having the narrative carried by Katie Rainey, who, friendly, somewhat wise, and neighborly gossip that she is, chooses to tell the reader, not her own story, but the story of King MacLain. It is a history of a man who, free from traditional morality, leaves his wife Snowdie only to return for few a hours every so many years to impregnate her as he has half of the women in the countryside. But it is also a history in which Katie and the whole community unwillingly partake, for, obviously, such behavior is a threat to community values. As Katie reports early in her narrative concerning King's comings and goings, "We might have had a little run on doing that in Morgana, if it had been so willed." It has not been "so willed," Katie implies, because she and her fellow townspeople have selected and reordered the events as they occurred. Katie's story concentrates not upon King MacLain's individual exploits, but upon the community conspiracy to keep the truth from Snowdie about King's penultimate attempt to return home, an occasion when his twin sons, dressed in masks for Halloween and wearing roller skates, unknowingly scared off their father. Although this story is hilariously comic, there are quite serious implications to it, for, as the story belies, Katie and the community have attempted to control the lives of those around them by converting individual action into history—a history which, like all histories, is created by the historian taking events in linear time and reinterpreting them according to his vision of reality. Katie may feel slightly guilty for the reinterpretation—she suggests that Snowdie "kind of holds it against me, because I was there that day when he come...." (p. 18)—but she believes that it is necessary in order to protect the community from the outside, from the world of threatening and chaotic modes of existence.

Indeed, even in telling her history, in her pretense of confidentiality, Katie attempts to draw the reader into the community; despite protestations that she tells her tale to the reader only because he is "a passerby, that will never see her [Snowdie] again, or me either" (p. 3), Katie invites, almost insists through sharing the reality behind her history, that he partake of the community sensibility.

On the other hand, in "Shower of Gold" one recognizes a pattern directly opposed to history, of which it is clear that Katie has little awareness. For Katie's narrative implies far more than she comprehends. She fears that Snowdie blames her for being there the day of King's return, but it is doubtful that she believes that Snowdie has any reason to blame her. While Katie sees that there is something special about King MacLain—as she says, "With men like King, your thoughts are bottomless" (p. 17)—she lacks the vision to see King in the proper perspective. In her historical view of reality she can only see King as a threat, as a special type of man, a "man with manners," of whom she cautions the reader to beware (p. 4). Fate, her own husband, the type of man she prefers, "is more down to earth" (p. 17). It is only in their literalness that events and people have meaning to her. When she asks her husband to describe what King looked like while riding with Governor Vardaman, where Fate claims he spotted King, she takes a broom to her husband for imitating "a horse and man in one" (p. 9). She has not the gift, the imagination to perceive that King has mythological qualities, that he may indeed be a centaur. And like many visionless people, she insists that it is others, not she, who cannot see. Snowdie, according to Katie, is a "blinky-eyed" albino who has never "ever got a good look at life, maybe. Maybe from the beginning. Maybe she just doesn't know the *extent*. Not the kind of look I got, and away back when I was twelve years old or so. Like something was put to my eye" (p. 7). Again, when she hears of people claiming to see King in New Orleans and Mobile at the same time, Katie responds, "That's people's careless ways of using their eyes" (p. 10).

Katie understands nothing that occurs simultaneously. From her historical perspective, "time goes like a dream no matter how hard you run, and all the time we heard things from out in the world that we listened to but that still didn't mean we believed them" (p. 9). She admits, in other words, that reality for her is like a dream, with several layers of meaning; but it is an enemy for that very reason, because she cannot make sense of it. She attempts, therefore, to outrun time, to make it into the past so that she can take away its dream-like quality and grasp it. But time always wins and confuses life. Thus, Katie suggests, things outside her narrow purview of experienced history cannot be believed. Reality exists only in the community, for the community is close at hand, and is the creator of history. The community unifies, regulates, and equalizes reality, and, in so doing, ends confusion, destroys simultaneity. Accordingly, after Snowdie meets King on the bank of the river and returns pregnant, looking as if "a shower of something had struck her" (p. 6), Katie fears for her. For even if she cannot recognize what has happened to Snowdie, she does perceive that, struck with that "shower of something," Snowdie is set apart. To keep Snowdie from being "by her own self," "Everybody tried to stay with her as much as they could spare, not let a day go by without one of us to run in and speak to her and say a word about an ordinary thing" (p. 8). It is no "ordinary thing," however, that has happened to Snowdie. As critics have pointed out, like Danaë, Snowdie has been impregnated by Zeus (King) in a "shower of gold." Thus, when years later on that day King tries and fails to return, in trying to protect her, in "fabricating," Katie and her friends cheat Snowdie out of partaking once more of another reality. As with Danaë, who was kept locked in a subterranean chamber, they keep Snowdie in their insulated chamber of community where time exists merely as the past.

In "June Recital" Cassie Morrison replaces Katie Rainey as historian. Like Katie, she tells a story from memory. Tie-dying a scarf in her room one summer afternoon, Cassie is made to remember by hearing a phrase of music. The phrase, from the recital piece titled *Für Elise*, recalls for her a scrap of language which, in turn, brings forth memories of her childhood piano lessons with Miss Eckhart, who had then rented out the bottom floor of the now-decaying MacLain house next door. Critic Zelma Turner Howard, in her chapter on time in *The Rhetoric of Eudora Welty's Short Stories*, has suggested that Welty is here using time in the Proustian sense, and, indeed, there are similarities. But, once again, it is not a personal history that Cassie recalls as much as it is a community one. For several of Morgana's children, including Jinny Love Stark, Parnell Moody, Missie Sights, the MacLain twins and, most importantly, Katie Rainey's daughter Virgie, also take lessons from Miss Eckhart, and it is their stories more than her own that Cassie relates.

The history of Miss Eckhart and her pupils is one of frustration and despair. Miss Eckhart, having come to Morgana for a reason no one knows, has spent her energy and accomplishment on the unpromising pupils such as Cassie, with only Virgie Rainey showing any particular talent. Thus, Cassie remembers the phrase, "Virgie Rainey, *danke schoen*," Miss Eckhart's continual sign of recognition and praise of her favorite, whom Miss Eckhart insists must "go out into the world," away from Morgana, to be "heard from" (p. 53). To the rest of her students Miss Eckhart reveals little evidence of any feeling save an unvarying strictness and a hatred of flies. As Cassie and her friends play, their teacher sits with flyswatter in hand, ready to come down upon their wrists if a fly should alight, otherwise entirely motionless and silent except for an occasional leaning forward to write on the child's music the word "slow" or "practice." The only other essential of Miss Eckhart's lessons is the presence of her metronome. As Cassie observes, "Miss Eckhart worshipped her metronome" (p. 40). It is that adoration which, among other things, makes Cassie and her friends suspect that there are other aspects of Miss Eckhart's personality. Virgie, who seems to be oblivious of Miss Eckhart's praise and love, one day refuses to continue to play another note if the metronome is not taken away; and thereafter, Virgie is made an exception to Miss Eckhart's metronome requirement. It is this event, and Virgie's general disrespect for Miss Eckhart, that enlightens Cassie concerning "changes" in her piano teacher:

> Anybody could tell that Virgie was doing something to Miss Eckhart. She was turning her

from a teacher into something lesser. And if she was not a teacher, what was Miss Eckhart?

There were times when Miss Eckhart's Yankeeness, if not her very origin, some last quality to fade, almost faded. Before some caprice of Virgie's, her spirit dropped its head. The child had it by the lead. Cassie saw Miss Eckhart's spirit as a terrifyingly gentle water-buffalo cow in the story of "Peasie and Beansie" in the reader. And sooner or later, after taming her teacher, Virgie was going to mistreat her. Most of them expected some great scene (pp. 41-42).

Indeed, a "great scene" does soon occur, although it is not one that any of them have foreseen. On a rainy day when Cassie, Virgie, and Jinny stay after their lessons in Miss Eckhart's studio-apartment to wait for a downpour to let up, Miss Eckhart plays a sonata which, Cassie reports, if it "had an origin in a place on earth, it was a place where Virgie even had never been and was not likely ever to go" (p. 49). The listening children, hardly daring to move, are made "uneasy, almost alarmed" by the performance, which they see as if "something had burst out, unwanted, exciting from the wrong person's life" (pp. 49-50). Later, when the local shoe salesman drowns—a man named Mr. Sissum whom the children recognize Miss Erkhart is "sweet on"—the community is presented with another "great scene" in which Miss Eckhart breaks "out of the circle" of mourners at the burial and is caught before going "headlong into the red clay hole" (p. 47). It is because of this demonstration of grief that the Morgana mothers begin to stop their children from taking lessons. Finally, some time after, Virgie's stopping lessons takes away "Miss Eckhart's luck for good" (p. 56), and she goes "down out of sight" (p. 58).

Cassie, like Katie Rainey, is unaware of what her history implies. She does not recognize in her memories of Miss Eckhart that she has witnessed a woman torn between a linear and a cyclical view of time. Cassie's view of time is, like Katie's, historical and linear, and, thus, she cannot comprehend her teacher's struggle. Cassie has never been able to play the piano without the metronome. It is only Virgie who can reject the bullying order of the metronome with its incessant reminder of time perpetually moving forward; it is only Virgie who can draw her teacher away from that narrow view of time which has come to rule Miss Eckhart's frustrated existence. Virgie is special. What Welty shows the reader through Cassie's memories is that, with Virgie's help, Miss Eckhart begins to loose herself from the exacting demands of historical time; that through the creative imagination, which among her students Virgie alone is sensitive of, Miss Eckhart comes to terms with a different kind of time, the kind of time of which Cassie had a glimpse when Miss Eckhart played for them on that rainy day, the kind of time which, like the music itself, is new and old at the same moment, like all music, made new each time it is repeated. It is the time of myth.

Cassie's failure to perceive this is at the heart of Miss Eckhart's frustration. Cassie, in her communal and historical view of the world, is  Miss Eckhart's enemy and yet akin to her. One may conjecture that Miss Eckhart's insistence that Virgie leave Morgana is an expression of new possibility for what she herself has attempted and failed. For it is implied by her origin that Miss Eckhart was once a wanderer like King MacLain. One suspects that she has stumbled into a cage of sorts where in order to survive she has imposed upon herself the strict order of the metronome. It may be, moreover, that in a world of Cassie Morrisons, a world of historicism, the use of the metronome is the only way to teach a concept of time. Miss Eckhart's flyswatter attacks of the wrists of her pupils is perhaps a subtle way of punishing them for their failure to grasp the idea of that other kind of time. Certainly, Miss Eckhart has been sensitive to myth all along. As McHaney points out, Miss Eckhart's recitals are clearly a rite of spring, and throughout *The Golden Apples* she is associated with mythological figures such as Circe, Eurydice, Perseus, and others. It appears that Virgie serves primarily as a catalyst for freeing Miss Eckhart once again from linear order, for opening her up to the life of the wanderer. But Miss Eckhart is too old to wander and, staying in Morgana, she is recognized as an individual opposed to communal history; her actions are interpreted to be a threat to social order.*** Cassie's suspicions concerning Miss Eckhart's disintegration prove correct. In the society where she remains, breaking "out of the circle" can only bring destruction upon her.

In "June Recital," then, Welty has, as in "Shower of Gold," brought together two sets of seemingly opposing forces: history and myth, community and the individual. But here she reexpresses these oppositions in the very structure of the story. While Cassie sits in her room and recalls the past, her brother Loch, in bed with malarial fever, observes the events of the present in the run-down MacLain house next door. Given his father's telescope because he is ill, Loch is able to watch the comings and the goings of several people, including Virgie Rainey, who with her usual precocity has a sailor in hand. They romp in the room upstairs while, unknown to them, Miss Eckhart, having walked into town from the old people's home, enters below; and there, after stuffing the room with torn newspaper, and setting out her once-precious metronome, she tries to burn down the house and accidentally sets fire to herself. Old Man Moody, the town Marshall, and Mr. Fatty Bowles also happen by (they have come to awaken Mr. Holifield, the night watchman, who has been sleeping in the house through the whole affair) and, after a farcical series of attempts, eventually put out the house fire and the fire in Miss Eckhart's hair, and take her away to the mental asylum, while the final caller on the old MacLain house, King MacLain, home again from his wanderings, looks on. In other words, it was Miss Eckhart herself playing the phrase of music which triggered Cassie's memory. Welty ironically demonstrates once more that Cassie has only memory; she is unable to look upon the present which has connections with all the past and future time. Loch calls to her from his room to come join him, but Cassie's answer is telling: "*I ain't got time.*" In fact, Cassie does not have a sense of time other than her historicism. She does not have the capability to look upon the multitudinous reality of the present.

Loch has that capability. Because he does not know as much of the past, he misinterprets the events which he witnesses; he is a poor historian. Nevertheless, he employs what he does know of the past to make sense of the present. The rest he fills in with imagination.

And, with these two, with history and imagination (which is at the heart of myth), Loch discovers a meaning which transcends the literal reality. As with the music of Miss Eckhart, he gives an order to the world in his especial and personal vision which is both old and new. To Loch, Miss Eckhart is logically the "sailor's mother" come to the house after her son who is upstairs, and, as she rips newspaper, he comes to believe that she is decorating the room as if for a party. Gradually, however, he perceives that, in the "splendor" with which the old woman continues to decorate long after everything seems "fanciful and beautiful enough," she is "all alone," that she is "not connected with anything else, with anybody. She was one old woman in the house not bent on dealing punishment" (pp. 27-28). Loch comes to understand that the old woman intends to burn down the house. At first he is vexed, not so much because of the loss of the house which he has come to claim for his own, but because she is going about setting the place on fire the wrong way: she leaves the windows shut tight, allowing for no draft. But when she takes out the metronome and sets it on the piano, Loch is newly fascinated by her slow, bird-like movements, for he now presumes that the box contains dynamite which will be set off by the fire in the piano. Old Man Moody and Mr. Fatty Bowles, men whom Loch recognizes, arrive just in time to put out the fire; but the other man, who happens along and watches Moody's and Bowles' antics through a window as if it were a show, Loch mistakenly identifies. Having no remembrance of King MacLain, Loch thinks he is Mr. Voight, an ex-roomer at the Mac-Lain house in the days of the piano lessons, who had promised Loch a talking bird that could say "Rabbits." Meanwhile, the two men inside discover the ticking metronome, and coming to the same conclusion as Loch, Fatty Bowles throws it out the window. The metronome falls into the weeds just below where Loch has crawled out onto a tree, and Loch retrieves the object. After examining it, he touches and stops its pendulum, takes away its key, pulls the stick into the box and secrets it away as if it were a prize.

What is noteworthy here is that, through his fevered imagination, Loch has made several conclusions which are closer to "reality" than is Cassie's history. Loch immediately makes a connection between the actions of the couple upstairs and those of the woman below, but he also perceives that, despite that connection, Miss Eckhart is terribly alone and separated from that couple. Loch's first belief, that Miss Eckhart is decorating the room as if for a party, is also not far from the truth, for Miss Eckhart's preparation for setting fire to the house is like a party; it is ritualistic. It is evident that in burning the house Miss Eckhart is attempting, in the mythological sense, to stop the flux of time, the time of history, and, with the destruction of what is left of the old, with the destruction of that history, to permit a rejuvenation, a beginning anew.**** Moreover, Loch's association of King MacLain with the man who had promised Loch a bird that could say "Rabbits" is not far from correct, for, as McHaney points out, King MacLain is associated throughout *The Golden Apples* with rabbits, a fact which will become more evident in the story titled "Sir Rabbit." Finally, and most importantly, Loch recognizes the destructive potential of the metronome, of time as seen merely in linear motion, and just as Virgie has previously been able to free herself from that time, so is Loch able to control it; he stops the metronome. As he sits in the sandpile with his new possession buttoned under his shirt, momentarily freed from that destructive rush of time, Loch hears "nothing ticking" but the repetitive music of the crickets—who keep the time of nature and myth—and the sound of "the train going through, ticking its two cars over the Big Black Bridge" (p. 77)—which suggests that in the future, in linear time, Loch will leave Morgana to become one of the special people, a wanderer who partakes of myth.

That evening, Cassie, having returned home from a community hayride, lies thinking in her bed. She recognizes that Miss Eckhart and Virgie Rainey are "human beings terribly at large, roaming on the face of the earth. And there were others of them—human beings, roaming like lost beasts" (p. 85), but Cassie also understands that she is unlike them. As Welty writes of Cassie earlier in the book:

> She could not see herself do an unknown thing. She was not Loch, she was not Miss Eckhart, she was not Virgie Rainey; she was not her mother. She was Cassie in her room, seeing the knowledge and torment beyond her reach, standing at her window singing—in a voice soft, rather full today, and halfway thinking it was pretty (p. 68).

Even as she has a glimpse once again of that other kind of being and time, even as she recalls Yeats' "The Song of the Wandering Aengus" (the poem central to *The Golden Apples* because it concerns the search for fulfillment through wandering and myth), even as the lines of the poem run perfectly through Cassie's head, the lines vanish as they go, the reader is told, "one line yielding to the next, like a torch race" (p. 85), exactly as life itself vanishes in the linear and historical view of time. In the middle of the night Cassie sits up in her bed and repeats out loud one of the lines, "Because a fire was in my head"; but no fire is in her head. The fire has been in Loch, sick with malarial fever, and in Miss Eckhart whose hair caught fire. Cassie falls back, "unresisting." The fact that was in the poem looks in only in her dreams, and, like Katie, Cassie cannot make sense of a reality which exists as dream.

From two different windows, Welty has made clear that there are two perspectives of time, and she continues to work with these perspectives through the rest of the book. The next story, "Sir Rabbit," perfectly counterpoints "Shower of Gold," for in "Sir Rabbit" the events which occur years apart are narrated not through the voice of a historian, but are seen rather through the eyes of Mattie Will as she is raped, first by the MacLain twins, and later by King MacLain himself. Mattie is not the only one who, like Snowdie, directly partakes of myth, but she is one who has heard the myth told and believed it from the start. "Oh-oh. I know you, Mr. King MacLain!" she cries," "I know the way you do" (p. 86). But it is not King the first time; it is his twin sons, who are the "spitting image" of King. And, although they may be somewhat lesser than King, Zeus himself, even Mattie seeing them as two "little meanies coming now that she'd never dreamed of, instead of the one that would have terrified her for the rest of her days" (p. 97), Mattie, nonetheless, obliges and, thus, partakes of myth. As she waits for the two boys to come at her, Mattie feels "at that moment as though somewhere a little boat was going out on a lake, never to come back" (p. 87). Like all experiences grounded in myth, the rape makes Mattie feel as if something is beginning anew, *from the beginning*. The sex act itself takes her back to the beginning, to "the Weakness," and being what King has left her, she will fulfill the patrimony of her maiden name, Sojourner; for, although she stays behind, married to Junior Holifield, she will always be a wanderer at heart. The aftermath of this rape is actually expressed in music, in what I have been suggesting is the perfect analogy of the mythical moment. Mattie sings a song which is concerned with that magical and mysterious world in which she has just participated:

> In the night time,
> At the right time
>   So I've understood
>   'Tis the habit of Sir Rabbit
>   To dance in the wood—(p. 97)

As Ruth Vande Kieft has suggested, however, there is something deprecating about the rhyme. Something has happened to the myth. King has grown older, and Mattie is aware that in his "affront of body" and "sense" there is something "frantic" about his existence. After sex King falls asleep, and is horrified to awaken and find Mattie watching him. And horrified he might well be, for during his sleep she has seen his body parts "looking no more driven than her man's now, or of any more use

71

than a heap of cane thrown up by the mill and left in the pit to dry" (pp. 96-97). For Mattie the myth has begun to disintegrate, perhaps because she has looked at it too carefully, perhaps because it has been fragmented. Mattie now looks upon the earlier experience with the twins almost with nostalgia. "For the first time," the reader is told, "Mattie Will thought they [the twins] were mysterious and sweet-gamboling now she knew not where" (p. 98). That previous participation in myth is for Mattie more meaningful than communion with the myth of which she has heard all her life. And, with that new look to the past, one perceives the beginnings of the transformation of myth to historicism. Perhaps Mattie has changed, or perhaps the times have.

In either case, it is clear in "Moon Lake" that the world has become more complex. The societal urge, which ruled Katie in "Shower of Gold," is more developed in this story, and the communal pressure is stronger, more ensnaring. All of this is made ironic because the action of "Moon Lake" takes place at a supposed retreat from society, a girls' summer camp. Jinny Love Stark, grown older (Jinny was much younger than both Virgie and Cassie on that rainy day when Miss Eckhart played a sonata), and Nina Carmichael are definitely the representatives of this social order, and the orphans, led by a girl named Easter, and the Blacks who work at the camp are clearly outcasts. The only person free from this dichotomous structure is Loch Morrison, now a Boy Scout and Life Saver, who has pitched a tent some distance from everyone else. Accordingly, Welty has set the stage for another encounter between history and myth. But this time the encounter is made more complicated through its occurrence in a world that is very self-aware. Previously, both Katie and Cassie could not always recognize differences between themselves and those with the ability to partake of myth; and to those in whom they did recognize that special awareness, they were protective or, at most, insistent in their attempts to draw them closer to the communal circle and the historical sensibility. But in this new age, Jinny and Nina, completely aware of distinctions, either reject the differences outright or try to possess them.

As Welty presents her, Jinny Love Stark is completely conscious of her role as societal spokesman. For example, Jinny suggests to camp councilor Mrs. Gruenwald, in "the cheerful voice she adopted toward grown people":

> Let's let the orphans go in the water first and get the snakes stirred up.... Then they'll be chased away by the time *we* go in (p. 101).

At another time when Easter suggests that Jinny, Nina, and she play "mumblety-peg," a game neither of the Morgana girls knows, Jinny asks, while "closing the circle," "Who would even want to know?" This "not wanting to know" is precisely Jinny's stance. For the society she represents no longer claims to have special vision; theirs is the *only* vision. Jinny knowingly rejects all realities save her own.

Nina, on the other hand, wants terribly to partake of those realities; she wants more than anything to possess the talents she sees in Easter. Indeed, the compulsion to possess seems the best way to describe the force which rules Nina. Just as she possesses her drinking cup which she permits no one to share, and of which Jinny says, "You don't know Nina.... You'd think it was made of fourteen-carat gold, and didn't come out of the pocket of an old suitcase, that cup" (p. 107), so must Nina possess Easter's ability to share in nature and myth, the capability, which Nina sees in Easter's open hand as she sleeps, to be one with the night:

> Easter's hand hung down, opened outward. Come here, night, Easter might say, tender to a giant, to such a dark thing. And the night, obedient and graceful, would kneel to her. Easter's calloused hand hung open there to the night that had got wholly into the tent (p. 123).

Pitably, Nina opens her hand, stretches it and tries intellectually to will the gesture. Inevitably she fails; she comes to recognize that the "night was not impartial. No, the night loved some more than others, served some more than others" (p. 124).

Earlier in the story, Nina attempts to share in the myth by following Easter into a swamp on the other side of the lake. Upon entering the swamp, which is "all enveloping, dark and at the same time vivid, alarming," she comes to see Moon Lake from "a different aspect altogether" (p. 113). But even in this primordial world, in this return to the beginning of time, Nina is unable to share in myth. She and Easter find a boat which Nina is determined to free, but upon pulling it out of the "sucking, minnow mud," she finds that the boat is chained to shore. For Nina, unlike Mattie Will of "Sir Rabbit," there is no journey in store. As much as she desires, she cannot become a wanderer.

Only Easter and, once again, Loch are destined to take part in that special experience. Every day all the girls are herded together to take their morning dip in the lake. Mrs. Gruenwald hoarsely sings, "Good morning, Mr. Dip, Dip, Dip, with your water just as cold as ice!" (p. 100), and, walking into the lake, she swims away. The girls feebly follow suit, but only the Morgana girls can swim, and even they do little more than stand around in the water holding onto the life rope, "hungry and waiting" until the time when Loch blows his bugle and they can all get out. Nina's sentiments express the girls' detestation of this daily ritual most clearly: "There is nobody and nothing named Mr. Dip; it is not a good morning until you have had coffee, and the water is the temperature of a just-cooling biscuit, thank Goodness" (p. 101).

One morning, however, something exceptional happens. Easter climbs onto the high diving board and, waiting there, suddenly falls into the lake as Exum, a black child, gives her heel the "tenderest, obscurest little brush" (p. 125). Loch swims to the rescue, but Easter is nearly drowned by the time he reaches her, and it takes some time before he successfully resuscitates her. Meanwhile, Miss Lizzie Stark, Jinny's mother, who visits the camp daily, arrives and ineffectively orders that Loch remove himself from the drowned girl sprawled atop the picnic table, while the girls look on, aghast that life-saving is so brutal, so "much worse than they had dreamed" (p. 129).

What they are witnessing is the fulfillment of the ritual in which they have daily failed to participate. Easter has truly gone for a "dip," which archaically means "to baptize by immersion." Easter undergoes a baptism, which mythologically permits the self-renewal which the name she has given herself signifies (her name is spelled Esther), and, through the girls' participation in the experience (they have no choice but to look on, and

Jinny Love even participates by fanning Easter with "a persistence they had not dreamed of" [p. 131]), Easter permits their renewal as well. It allows for a new beginning, for an opening up of the minds of the girls at Moon Lake Camp to the greater awareness of life and death. What Miss Lizzie, the social leader of the community, cannot tolerate, understandably, is Loch's life-saving—which is a metaphorical acting out of a confrontation with the world outside of the community, with chaos, with death. The life-saving act also symbolically represents the sex act, the implantation in Easter of a new seed of life. Now, as Nina observes, all present share in the time of myth: this is a time "far, far ahead of her—...without time moving any more" (p. 134). Miss Lizzie Stark's historicism has no power here. As Parnell Moody tells her: "Can't any of us help it, Miss Lizzie. Can't any of us. It's what he [Loch] came for" (p. 130). Again, Nina sees things momentarily from an entirely different aspect. She faints, loses the consciousness which has prevented her previously from partaking of myth. By the end of the story even Jinny thinks in terms of the future. But her prediction that Nina and she will always be old maids is wrong. She belongs too much to historical time to have vision. Nina and she turn back from their walk to join "the singing" (p. 138), but it is clear that their song will be dictated by the metronome.

While the girls' summer camp still contains some

possibility for myth, Morgana, several years later, does not. Ran MacLain, one of the twins, is now married to Jinny Love Stark, and has left her because she has had an affair with Woody Spights, which, as the title of the story presenting Ran's impassioned plea to his still-missing father suggests, "the whole world knows," at least *his* world, the world of Morgana. And, since the events have already been subsumed into community history, Ran's life is taken over by the community as well. As Miss Perdita Mayo, who daily visits Ran at work in the bank, reports:

> My Circle declares Jinny's going to divorce you, marry Woodrow. I said, Why? Thing of the flesh, I told my Circle, won't last. Sister said you'd kill him, and I said Sister, who are you talking about? If it's Ran MacLain that I knew in his buggy, I said, he's not at all likely to take on to that extent (p. 146).

But Ran *is* ready to kill. Trapped in space, as Miss Eckhart once was, working in a bank caged behind bars, living in a hot rented room in the same house where Miss Eckhart gave piano lessons—perhaps living in the same room—the same house wherein he grew up, and having no place to go but to drive up and down the main street, Ran, at least imaginatively, plots Woody's murder. His mother, Snowdie, exhorts him to move to MacLain, the neighboring town where she now lives, the town where, as its name suggests, myth is still possible; but Ran is too much in love with Jinny and all that she represents to leave. Snowdie warns him, "Son, you're walking around in a dream" (p. 145), but Ran no longer recognizes the significance of that statement and, like Katie and Cassie before him, despairs that the world is made no clearer. He focuses all of his awareness on one event in the past: his wife's infidelity. Ran has no Virgie to help free him from his historical perspective, but he does have Maideen Sumrall, an unimaginative farm girl who has come to town to work at the Seed and Feed store. It is on her that Ran takes out his vengeance. They drive to Vicksburg, and eventually end up in a motel where Ran takes out his father's pistol and, putting the gun to his head, pulls the trigger. The gun is empty. But Maideen is not so fortunate; after the sexual encounter that follows Ran's attempted suicide, she kills herself in the store where she works. Unlike Ran, Maideen acts, and her act has significance. Her mother's maiden name is the same as Mattie Will's, Sojourner. Thus, in a small way, she too is connected with myth. Her death is a sacrificial death which again permits a renewal. We discover later that Ran, after Maideen's death, is reunited with Jinny. The farm girl's suicide even gets him elected as mayor years later. But Ran himself is lost forever to historicism. His existence, like the tale which he tells, lies already in past despair. And, as Welty implies, it is a despair which now "the whole world knows."

Certainly Eugene, Ran's twin brother living in San Francisco, knows that despair. In "Music from Spain" Welty describes the conditions which lead him one morning to slap his wife across the face and leave the house, unconsciously seeking and finding an experience which will permit him again to share in myth. Emma, his wife, is described as a woman with a historical sensibility. She is obsessed by the death of her only child, Fan, and therefore is able to do very little in the present except sit and talk with a neighbor. Eugene himself works at a job of putting together clocks, at a job defined by clock time; waiting at the door is the jeweler's son, watching to see that no one arrives to work late. But on this special morning, Eugene slips past him and comes across the Spanish guitarist whom he and Emma had seen in concert the night before (in one of their only nights out since Fan's death). Eugene saves the guitarist from being hit by an automobile. Through that act a special kinship arises between them, and Eugene and the Spaniard wander together throughout the city all day without being able to speak a word of each other's language.

If the incidents of this story seem unbelievable, it is perhaps because on this special day the events which occur to Eugene are not of that literal and historical world. To the non-visionary they appear as in a dream, but to one who participates in myth they, like all the events which occur in the time of myth in *The Golden Apples*, have great significance. For the Spaniard to whom Eugene attaches himself is another wanderer. As McHaney points out, the Spaniard's face, having "the enchanted presence of a smile on the face of a beast" (p. 173), seems to be the face which looked in at Cassie in her dreams. And, like Miss Eckhart, the guitarist plays a music from far off, some "unbearably rapid or subtle songs of his own country" (p. 183), a music "most unexpected" (p. 173) which makes Eugene feel as if on a "visit to a vast present-time" (p. 174). So it is to be expected that Eugene's journey with the guitarist to the top of a hill overlooking the ocean—where the two men battle, clinging to each other as if they were in love (the entire story is bathed in homoerotic imagery), and where the Spaniard lifts Eugene out over the edge of the cliff, wheeling him in air as if to throw him over before setting him down again—should end in renewal, in a "vision—some niche of clarity, some future" (p. 197-8), some hope for him and Emma. But, as for Ran, the renewal is only temporary. Returning home, Eugene is not met by Emma running to him as he has imagined she might; rather, she sits in her kitchen "talking-away" to her "great friend, Mrs. Herring from next door..."

(p. 201), and together the two women condemn the Spaniard for not fitting their societal requirements: for his long hair, for his laughing out loud at church where he was supposedly seen that morning with a woman by Mrs. Herring, for his "bad taste" (p. 202).

"The Wanderers" takes the reader back to Morgana where Katie Rainey, who began the book, has just died. But Katie is not the only one to die or about to die in this story of the dead. Eugene's body has been sent back to Morgana for burial; Cassie's mother has died, committed suicide some years after her husband's death (Cassie, true to her ability only to remember, memorializes the death by spelling her mother's name in hyacinths); Miss Lizzie Stark is now an old woman, too old even to lay out Katie's body; Snowdie, who lays out the body in Lizzie's stead, is nearly 70; and King, Zeus himself, who has come back home, is terrifying now because he is "too old" (p. 246). The whole town has radically aged. The road by which Katie waited like all the town's old people, "...watching and waiting for something they didn't really know any longer, wouldn't recognize to see it coming in the road" (p. 205), where she waited out her "remaining space of time" (a metaphor which clearly defines time as linear) (p. 206)—that road, everyone says, now "goes the wrong way," which means evidently that the "wrong people" go by on it, those "riding trucks, very fast or heavily loaded, and carrying blades and chains, to chop and haul trees" (p. 213) as they deplete Morgan's Woods. The old myths and their incarnations and even the sacred places have fallen, and those who perceived only in terms of history have become history themselves, replaced by a people who move faster, who are more willing and able to outrun time than Katie, who tries once more, however, just before her death by listing "faster and faster" all the flowers she can think of (pp. 207-8).

Thus Virgie is alone in a house of dead people, alone in the midst of almost all of those who come to the wake and funeral, those who keep her from partaking even of that last ritual left her, death itself. They fondle her, reassure her, protect her as always; but for Virgie, as well as the reader, they are now only ghosts. As Juba, Miss Lizzie's black servant sent to help Virgie, says: "I seen more ghosts than live peoples, round here. Black and white. I seen plenty both. Miss Virgie, some is given to see, some try but is not given" (p. 237). Only King shows vestiges of life. While all listen to the funeral music, he pushes out his "stained lip" and makes a "hideous face at Virgie, like a silent yell. It was a yell at everything—including death, not leaving it out—and he did not mind taking his present animosity out on Virgie Rainey; indeed, he chose her" (p. 227).

King chooses Virgie because he knows that she is one "given to see," that only she can understand that his hideous face is made from the horror and anger that he knows since he can no longer participate in myth. It is a face that Virgie sees and carries with her, not in her dreams, but in her awakened and active mind. After the wake, Virgie crosses the road to the old MacLain place and walks back into the pasture and down to the river. She undresses and lets herself into the water, where after a few moments she hangs "suspended in felicity" (p. 219). So she purifies herself; she is reborn, which in this book of myths one has seen occur time and again. She is now free to lead the life of a wanderer.

After the funeral, she packs, gets into her car, drives to MacLain (still the town connected with myth) and, as it begins to rain, stands under a tree where she suddenly remembers Miss Eckhart and her lessons. But what Virgie remembers is a picture which hung in the studio, Perseus with the head of Medusa. What Virgie perceives about the picture is not merely the heroic act, the act of order which makes visible "a horror in life... a horror in love...the separateness," but, because Virgie "sees things in their time," "she must believe in the Medusa equally with Perseus." Virgie sees the "stroke of the sword in three moments," which occur over and over again in time like music: "Every time Perseus struck off the Medusa's head, there was the beat of time, and the melody. Endless the Medusa, and Perseus endless" (p. 243). Because Virgie sees things not as in a dream, an image of reality, but recognizes and accepts things in their multitudinousness, she sees life in all of its fullness: in the past, present, and future simultaneously. And seeing that, the very structure of time is revealed to her, revealed as a cyclical time. As Welty has written of Faulkner's *Intruder in the Dust*, life is "full of riddles and always starting over" (Welty, "In Yoknapatawpha," *Hudson Review* I [Winter 1949], p. 596).

As Virgie waits under that tree with an old black beggar woman, it is no longer certain whether she will leave or stay. It does not matter. For Virgie, unlike anyone else in the book—except perhaps for Loch on that one summer afternoon—has in that revelation learned how to wander without moving. Remaining where she stands, Virgie listens to the "magical percussion":

> ...the running of the horse and the bear, the stroke of the leopard, the dragon's crusty slither, and the glimmer and the trumpet of the swan (p. 244),

a world where history is embraced by myth.

---

*I emphasize that I am using the word "history" here in its most limited meaning. History, understood properly, is also a thing of flux; the historian is as much a creator as the artist. But here I am using the word "history" to suggest a sensibility which, looking to the past, sees time as progression, as spatialized.

**Actually, the events narrated by Katie Rainey in "Shower of Gold" begin much earlier than this time-span. She reports that her husband Fate claims he saw King MacLain riding in the inauguration parade with Governor Vardaman to the new capitol building. The new capitol was dedicated on June 4, 1903, and Vardaman was elected governor in September of the same year. However, the work actually "begins" a few days after the Halloween day when the MacLain twins frighten away their father and Katie's daughter, Virgie, swallows a button. By the end of this book, Virgie is in her 40s.

***This idea is emphasized by the fact that, when Miss Eckhart is raped by a black man, the community cannot fathom why she does not move away. Again, by staying, Miss Eckhart reminds them of another, more dangerous reality that lies outside of community order.

****Mircea Eliade describes just such a ritual in his *Myth and Reality* (New York: Harper, 1963), pp. 50-53. He calls it the "perfection of the beginnings," for in the myth the "flux of Time implies an ever greater distance from the beginnings," and hence "loss of the original perfection." This implies a complementary idea, he suggests, "That, for *something genuinely new to begin, the vestiges and the ruins of the old cycle must be completely destroyed.*"

WASHINGTON, D.C., 1977
Reprinted from John F. Desmond, ed., *A Still Moment: Essays on the Art of Eudora Welty* (Metuchen, New Jersey: The Scarecrow Press, 1978).

*For several years, I had been trying to watch Max Oph-
uls' great film* The Earrings of Madame de.... *I purchased
a video of the film, but the condition of the print was
so scratchy that I could hardly see the images, let alone
read the subtitles. In late August of 2008, the Los Angeles County Museum of Art showed the film, which I
tried to attend, but preparations for prostate surgery in-
tervened. Just before I went into the hospital, however,
Criterion Films announced a new edition of the film on
DVD, which I ordered. Upon my return home, the film
was waiting for me, and I quickly viewed it and wrote the
essay below which seemed a perfect fit for my concerns of*
My Year 2001.

On the Periphery

MARCEL ACHARD, MAX OPHULS, AND WADEMANT
(WRITERS), BASED ON THE NOVEL *MADAME DE* BY
LOUISE DE VILMORIN, MAX OPHULS (DIRECTOR)
MADAME DE... (THE EARRINGS OF MADAME DE...) /
1953

THE COMTESSE LOUISE DE... is represented in the first
moments of Max Ophuls' *Madame de...* (*The Earrings*

of Madame de...) by only her hand and arm—a fragmented and disembodied being—at home with the objects which she is apparently reviewing, the boxes of jewels and her closets of elaborate gowns and furs. We soon discover that she is choosing from among these precious objects something to sell—and as her entire body slowly comes into perspective, we comprehend that she is attempting to raise money to pay outstanding debts.

She is, so Ophuls tells us, a pampered and frivolous woman, who might have continued her life in such isolated luxury had she not selected to sell a pair of diamond earrings, given to her by her husband. Among her cherished gems and clothes, the earrings are, apparently, her least favorite thing—also an indication, perhaps, of her position regarding her husband. Apparently, she has had neither the courage nor the trust to tell him of her financial situation, even though it soon becomes clear that he would have quickly resolved the problem and overlooked her financial indiscretions.

Once we have glimpsed Louise we see the beautiful woman so attached to these things. Indeed, throughout the film, Ophuls shows off Danielle Darrieux's beauty through her exquisite gowns and jewels in a manner almost reminiscent of today's "fashion" films such as the recently issued *The Duchess* (2008). Ophuls has been neglected, in part, precisely because of the elegance of his films; particularly in the 1950s atmosphere of abstract expressionism and discordant 12-tone music, Ophuls' highly narratively framed histories of sexual indiscretion and innuendo seemed old-fashioned and out of place. Even in his otherwise positive review of this film, Roger Ebert summarizes one standard view of Ophuls' world: *The Earrings of Madame de...* "...is one of the most mannered and contrived love movies ever filmed." As the reader of my essays on film will recall, I am a great admirer of theatrical filmmaking. But I would argue that, except for the *MacGuffin*, the reappearing earrings, the love story Ophuls tells, in terms of the great romances of fiction, is not nearly so contrived and mannered as it may seem.

One must also recall, of course, that any focus on women in 1953 might have been seen, in the testosterone- and smoke-filled rooms of journalism, as simply uninteresting. Critic Molly Haskell summarizes that position best through Richard Roud's comments: "What are Ophuls' subjects? The simplest answer is: women. More specifically, women in love. Most often, women who are unhappily in love, or to whom love brings misfortune of one kind or another."

Obviously things have changed some since those evaluations, and Ophuls' film, thanks to intelligent analyses by critics such as Andrew Sarris, his wife, Molly Haskell, and Pauline Kael, is now recognized as a masterwork, even though, as Haskell notes, it "never seems to attain the universal accolade of 'greatness,' automatically granted to movies like *The Godfather* or *Citizen Kane*."

Ophuls clearly loved Louise de Vilmorin's 1951 novel *because* of the recurring theme of the earrings. It provided him with a structure against which the "real" story, the love between Madame de... and Baron Fabrizio Donati (handsomely played by film director Vittorio De Sica), develops. But in order to even comprehend this structural device, we need to attend not only to the seemingly isolated and pampered world of Louise, but the society of the male characters, represented in an almost dichotomous manner by Louise's husband, Général André de... (Charles Boyer), a military figure who seems to have stepped right out of a book by Ophuls' favorite writer Arthur Schnitzler, and the romantically-inclined ambassador Baron.

Proud, loyal, and outwardly loving of his wife, André is, nonetheless, a man of action. Although he appears to easily forgive his wife's indiscretions, he can do so only because he believes all women to be inferior and irrational beings. They are to be petted and forgiven, never openly chastised. Like Louise's jewelry and furs, they are not worthy of the passion of anger; they are, rather, *possessions*, like a military decoration one wears on one's lapel. It is strange that, although most critics make a great fuss about Louise's relationship (apparently a love affair that is never sexually consummated) with the Baron, they speak little of André's mistress, Lola (described in de Vilmorin's original book simply as "a Spanish lady"). In the French society of the day (perhaps still today) men were expected to have mistresses, but women were shamed for behaving similarly.

If Louise is insensitive about her husband's expensive gift of the earrings, so too is he to his wife—once he has repurchased them from the jeweler to whom Louise has sold them—by presenting them as a parting present to his mistress. Moreover, Ophuls' revealing scene of Louise's and the Général's living arrangements, each bedded in adjoining rooms into which they shout their bed-time messages, demonstrates that, although André may be a man of valor, he is most definitely not a man of passion. As we discover later in the film, he does not even believe in emotions: "Unhappiness," he declares, "is an invented thing."

Is it any wonder then that all of Louise's friends, the society world into which she is cocooned, wish her a better companion: the Baron Fabrizio Donati, a man whose life is devoted to social skills? Ophuls literally whirls the couple into a relationship as he employs Strauss' dizzying waltzes as the *modus operandi* of their romance. Warned never to hope—the Madame is known for leaving all of her hopeful suitors in the lurch—the Baron insinuates himself into Louise's world less as a male intruder than as an expert thief of the heart.

How different is Louise's reaction to his gift of the same diamond earrings compared with the gift from her husband. Now, it appears, the earrings—which he has purchased in Constantinople, where Lola has given them up to pay a gambling debt—are among Louise's most cherished things; she sees them with different eyes.

Pretending to rediscover them in the confines of one of her gloves, Louise proudly wears the earrings to a ball, only to have them snatched away again, this time by her husband, who recognizes in his wife's sudden admiration of them how deeply she has fallen for the Baron. His insistence that she give them up to her baby-bearing niece helps us to realize just how out-of-touch the Madame is with everyday life. Tormented by the loss of her jewels, Louise bends briefly to coddle the

new baby as she breaks into tears. But the tears, quite clearly, have nothing to do with the child, but with the loss of her baubles. For Louise is herself still a child, and will never be able to share the fulfillment of motherhood and adult love.

The Baron may be an expert romancer, but he is, after all, still a diplomat, and with Louise's various indiscretions—her white lies to him, her husband, and even to herself—he has little choice but to break off their relationship. Suddenly the object of so much love and attention is utterly abandoned, without even an escape from the life she was destined to live out. In the beginning of the film Louise declares that she wishes her mother were still living to help her in her decisions. Now she is left only with La Nourrice, her loving and protective nursemaid who tries to draw her into a darker and even more isolated world of tarot and magic. The violence and anger, lurking just below the surface of André's seemingly calm demeanor, explode as he challenges the Baron to a duel—a duel which says nothing of his wife, but is superficially based on the Baron's opposition to the military.

Against love and diplomacy violence often wins

out. Louise, attempting to halt the duel, remains on the periphery of the action—outside of history and event—as she has been all her life, unable to catch her breath. For one of the first times in her existence, her fainting spell is real, as she suffers what most of Ophuls' heroines ultimately suffer, a heart-attack, a breaking of the heart!

LOS ANGELES, SEPTEMBER 24, 2008
Reprinted from *N^th Position* [England] (October 2008).
Reprinted from *Reading Films: My International Cinema* (2012).

Diving into History

ANETTE WADENANT AND MAX OPHULS (ADAPTATION FROM A NOVEL BY CÉCIL SAINT-LAURENT), JACQUES NATANSON (DIALOGUE), MAX OPHULS (DIRECTOR) **LOLA MONTÈS** / 1955, USA 1959

I SAW THIS FILM when I was a college student. Fortunately I recall hardly anything from that early viewing—maybe a version of the butchered English-language film cut down from the original 114 minutes to 90 minutes and presented almost completely in chronological order; but more likely, while I lived in New York, the Pierre Braunberger restoration, in which the movie

had been expanded to 110 minutes and rereleased at the New York Film Festival in 1969, with a commercial release following across the US.

Fortunately, Criterion has finally released a newly restored version (2009) by Tom Burton and others that is about as close to Ophuls' original as one can get.

It is odd even to think that the original audiences were so insensitive to this beautiful film. True, the 1950s filmgoers might not have been prepared for a work that is so obviously artificed, and that reveals much of its story through tableaux vivants and circus acts. Today, Ophuls' masterpiece—a word I rarely use in writing on film—seems to bear a closer relationship to Baz Luhrmann's *Moulin Rouge* than to any Hitchcock thriller of the day. Certainly Ophuls use of color out-does even Luhrmann's vivid palette. More obviously, Ophuls' work is not a coarse frenzy of action, but a carefully nuanced movement of the camera and actors that almost literally cuts and shapes the work before our very eyes. Moreover Ophuls' work fits very nicely with both the thematics and artificed "reality" of theater played out in Jean Renoir's theatrical trilogy: *La Carousse d'Or* (1952), *French Cancan* (1954), and *Elena et les hommes* (1956). So why did Ophuls' work displease its original audiences?

I was not there, and I suspect any speculation I might make could be met with more knowledgeable

suggestions. What is obvious is that Renoir's relationship with strong, sexual women within highly theatrical settings is located almost entirely in the past. There is almost a kind of nostalgia, lovely as it, in Renoir's films. The forceful courtesans of his works, it is clear, do not, *cannot* exist in contemporary life.

Ophuls' *Lola,* on the other hand, although clearly demonstrating events of long ago, is cinematically placed in a mishmash of time, moving non-chronologically through time and space—from her early affair with Liszt, returning to the present of the story played out with circus trappings, then going even further back to her early teenage sexuality, forward again to the circus where the doctor expresses his fears for her future, then back in time to the more recent seduction of Ludwig I, King of Bavaria. Others of her liaisons—with Wagner, Chopin, Dumas, and Alexandre Dujarier—are only hinted at or not even mentioned. In short, the film does not attempt to focus on her entire life, but only upon almost accidental encounters, memories that flash out before her on this one particular night. Rather than traveling through history, Ophuls shows Lola diving, almost at random, into the fragments of her life. There is, one might argue, no truly historical perspective possible for her, only an emotional and sexual one.

So too does Ophuls, using his somewhat stolid and stony-faced actress Martine Carol in a variety of ways, present Lola in numerous opposing positions. She first appears almost as a kind of statue, a representation of herself sitting atop spinning platters at the circus, then lounging as a supine trophy in Liszt's coach, unhappy with her state. Through nearly all the Liszt scenes she lies in bed, bored or pretending to sleep.

Yet later Ophuls and his camera follow her movements vertically and horizontally as she moves straight up, at angles, and out upon the trapeze from which she will eventually make her final dive, which, we fear, may end her life.

Although she is described as a dancer, we never see her dance. She glides in and out of rooms—at one point her future circus master, Peter Ustinov, demanding that she stand still—she floats into chairs and sofas or into benches of her coach. She hovers over the shoulders of her ardent lover, Ludwig. But only once does she even hint that she can dance (and Ustinov, in his brilliantly acted visit to her, outrightly denies that she can). No matter how great of a performer the real Lola might have been, the film Lola clearly performs best in bed. It is difficult to feel sympathy, accordingly, for the emptiness, the loneliness of Lola's current life, even if her loves are less those of a money-grubbing courtesan than those of woman seeking true romance.

I would not suggest, however, that Ophuls really asks for sympathy, even empathy. All that is wondrous about Lola is that she is nearly unstoppable, that she turns the world into action, immediately leaving anything that is dying or dead behind. Like Ophuls' ever-moving camera, she is a life force, willing to put her own being, every night, on the line. In the end, she dives to survive once again. Our final glimpse of her is behind a cage-like construction to where the males of the circus audience are invited to come forward and kiss her hand, as if the very touch of her might regenerate their lives.

It might be useful to remember that the real Lola Montès, after having lived an even busier life than that depicted upon the screen, died at the early age of 42.

LOS ANGELES, NOVEMBER 14, 2011
Reprinted from *World Cinema Review* (November 2011).
Reprinted from *Reading Films: My International Cinema* (2012).

THREE FILMS BY BUDD BOETTICHER

I must admit that of all film genres, my least favorite, at least as an adult, has been the Western. Of course, I recognize those masterworks of John Ford and the works of the later career of Howard Hawks. I too love the great showdown of High Noon. *But by and large, the film Western seldom appealed to me.*

When filmmaker Budd Boetticher died on November 29, 2001, however, I determined to discover why he was so admired for films that were described as grade-B Westerns. What I discovered quite amazed me, and I have become a true fan of his cinematographic gifts and of Randolph Scott's acting abilities. The films I saw were on badly deteriorated tapes, but in 2008 Boetticher's four great films—three of which I write about below—were published on DVD.

In the Middle of Nowhere

BURT KENNEDY (SCREENPLAY), BASED ON A STORY
BY ELMORE LEONARD, BUDD BOETTICHER (DIRECTOR)
THE TALL T / 1957

ON HIS WAY into town to buy a bull, homesteader
Pat Brennan (Randolph Scott) stops by the stage-
coach waystation to visit his friend Hank Parker and
his young son. In this early scene we already sense the
dangers and tension in director Budd Boetticher's vision of the frontier, as, observing someone riding his
way, Parker immediately grabs his rifle. The boy, however, has better eyes than his father and recognizes the
man immediately as their friend, ignoring the calls of
his father warning him to remain still, instead running
forward with anticipation. As Parker soon after tells
Brennan, living "stuck out in the middle of nowhere,
all by yourself, knowin' nobody but stage drivers and
shotguns" "ain't no fit life at all"; certainly it is not a life
he wishes for his son.

The child asks Brennan to bring him some candy back from town, a task to which the laconic and kindly farmer readily agrees. But once in town he is tricked by his former employer—a man who would like Brennan to return to work with him—to bet his horse against his ability to break the bull, which if he succeeds he will receive for free. Tossed into a nearby watering trough, Brennan comically loses, forfeiting his horse. After a quick visit to the candy shop, he is forced to walk the several miles back to his farm. While on route, how-

ever, the stage, driven by his friend Ed Rintoon, passes him, and he hails a ride—over the protests of the couple who have hired it—back to the stead.

Within the coach sit a cowardly bookkeeper, Willard Mims, and his new bride, a severely plain woman (Maureen O'Sullivan) who is the daughter of a wealthy copper miner. Clearly, the bookkeeper has married for money, and although the daughter may look plain, we see her through the eyes of Brennan as a quietly beautiful woman (she is after all Tarzan's beloved Jane). Thus far, accordingly, Boetticher has set up the structure of a seemingly typical Western. We know love will blossom between the lonely Brennan and the miner's daughter; it is just a question of when or how.

But Boetticher's Westerns are not usually what they seem, and a few seconds later we enter an entirely different world, where simple black and white values suddenly disappear. When the stage reaches Parker's station house, we see it has been taken over by three men, Frank Usher (Richard Boone) and his quick-to-draw partners Chink and Billy Jack. Parker and his son are nowhere to be seen, and we suddenly perceive that what we are about to witness in the next hour is a terribly dark vision of western life. Chink shoots the coach driver dead; upon Brennan's inquiry into the whereabouts of Parker and his son, he is told that their bodies have been tossed into the well where a few hours earlier Brennan had watered his horse.

Before we can even catch our breath from this horrific announcement, Usher orders Mims' wife to the house to cook, while Mims quickly strikes a bargain to leave his wife behind while he goes back to demand a ransom payment from her father. Accompanied by Usher, Mims speeds away, while the nearly speechless Brennan—the only one of the group who recognizes it may be best to hold his tongue—and Doretta Mims are cornered into a small cave-like shack from which any attempt to exit is met with gunshots.

Mims and Usher return with the news that the

miner will be sending ransom by the next day; but if there is hope for salvation in that fact, one of Usher's men quickly shoots Mims dead. While Brennan has hidden the truth from the wife that Mims has offered her up for ransom, Usher and his boys now make it clear just how disgusting his role has been, and Doretta beaks down into fearful sobs. Later, Brennan, trying to help her regain her equilibrium, discusses the ridiculousness of her marriage:

PAT BRENNAN: Did you love him?

DORETTA MIMS: I married him.

BRENNAN: That's not what I asked.

DORETTA: Yes! Yes, I did.

BRENNAN: Mrs. Mims, you're a liar. You didn't love him, and never for one minute thought he loved you. That's true, isn't it?

DORETTA: Do you know what it's like to be alone in a camp full of roughneck miners, and a father who holds a quiet hatred for you because you're not the son he's always wanted? Yes, I married Willard Mims because I couldn't stand being alone anymore. I knew all the time he didn't love me, but I didn't care. I thought I'd make him love me...by the time he asked me to marry him, I'd told myself inside for so long that I believed it was me he cared for and not the money.

Such language seems to belong more to the psychological stage dramas of the day—works by William Inge and Tennessee Williams—than the adventure genre of Western movies.

Soon after, moreover, Boetticher's screenplay writer, Burt Kennedy, takes the drama even further into new territory as the cruel murderer Usher reveals in a conversation with Brennan that he hopes one day to get himself a place, "something to belong to," and settle down. Usher goes so far as to insult the two men with whom he rides as "nothin' but animals." Brennan sees through the murderer's self-delusions, however, reminding Usher, "You run with 'em." "Nothin' you can do with 'em," Usher replies. "Nobody ever tried," rejoins Brennan.

Indeed, there is something almost homoerotic about Usher's controlling and manipulative relationship with the two younger villains. And in this fact, there is also a quality in Usher—in his inability to control his own apparent instincts despite his ideals—that makes him oddly likeable, as if given half a chance he might have turned into a man more like Brennan.

We know however, despite Brennan's absurd assurances to Mrs. Mims ("Come on now. It's gonna be a nice day."), that if he does not act quickly they too will be destroyed. As Usher rides off to collect the ransom,

Brennan tricks Chink into believing that Usher intends to leave without them, and the young man quickly rides after Usher. Suggesting to Billy Jack that he "look in on the woman," he captures the boy's gun and kills him. When Usher and Chink return, Brennan shoots them dead, walking off into the sunset with Doretta Mims. He will no longer be alone in "the middle of nowhere."

There is something so dark and grandly absurd about this work that one recognizes its influence upon the work of a contemporary, postmodern dramatist such as Sam Shepard.

LOS ANGELES, OCTOBER 17, 2008
Reprinted from *American Cultural Treasures* (January 2010).
Reprinted from *Reading Films: My International Cinema* (2012).

Burning the Past

BURT KENNEDY (WRITER), BUDD BOETTICHER
(DIRECTOR) **RIDE LONESOME** / 1959

BOETTICHER'S *RIDE LONESOME* begins where most Westerns end, with its bounty-hunter hero Ben Brigade (Randolph Scott) catching up with the murderer Billy John (James Best). Billy, thinking he has outwitted Brigade, is waiting for him, threatening a showdown before revealing he has hidden his men behind nearby rocks, and warning Brigade that if he doesn't turn around and leave, he'll be killed. The wily Brigade, however, admits that he may die, but not before he "cuts" Billy John "in half."

The dim-witted criminal calls off his men, commanding them to tell his brother and his gang that he has been captured, and throughout the rest of the movie, we await the arrival of Frank and his men to save his younger brother.

Meanwhile, Brigade moves forward with his pris-

oner to the nearby way station. But as in *The Tall T*, they realize that something is wrong as they discover two other outlaws, Sam Boone and his long-time partner Whit (James Coburn), have taken charge of the place. Inside waits Mrs. Carrie Lane, before she enters the dramatic scenario, rifle in hand, in an attempt to run them all off; her husband, evidently, has gone to round up some missing horses, leaving her alone. She obviously is a hardy and seemingly unintimidated pioneer woman, ready to defend her domain—until a coach comes crashing into the station, its driver and passengers killed, evidently, by the nearby Indians. Suddenly, it is apparent that her husband is in danger, and that, if Brigade wants to move forward to Santa Cruz with his prisoner, he must join forces with the outlaws.

An overnight stay at the way station reveals the increasing attraction of the men to Mrs. Lane, in particular Boone, who has "seen...in her eyes" that she is "the kind that got a need." To Boone's description of Carrie as a beautiful thing to look at, Brigade replies, with the laconic wit of Burt Kennedy's writing, "She ain't ugly."

While the group awaits the Indians, it becomes apparent that Boone and Whit have gathered at the way station to await Brigade; Boone wants to take Billy John in for the reward, not of money, but of *amnesty* (a word which has taken him a long time to comprehend). For like Usher in *The Tall T*, Boone wants to settle down on a small ranch he's purchased ("I got me a place. Ain't much—not yet it is."); amnesty will free him from his past crime and his role as a gunfighting outlaw; but, obviously, before they can take in Billy John it is clear that Boone must kill one more time.

When the Indians finally arrive the next morning, it is not to fight but to trade a horse for Mrs. Lane. Brigade pretends to play along with them, hopeful that when he refuses the horse as an insufficient price, they will ride off. Warning Carrie not to show any fear in front of the Indians, they ride forward in pretense of the trade; when the chief presents the horse, however, Carrie suddenly breaks down: the horse, she recognizes, is her husband's.

Brigade and his small group ride off, hoping to outrun the Indians, to another burned-out way station, a feat they achieve, killing the Indian chief as the other Indians escape. In the run, however, Carrie's horse has fallen, and Ben spends the night watching the horse, hoping that he can convince it to stand again, while the others urge him to simply shoot it. When, come morning, it finally stands, Boone summarizes the situation: "Looks like we don't need to shoot him either."

Their leisurely movements forward brilliantly reveal the potential dangers through composer Heinz Roemheld's music, which begins as an almost familiar tune accompanying the movement of an ambling horse, but which gradually, sickeningly spirals down into the minor scale before returning to its original cowboy-like melody. Repeated over and over throughout the movie, the music sums up the dread of all those concerned.

When the group finally beds down near an old hanging tree, Boone realizes he must act. He tries to explain to Carrie his position:

BOONE: I got 'a kill him.
CARRIE: Two dogs fighting over the same bone.

Yet Boone and Whit have come to realize that Brigade's trip to Santa Cruz has been an inordinately slow one, as he meanders toward his desti-

nation in the open, for all—Indians and Frank and his gang—to witness. In a conversation with Carrie, Brigade's actions become apparent: it is not Billy John in whom he is interested, but his brother Frank, who years earlier—when Brigade was sheriff—abducted Brigade's wife, hanging her on the tree beneath which they now stand.

When Frank and his men finally do catch up, Brigade has strung Billy to the same tree and is ready to hang him if the elder brother does not come forward alone. Frank has little choice: if he shoots, Billy will be hung, and if he doesn't, he will be killed by Brigade. The outcome is inevitable.

To his horrific crime of the past, Frank has nothing to say but, "I 'most forgot." History, as it is for Boone and Whit, is something to be forgotten. Only moral men such as Brigade can allow memory to guide their acts.

Having achieved his goal, Brigade allows Boone to take in the prisoner and possibly redeem his life, and, as Boone and Carrie ride off to the civilized world, Brigade can be seen burning the hanging tree: the past is laid to rest at last.

LOS ANGELES, OCTOBER 14, 2008
Reprinted from *Reading Films: My International Cinema* (2012).

Amounting to Something

BURT KENNEDY (WRITER), BUDD BOETTICHER
(DIRECTOR) **COMANCHE STATION** / 1960

THE LAST OF Budd Boetticher's Westerns with actor
Randolph Scott, *Comanche Station,* presents a familiar
pattern for those who have seen his films. Although
the movie begins with hero Jefferson Cody seeming to
be captured by Comanche Indians, it soon again becomes apparent that the more dangerous enemies are
the renegade cowboys. For Cody has purposely sought
out the tribe to trade for a white woman whom they
have captured. Although we are not told until late in
the film, we discover that Cody's wife has been taken
10 years before, and during the lonely years since he has
continued to seek her out, trading for the lives of many
captured pioneer wives.

It only takes a few minutes after the woman's release
before writer Burt Kennedy and director Boetticher
begin a series of humorous and, at times, near-absurd

dialogues that pepper their cinematic collaborations. In response to Cody's bemused question, "All right, what's your name?" the woman answers straightforwardly, "Nancy Lowe," to which Cody oddly replies, "I should have known." A few minutes later, Nancy says, "So you came after me. Why?" "I thought it was a good thing," wryly responds the former soldier. It is often the verbal wit of these films more than the inevitable action scenes that makes Boetticher's works so original.

As the two ride into Comanche Station, a way station typical of the Kennedy stories, they are met with three outlaws, Ben Lane (Claude Akins) and his younger partners Frank and Dobie. Cody has known Lane from army life of long ago, when Lane had so brutally killed Indians that Cody, then a major, testified against him, resulting in a court martial for Lane. Lane and his followers, it seems, have been on the track of Mrs. Lowe, determined to bring her back for the re-  ward of $5,000 offered by her husband.

It soon becomes apparent that, in order to claim the money, Lane and his boys will have to kill Cody and, in order to escape suspicion, Mrs. Lowe as well; af- ter all, her husband has offered the money for his wife, dead or alive! But since they must first pass through the remainder of Comanche country, they now need Cody's help, and Cody needs them to help get him and the woman back to civilization.

In several of the films of this series, the Randolph Scott figure, in his need for temporary friendship, seems almost to admire some of the young villains he encounters, and a kinship is often established between the obviously "good" cowboy and the "bad" men. Do- bie recognizes Cody immediately as a good man, a man of the type his father had wished he might become, a man who to his way of thinking has "amounted to something":

DOBIE: A man does one thing, one thing in his
life he could look back on...go proud. That's
enough. Anyway, that's what my pa used to
say.
FRANK: He talked all the time, didn't he.
DOBIE: Yeah. He was a good man. Sure is a shame.
FRANK: Shame?
DOBIE: Yeah, my pa. He never did amount to
anything.

Unlike the other villains of this series, however,
Ben Lane has no intentions of giving up his evil ways
and settling down to farm life. Accordingly, he is perhaps one of Boetticher's least appealing villains. But the
other two men, particularly the young, "gentle" Dobie,
who cannot abide the idea of killing the woman, offer
Cody more kinship.

Dobie would clearly like to fulfill his father's desire. And in his profound loneliness, Cody offers him a
way out that is as close to an offer of deep friendship —
and an obviously homoerotic relationship —as we have
seen in this genre to date.

DOBIE: Me and Frank were riding together up Val
Verde Way. Frank was alone, same as me. And
we heard about this fella who was looking for
some guns. We've been with him ever since.
JEFFERSON CODY: You'll end up on a rope, Dobie.

You know that.

DOBIE: Yes, sir.

JEFFERSON CODY: You could break with him.

DOBIE: I've thought about that. I've thought about that a lot. Frank says, "A man gets used to a thing."

JEFFERSON CODY: Dobie, when we get to Lawrenceburg, you can ride with me for a ways. A man gets tired being all the time alone.

The boy practically gushes in appreciation like a courted maiden. Sadly, fate determines that Dobie will not escape. While on lookout, Frank is killed by the Comanches, and Dobie is forced to stay with Ben. After crossing Comanche territory, Cody steals their rifles and sends them off into the wilds in order to protect the woman and save his own life.

As we have already been told, however, Lane has a plan. Having hidden away another rifle, he insists that Dobie wait for him at a point past where Cody and Mrs. Lowe will have to pass. When Dobie refuses to participate, Lane shoots him in the back.

The resounding murder, however, saves Cody and the woman, and the inevitable showdown ends with Lane's death. Mrs. Lowe is returned to her husband, who we discover has not himself come to save her because he is blind. Her physical beauty, so readily observed by the other men, has meant nothing to him: like Cody, John Lowe's love is clearly a love that transcends.

The final view we have of Jefferson is as he passes behind a large domed rock, coming into view again at a far lower elevation from where we have just observed him. It is as if Cody, a man who once amounted to something, without wife or even someone "to ride with," has collapsed into the landscape over which he formerly prevailed.

LOS ANGELES, OCTOBER 19, 2008
All three essays reprinted from *Nth Position* [England] (October 2008).
Reprinted from *Reading Films: My International Cinema* (2012).

The Making of Allen Ginsberg

ALLEN GINSBERG **JOURNALS: EARLY FIFTIES,
EARLY SIXTIES**, EDITED BY GORDON BALL (NEW YORK:
GROVE PRESS, 1977)

IN MARCH OF 1952, at 26 years of age, Allen Ginsberg could look back upon an active if checkered past: suspension (for writing an "obscene" word on his dorm window); reinstatement and graduation from Columbia University; close friendships with writers Neal Cassady, Jack Kerouac, Herbert Huncke, and William Burroughs; an epiphanic vision of a metaphysical sign accompanied by the voice of William Blake; arrest for possession of stolen goods; and incarceration in the New York State Psychiatric Institute for eight months.

As Ginsberg, only half in jest, writes:

"At 14 I was an introvert, an atheist, a Communist and a Jew....

"At 23...I was already a criminal, a despairing sinner, a dope fiend....

"At 26, I am shy, go out with girls, I write poetry, I am a freelance literary agent and a registered democrat...."

The reader of the *Journals* is thus greeted with what might be unexpected; this is no fiery rhetoric of a revolutionary youth, but a mature voice from a poet who has already "come through" a great many experiences, a poet oppressed by his own "inaction and cowardice & conceit & cringing, running away..." who admits that "I want to find a job," and who asks, "What will I *make* happen to my life?"

Only a decade later, when these journals end, Ginsberg had been transformed—at least in the public consciousness—into a symbol of radical youth, and, soon thereafter, would come to stand as the prophet of the drug culture and mid-'60s hippiedom.

What happened to Ginsberg in those 10 years out of which came both his great poems—*Howl* and *Kaddish*—cannot but be fascinating to anyone interested in American cultural life. But for those seeking such information, Ginsberg's *Journals* may seem to be a great disappointment. A collection of fragmentary descriptions

(mostly of dreams), incomplete poems, brief exposi-
tions. and seemingly unimportant facts, these journals
seldom explain and even less often reflect the public
Ginsberg most of us want to know about.

Ginsberg is not being coy. As he had learned from
haiku, "Never try to write of relations themselves." And
in fact these journals are illuminating when this is taken
into account—illuminating not so much in terms of
what happened to Ginsberg in a social or political context, but in terms of the personality behind the cultural
events.

This is not to say that the *Journals* are merely in-
trospective. All of the five notebooks published here
deal with some aspects of Ginsberg's social and political actions. And two of the largest notebooks, written on travels to Mexico and later to France, Tangier,
Greece, Israel and back to Africa, are often most effec-
tive in their lyrical poetry and descriptive prose. Other
notebooks, moreover, contain a wealth of literary and
political memorabilia, including a conversation with
Ginsberg's hometown poet and friend, William Carlos
Williams, brief descriptions of encounters with Dylan
Thomas, T. S. Eliot, and Eleanor Roosevelt, and, of
course, vignettes of Ginsberg's relationships with close
friends and lovers such as Corso, Cassady, Orlovsky,
and Kerouac.

But the importance of the journals lies in their revelation of Ginsberg's innermost perceptions and fears rather than in outward events. And it is in the dream— and the dream made public through poetry—that Ginsberg comes alive as an individual, as a compelling and compelled man. The most important thing about dreams, Ginsberg explains, "is the existence in them of magical emotions to which waking Consciousness is not ordinarily sentient." What these journals make clear is that above everything else, even political change, it was these dream-like emotions which in these years Ginsberg most sought. If, on the one hand, like Ezra Pound, Ginsberg saw in language's "worn out" abstractions the need for "objective images" which when put haiku-style next to one another made for new relationships in the universe, on the other hand Ginsberg was (and is still) an avowed Romantic, a surrealist poet who, through the unconscious, attempts to uncover the mysteries of the universe present and past.

What these journals reveal then is a poet trying to change objectively the culture in which he lives, while simultaneously coming to terms with a self that fears change and is constantly in search of the security of identity and love. From the beginning of these journals to the last pages written in Mombasa, Ginsberg's dreams betray the conflict. The editor, Gordon Ball, describes the pattern in terms of what he calls "The Room Dreams": Ginsberg dreams of finding himself in a strange room, building or street and attempts to get back to a place of security. Associated with the dream is the presence of an older male, often Ginsberg's brother or close friend, or occasionally poet Louis Ginsberg, the father himself. Always Ginsberg is confused or endangered in these dreams and most often the safety or security he seeks is associated with his past.

Not surprisingly, in the most political period represented in these journals (January 4, 1959–March 16, 1961), in the period in which Ginsberg was writing one of his most personal poems, *Kaddish*, and at the same time composing his political poems as represented in the journals, the dreams increase (accompanied by heavier use of drugs) and are filled with paranoiac fears of the police and the police state in which the dreamer often finds himself. Again and again, the conflict is replayed; the insecure individual must do nightly battle with the artist and his political acts. Even the conscious artist is not free from the fight. As Ginsberg observes at the end of his political poem "Subliminal": "I shouldn't waste my time on America like this. It may be patriotic / but it isn't good art. This is a warning to you Futurists and you Mao Tse-tung...."

Ginsberg obviously found a middle ground in his role as prophet, as one who could speak to the culture of its wrongs, but could also foretell the future, and with that knowledge protect himself from the change it brought. And there is certainly enough evidence to believe that in his role of prophet Ginsberg discovered his true self. The recent disclosures of the CIA and the FBI show Ginsberg's paranoia and political accusations often seem to have been justified; moreover, Ginsberg's October 1959 description of presidential candidate John F. Kennedy—"He has a hole in his back. Thru which Death will enter."—and his November 1960 dream of Richard Nixon—in which Nixon is described as "an abused prisoner alone in his breakfast nook nervously being self-contained reading the papers"—all help the reader to believe in Ginsberg's prophetic powers.

Ultimately, however, the Ginsberg that is most convincing is the man: the highly intelligent, self-questioning critic of his country who, perceiving himself and his countrymen running headlong into destruction, desperately seeks for a shared freedom and peace. This is a difficult book, often unrewarding, and it has a few editorial problems—a confusion in the introductory pages, an erratic use of footnotes and the lack of an index—but for its utterly fascinating revelations about one of our most important poets, it is a remarkable work.

COLLEGE PARK, MARYLAND, SEPTEMBER 1977
Reprinted from *The Washington Post Book World*, October 2, 1977.

Book World *editor Bill McPherson reported to me that soon after this review Ginsberg sent him an angry letter in response. In retrospect, it is clear that I focused too heavily on Ginsberg's doubts and paranoia as opposed to his poetic achievements, but* Journals *also was not centered on that aspect of his work. Over the years I have continued to have ambivalent feelings about Ginsberg's writing, in part because of its insistence upon self-mythology and, ultimately, out of agreement with Allen's own assessment that political writing does not always lead to good art. Yet I cannot imagine the 1950s without the clarion call of* Howl. *And there were wonderful works throughout his entire career.*

About a year after the above review, I delivered a paper on manifestoes at the Modern Language Association, discussing at length the statements of various American poets, Ginsberg among them. Ginsberg was in the audience, and, in the question and answer period, expressed his appreciation that I had at least sought out what poets were attempting through their own comments on their poetics. Afterwards, I personally expressed my admiration of his work. By this time his publisher had used a comment from my review on the back cover of the paperback edition of Journals. All, apparently, had been forgiven— or perhaps Ginsberg recognized that the review I'd written was basically a positive one.

I have previously written in the 2005 volume of My Year about Ginsberg's and my relationship at The William Carlos Williams Centennial Conference in Orono, Maine in 1983.

In November 1996, not long before his death in April 1997, I encountered Allen at the Los Angeles County Museum of Art, in conjunction with a photographic show on William Burroughs. For a few minutes, Ginsberg could not place me, but as soon as he was able to remember who I was, he kept shouting over at me that I should publish Antler. "Antler! He's the great poet. Antler! You need to publish Antler!"

Even nearer his death, Ginsberg sent me a poem (dated 7/5/96) for my "calendar project" that never came into existence. That poem, it seems to me, clearly summarizes his life:

Multiple Identity Questionnaire

"Nature empty, everything's pure;

Naturally pure, that's what I am."

I'm a Jew! A nice jewish boy?
A flaky Buddhist, certainly
Gay in fact pederast? I'm exaggerating?
Not only queer an amateur S & M fan, someone
        should spank me for saying that
Columbia Alumnus, class of '48.
Beat icon, students tell me.
White, if jews are "white race,"
American by birth, passport and residence
Slavic heritage, mama from Vitebsk, father's
        forbears Kamenetz-
Podolska near Lvov.
I'm an intellectual! An anti-intellectual, anti
        academic
Distinguished Professor of English, City
        University of New York,
Manhattanite, Brooklyn College Faculty,
Another middle class liberal,
But lower class second generation immigrant,
Upperclass, I own a condo loft, go to art gallery
        Buddhist vernissage dinner parties with
        Niarchos, Rockefeller, and the Luces
Oh what a sissy, Professor Four-eyes, can't catch
        a baseball or drive a car—courageous
        Shambhala Graduate Warrior!
Still student, chela, disciple, my guru Gelek
        Rinpoche,

Myself addressed "Maestro" in Milan, Venice,
 Napoli
Because Septuagenarian, got Senior Citizen
 discount at Alfalfa
Healthfoods New York subway—
Mr. Sentient Being!—Absolutely empty Non-
 being Non not-being neti neti identity, Maya
 delusion, Nobodaddy, a nonentity

7/5/96 Naropa Tent,
Boulder, CO

LOS ANGELES, SEPTEMBER 20, 2003

Keeping History a Secret

SUSAN HOWE **SECRET HISTORY OF THE DIVIDING LINE** (NEW YORK: TELEPHONE BOOKS, 1978)

IN 1976 *The Western Borders* (Tuumba Press) introduced its readers to the curious wordscapes of Susan Howe, a writer who, in her unusual blend of poetic and narrative elements—a combination that Jonathan Culler has perceptively described as a rapidly emerging "non-genre"—both confuses and intrigues. Like that of the "language poets" (Bruce Andrews, Charles Bernstein, Ray DiPalma, Ron Silliman, Barrett Watten, and others), Howe's work often focuses on language wrenched from the context of the sentence, phrase, even the word itself, and arranged in somewhat unusual typographical configurations on the page. Yet, in antipathy to "language" concerns, the language of *The Western Borders*, fragmented though it was, moved always in the direction of narrative, towards legend, dream and myth. Now, in *The Secret History of the Dividing Line*, Howe not only demonstrates that she has not abandoned this seeming contradiction, but that it is at the very heart of her eccentric vision.

I describe Howe's work as "eccentric" not because it is particularly peculiar or odd, but rather because, in the best sense of that word, her concerns are "out of the ordinary," in fact, are extraordinary. Howe is one of a special breed of authors (I can think of only one other contemporary writer, Bernadette Mayer) who thoroughly explore the terrain between utterance and gesture, between word and act, that narrow gap, as she puts it in *Secret History*, between "salvages or savages."

Indeed, Howe's work suggests the world as actualized *is* a savage one; man in motion is a terrible pagan, battling, plundering, raping his way through history like the Vikings. Any chronicle of man inevitably is filled with terror. Man is a warrior, thus his history is always a tale of war; as Howe writes, "I know the warwhoop in each dusty narrative." Storytelling, then, becomes an act of recreating that horror.

I search the house

hunting out people for trial
. . . .

Needles fell in strands
Daggers like puppets scissored the sky

Millions faced north
the Emperor's last Conscription
the year One.

Some craned away
some used their elbows for meat
families knocking their heads together
and thanking the Gods outloud.

Even in sleep mankind moves through its dreams, in Howe's imagination as "troops of marble messengers," "half grotesque, half magical," enchanted speaking beasts "acting out roles."

Simultaneously, however, Howe implies that the very language that evokes this horrific vision, the very words that chronicle man's mad actions, are also his salvation, a potential salvage. With man's enchantment, with his amazing ability to record his own actions in speech, comes the gift of creation, which, in turn, momentarily stops that flow of meaningless acts through time and space. "Our law," Howe observes, resides in "vocables / of shape or sound." Hence, language must be recognized as a thing apart from nature, as separate from man's headlong rush into chaos. For Howe, just as for the "language" poets, "words need always be torn away" from the "icy tremors of abstraction," from their old associations, and brought to life instead as objects, as things existing in reality in their own right. If language is to have any power, a word must be recognized as a *thing*, as "an object set up to indicate a boundary or position," a "mark/border/bulwark...." Only then can the word be used to heal the devastation like an "anecdote."

Accordingly, the narratives of *Secret History* are purposely attenuated; the history is kept at arm's length, even thwarted. History *must* be kept a secret; it cannot be permitted to dominate, for that would be to abandon the work to chaos, to the mere recounting of man's terrifying inhuman acts. At times in *Secret History* it is almost as if the teller of the tale has been metamorphosed into a stammering, absent-minded historian, as the tale, once present, fortuitously is lost to the sound of human speech:

O
where ere
he He A

ere I were

wher

father father

O it is the old old

myth

......

As Howe has put it in a more recent poem (in *Hawk-Wind*, no. 2 [1979], p. 19), "the real plot was invisible."

On the other hand, Howe recognizes that she must be careful always to walk a fine line between story and speech. If she is to continue to explore that dividing line between chaos and order, she cannot afford to give up the tale. To do so would be to see man as a debilitated schizophrenic, as a creature doomed to act in one way and to think (for to speak *is* to think) in another. Moreover, Howe recognizes language as an object that can be a dangerous thing to a creature in such continual motion; the mark, border, bulwark can suddenly become a boundary, impaling the animal "in a netting of fences." The two, she indicates, must always be superimposed: language, existing in its own space, necessarily must coexist. "The Fortunate Islands," Howe perceived in *The Western Borders*, "are in The Sea of Darkness."

Such a controlled tension invariably results in a certain degree of coyness; and behind that there even may be a kind of fear of permitting the artist his full range as both actor and creator. Yet one is reminded in this of the painfully brilliant fictions of Jane Bowles, a writer who, like Howe, attempted to describe those subtle relationships between act and speech. The tensions inherent in works by writers such as Howe and Bowles stem less from fear than from these authors' commitment to their art, their absolute belief in language and in its ability both to repeat and *make* new reality. One can ask no more of any writer. That Susan Howe has so incredibly combined the tasks of both remembering and creating is an added reward for her readers.

COLLEGE PARK, MARYLAND, 1980
Reprinted from *American Book Review*, II, no. 6 (September-
October 1980).

In 1980, as I recall it, I was assigned by Rochelle Ratner or someone else at The American Book Review *to write about* Secret History of the Dividing Line. *I had not previously read the work of Susan Howe, but as is apparent in the above review, I was very taken with the writing, and I followed her work closely after that, ultimately republishing three of her works—* The Liberties, Pythagorean Silence *and* Defenestration of Prague—*as* The Europe of Trusts *in 1990.*

Coincidentally, soon after this review was published, I was invited to read my own poetry at St. Mark's Church in New York with Susan, to which I readily agreed. As I remember it, that afternoon I attended a concert of music by Steve Reich, where I ran into my friend Peter Frank. After the concert, Peter and I went backstage to talk to Steve, and from there we decided to go out to dinner before the 7:00 o'clock reading. Anyone who knows Peter will confirm that he is often late for events, simply because he packs so many events into one day. After a long dinner, we started out on our voyage to the Church, but Peter insisted that we dart into three art galleries along the way, despite my pleas that I had to get to my own reading. I arrived at St. Mark's about 10 minutes before the reading—with plenty of time, as I saw it. But anyone who knows and loves Susan also knows that she—at least at that time in her life—was rather emotionally high-strung and nervous about public performances. She was in a near frenzy by the time I breezed in. Her first impression of me, accordingly, was not a good one. We later, however, developed a solid friendship.

LOS ANGELES, DECEMBER 12, 2003

When You Feel Like You Can't Breathe

MILO ADDICA AND WILL ROKOS (SCREENPLAY),
MARC FORSTER (DIRECTOR) **MONSTER'S BALL** / 2001

IF FOR NO other reason, *Monster's Ball* deserves our notice simply for devoting its first hour and a half to a series of nearly unbearable events, beginning with the execution of a penitentiary prisoner (played by Sean "P. Diddy" Combs), and followed soon after by a series of racist acts played out by the movie's major figure, Hank Grotowski (Billy Bob Thornton). Then comes a fight between Grotowski and his son, Sonny (Heath Ledger), Sonny's suicide, and the death, by a hit-and-run car, of the child of the executed prisoner. And that's only the beginning: the dead prisoner's widow's car breaks down, she (Halle Berry) loses her job and faces eviction from her apartment.

While all these events are painfully riveting (tears rolled down my face for much of the film), the writ-

ers of this work, Milo Addica and Will Rokos, have embellished their characters with so many dilemmas, along with layers of guilt, silent suffering, and social and political injustices, that it is difficult, at moments, to see through to their humanity upon which the rest of the film depends.

Like his own father, Hank has remained a tower of strength by refusing to face anything coming close to friendship or love. He is a silent loner, choosing not even to face the prostitutes he fucks, rejecting any demonstration of love to his son, and, following in his father's footsteps, ignoring any of the strides of equality made by Blacks in the South. Leader of the correctional officers at the local State prison, he determinedly employs protocol as they prepare to execute their prisoner, urging his men, including his own son, to put all feeling behind them: "You can't think about what he did or anything else about him. It's our job."

Yet through a meeting with the prisoner, his son and wife, and with the focus of the camera on the suffering prisoner (who, for a few dreadful moments, cannot catch his breath for fear of his approaching death), one very much does wonder about what he *did* and gets caught up with his life. One readily comprehends why, as they take the prisoner on his "walk of death," Sonny vomits; but it is for the other officers an unforgiveable act of personal expression.

After the tor-turing series of elec-tric shocks are sent through the pris-oner's body, Hank  confronts his son, leading to an intense fight. The next morning he orders him out of the house. The younger man threatens him with a gun, ending in the down-stairs living room, where he challenges his father: "You hate me?" When Hank admits, "Yeah, I hate you. I re-ally do," the son wails back, "Well, I always loved you," as he puts a bullet through his own heart. When at the funeral the priest asks if Hank would like to read a par-ticular passage from the scriptures, the father vengeful-ly replies: "All I want to have is that dirt hit that box."

It may be a stretch for the viewer, accordingly, to understand why this martinet of a man suddenly quits his job, and soon after, develops a relationship with a Black waitress—the wife, it turns out, of the man who he has just executed—beginning with his decision to help her rush her dying son to the hospital and fall-ing, a few frames later, into a frenzied sexual union in which the couple release their pent-up tension, anger,

 and hate. Upon discovering her identity through a photograph of her husband and a sheaf of drawings she shares with him, he, like his son, vomits out of sympathy and self-disgust. They both have experienced moments, as Hank suggests, when you feel like you can't breathe.

Leticia visits her new lover's house, gift in hand, in response to which Hank's father attempts to displace her with a racist comment. In reaction, Hank places the old man in an assisted living facility, inviting Leticia into his house and bed. They both, presumably, have been born again; yet we have a hard time understanding their transformations, for we are allowed to witness only the aftermath. Such miracles may indeed happen, but in order to sympathize with these new beings, we have to first comprehend them as humans instead of the typological characters to whom we have been introduced.

It appears that even the filmmakers are not sure their characters' sudden love will survive. As Hank goes to fetch ice cream in celebration of their new life together, Leticia wanders to the attic, where she discovers the drawings her husband has made of Hank and his son on the last night of his life. The secret history of her lover is suddenly revealed, and her passionate response is, understandably, fury. When he returns, however, and she is invited to join him on the porch, she says nothing about her discovery, as he quietly speculates: "I think we're going to be all right." Perhaps history, in a world such as the one these two beings have inhabited, *is* best forgotten.

LOS ANGELES, DECEMBER 29, 2001
Reprinted from *Green Integer Review* (December 2001).
Reprinted from *Reading Films: My International Cinema* (2012).

Up in Smoke

LEONARD BERNSTEIN (LIBRETTO AND MUSIC)
TROUBLE IN TAHITI, PREMIERED AT BRANDEIS UNIVER-
SITY ON JUNE 12, 1952 / WHAT I DESCRIBE BELOW WAS
PERFORMED BY THE CITY OF LONDON SINFONIA CON-
DUCTED BY PAUL DANIEL, IN A FILM VERSION DIRECTED
BY TOM CAIRNS / 2001

I HAVE ALWAYS been a great admirer of Leonard Bernstein's short opera *Trouble in Tahiti,* and, accordingly, I was delighted when my companion Howard recently brought home from the library the 2001 DVD cinematic recording, performed by the City of London Sinfonia and directed by Tom Cairns.

Using iconographical advertising images of the early 1950s, and moving the opera between each of its seven scenes into the city streets, Cairns presents a fantasy-like vision of suburbia in Bernstein's "pop"-art conception of the period.

But behind the postwar paean to the joys of suburban life, sung mostly by the three-person chorus—

> Mornin' sun kisses the windows,
> Kisses the walls
> Of the little white house;
> Kisses the door-knob, kisses the roof,
> Kisses the door-knob and pretty red roof
> Of the little white house in Scarsdale.

—there is a crueler reality that shares much with the writings of the period by J. D. Salinger, Vladimir Nabokov, Allen Ginsberg, and, later, Edward Albee. Dinah and Sam have seemingly everything they might want, he a good job, she a beautiful home with the latest appliances, and a child right out of a Norman Rockwell catalogue, shown in the first scene dressed in a cowboy suit, watching a cartoon that seems to be teaching the important lesson of American accumulation of goods. The couple begins their interchange with full hostility, Sam (Karl Daymond) singing, "How could you say that thing that you did in front of the kid!," Dinah (Stephanie Novacek) reacting, "You were the first to go up in smoke." Both are "sick of this life," the humiliations, "the nagging," the impossibility of having a friendly conversation.

Together they seem oblivious of their son, who slips away at the first sign of the argument. Sam hasn't even time to attend an evening play in which Junior acts; a handball tournament at his gym is of greater importance; and despite her  criticism of his values, Dinah too, we later discover, misses the event.

The couple are both trapped in their own worlds: Sam in a job that keeps money away from some while openly giving it to others through a value system where, he argues, some men "are flabby and some men are thin," Dinah torn between sentimental self-analysis (her beautiful aria "A Quiet Place" is little more than a dream of desire instead of a deep subconscious revelation) and total fantasy, wonderfully acted out in a drunken retelling of the plot of the movie "Trouble in Tahiti." Both are adult children who live in a world no more real than the Technicolor advertisements surrounding them. Even as they encounter one another on the street, they lie to escape each other's company. Their promised "talk" turns into another trip to the "Super Silver Screen." Any possibility of real communication

vanishes like smoke as they truly "Skid a lit day" (one of the scat phrases sung by the chorus).

In short, there is no real solution possible in this short satire, and we understand why Bernstein would want to revisit this material in his more substantial late opera *A Quiet Place*, wherein Dinah has just died, and Sam's two children, Junior and Dede, return home, along with Dede's husband and Junior's former boyfriend, Francois. These figures are no freer from angst than Sam and Dinah had been, but they do find, by opera's end, at least a temporary release from their own histories, signified most clearly by Junior's tossing the pages of Dinah's diary (in which she has revealed both her hate of the marriage and her love for her family) into the air, after which a short-lived quietude descends upon "the little white house in Scarsdale…Highland Park, Shaker Heights, Michigan Falls, Beverly Hills, Suburbia."

It is interesting to note that Bernstein's own parents were named Sam and Dinah. And one wonders, despite Bernstein's more successful marriage, how much the tensions between man and wife are an expression of his own homosexual desires. He was himself a man torn between a need for a quiet life in which to compose and the reality, as an internationally renowned conductor, of a completely public one.

LOS ANGELES, DECEMBER 20, 2009
Reprinted from *American Cultural Treasures* (January 2010).

In early April 2012, my companion Howard heard on the radio of a young Los Angeles opera company's plans to revive their first operatic production, Trouble in Tahiti, *in a small theater space in a Santa Monica park. He immediately called for tickets.*

On Sunday, April 15th, the day after we had watched the HD-live production of the MET's La Traviata, *Howard and I attended this amateur production of the Pacific Opera Project. The singers, all of whom had performed in small companies and in lesser roles in professional opera groups, introduced themselves, first performing—almost as a sort of bonus and promotion for their upcoming production, in Pasadena, of* Cosi Fan Tutte—*a medley of works from the Bernstein songbook, including numbers from* Wonderful Town *and* West Side Story. *Although their performances were certainly competent, the actors hammed-up their numbers a great deal, and their vocal ranges were not always best suited for the musical theater numbers they performed.*

Their performance of Trouble in Tahiti, *however, was near perfect—at least vocally. Using a minimal set of interlinked, painted walls, the trio of the girl (Tara Alexander) and two boys (Robert Norman and Ryan Reithmeier) perfectly captured Bernstein's jazz-inspired riffs on "the little white house" in the numerous American suburbs where they exist. Jessica Marmey and Phil Meyer expertly played the central couple, Dinah and Sam, as they fight, battle, and wander through a day in their tortured lives, each escaping into fantasy worlds—Sam into his vision of male-bonded power-brokers and Dinah into the romance of the movie she has seen, loved, and yet mocks. Her lovely aria of a dream of "a quiet place" was particularly well done; such longing almost breaks the heart. But*

this is a couple, after all, who both make up excuses, when they encounter each other in the city, for why they cannot share lunch, only to sit, each of them, lonely and unfulfilled.

The remarkable thing about this small production is that, playing where it did, in a small local park in an intimate theater with about 60 audience members, it still absolutely charmed its audience in way that, after experiencing so many years of professional theater and opera, one begins to forget is at the heart of the art. It is a bit like attending a high school performance of a musical or opera about which one has little expectations, only to be suddenly astounded by the freshness and resplendent originality of the work. While the film version I review above was brilliantly conceived and performed, this smaller production seemed somehow to get at the very heart of Bernstein's simple two-piece operatic melodrama, and we both left the theater filled with a new kind of wonderment for both the piece and these young performers. Sometimes one simply has to go back to the roots of how one came to love theater and opera in the first place to rediscover the simple marvel of talented individuals standing upon—in this case—a *nearly empty stage and opening their mouths to sing out the pleasures and sorrows of life. Unlike all the productions of operas we have recently seen, the singers of this* Trouble in Tahiti *stood outside the entrance to the theater after the performance like the minister and chorus of a small town church to greet their congregation. We all shook hands and went home spiritually uplifted.*

LOS ANGELES, MARCH 21, 2012
Reprinted from Green Integer Blog *(March 2012).*

Truth-Telling in a World Of Lies

JUAN GOYTISOLO **THE GARDEN OF SECRETS**,
TRANSLATED FROM THE SPANISH BY PETER BUSH (LON-
DON: SERPENT'S TAIL, 2001)

LIVING IN MARRAKECH'S me-
dina, Spanish novelist Juan
Goytisolo has published at least
15 works of fiction in English.
The most recent, *The Garden of
Secrets*, like most of his preced-
ing works, is in part an attack
on the author's native Spain
and, in particular, on Franco and
the Fascists. Indeed, like James

Joyce, Samuel Beckett, Thomas Bernhard and other
great writers who lived in exile and often loathed their
homelands, Goytisolo has spent most of his life attack-
ing the values present and past of his own country. His
most recent novel, *Carajicomedia* (A Cock-Eyed Com-

edy)—now a bestseller in Spain—attacks the Spanish Catholic Church and its ancillary secret society, Opus Dei.

In part, Goytisolo's literary warfare with Spain has much to do with the general Castilian oppression of the Catalan minority. As a recent interview with Goytisolo revealed, his Catalan mother's parents were not permitted to speak to the family in their own language. His father, a chemical company executive, supported Franco and was later imprisoned by the Republicans; his mother was killed by Franco's bombs in Barcelona, the Catalonian capital, which, until 1939, remained the Loyalist center of the Spanish Civil War and was accordingly severely punished by Franco and his forces. The young Goytisolo was forced into exile. Over the years, living in Paris, Morocco and elsewhere, Goytisolo came to be a passionate supporter of Arab culture, and in his novels and other writings he argues for the Spain of Moorish and Jewish roots. His struggles against fascism are not directed merely at the Franco past of his country but also at the Serbian nationalism of Slbodan Milosevic, the Russian treatment of the Chechens, and Israeli relations with the Palestinians (his book *El País, Landscape of War: From Sarajevo to Chechnya* was published by City Lights Books last year). Once a supporter of Cuban Communism, he later disavowed his support after visits to that country in which he witnessed the oppression of the African and Asian cultures as well as of homosexuals. Moreover, Goytisolo's own bisexuality, which he discusses in his two-volume autobiography, *Forbidden Territory* and *Realm of Strife,* has led him to strong moral statements against sexual tyranny as well. He claims his true mentor to be Jean Genet.

All of these issues merge in *The Garden of Secrets*, which tells the fictional life of a Spanish poet named Eusebio—a homosexual friend of the great authors Federico García Lorca and Luis Cernuda—who is arrested by Franco's forces and imprisoned in the military psychiatric center in Melilla at the beginning of the 1936 rebellion. But this is not an ordinary fictional biography, told in the third person. Like Orson Welles' exploration of the life of Charles Foster Kane in *Citizen Kane*, Goytisolo's is a Rashomon-like tale with 28 tellers, one for each letter of the Arabic alphabet. Sitting in their garden, which one of the figures describes as "make-believe," the Readers' Circle meets for three weeks, each member telling his or her own version of stories about the mysterious poet, his arrest, escape, and later life. Obviously, they are attracted by the rumors and myths surrounding Eusebio just as American readers have been attracted to figures like Charles Bukowski, Jack Kerouac and—in a previous generation—William Randolph Hearst.

Unlike *Citizen Kane*, however, Goytisolo supplies

no Rosebud to draw his themes—his multifaceted version of reality—together. As in all the works of this great experimental writer, there is no single truth. Part of the joy of reading the novel, in fact, is in the various styles, from high poetic diction to the ribald language of sex films, as well as in the methods and genres that the members of the group employ. Some are highly factual, recounting Eusebio's surprise arrest, his imprisonment and tortures; one teller extracts the supposed interrogation of the prisoner with regard to an inquiry into the sexual proclivities of the military leaders who imprisoned him. Some members of the group are of the belief that Eusebio, dressed as a woman, escaped to Morocco; others argue that he escaped through the intervention of his brother-in-law, an officer in the fascist army. The story, popular with many members of the group, is that he fell under the sway of the Falange leaders Veremundo and Basilio, who engaged in all-male orgies in the army camp, and that he escaped through their help; one member of the "secret garden" even presents a film proposal—in the manner of Luchino Visconti's *The Damned*—of these sexual events.

One reader proposes that, after Eusebio's escape, he lived with the everyday citizens of Marrakech as a servant to a woodcutter. Another suggests he became a religious man and is still seen as the holy man by some. Several argue that he involved himself with the wealthy

Madame S., and one reader—in complete abandonment of the character—tells the story of Madame S.'s cook. Taking the subject in yet another direction, one woman reader, "just wild about novels and stories seething with colorful characters and awesome incident," ends her investigation of Eusebio and tells a magical-realist tale of a man who transforms himself into a stork in order to spy on his wife and her lover.

Later in the fiction, others conflate Eusebio with bizarre figures such as Alphonse von Worden, a Polish aristocrat who lives with a Filipino lover, watches old movies night and day and dresses in drag. In bringing that name into his narrative, Goytisolo opens up a Chinese box-like association that is remarkably similar to the Polish count Jan Potocki's *The Saragossa Manuscript*, a fiction like the *Arabian Nights* in which the hero, similarly named Alfonso von Worden undergoes a number of tests to prove his courage; at the castle of a mysterious magician, he is told a series of sometimes contradictory stories not unlike those in Goytisolo's own novel.

Several antithetical stories are told surrounding Goytisolo's von Worden figure, whose outrageous behavior ends in his murder at his own doorstep. One of the members of the garden group gets booed off the floor for his academic rendering of his own arrival in Marrakech, which absolutely overflows with obscure

Arab words and numerous scholarly footnotes.

The penultimate story is told, from the grave, by Eusebio himself, who pleads not so much for a reconsideration of his own portrayals—although he describes the Readers' Circle as "a monster with repulsive heads"—but for better portraitures of his beloved sister and Madame S. But his arguments shed no more light on matters than any of the other fictions the group has created. In their final act, the group creates the author himself, toying with several names ("Goitisolo," "Goitizolo") until they come upon the one they choose: "Goytisolo...Juan...Lackland, Landless, the Baptist, the Apostle"—all references to phrases and titles in Goytisolo's other works.

Goytisolo's tale is not just about a fictitious poet but also about the nature of storytelling, and concerns the whole milieu of a culture that destroys men and women "in a climate of fanatic hysteria and persecution." It is about a world that perceives homosexuality, for example, as "odious to God and his angels, responsible moreover, as in other years, for the fatal decadence of the nation, the ruination of Spain," about a world that describes poems that do not praise God and the fatherland as the writing of "the perverts' perineal muse, coarse sand-swept desert songs, demagogic hot air without the pulse of poetry, oozing plebeian pores, unnatural thrills, forbidden pleasures."

Such a milieu is, quite obviously, something endured not just by Spain and Goytisolo's Eusebio, but suffered by those under any fascist or dictatorial rule throughout the centuries. And in this context, in which everything is turned on its head, there can be no truth. One cannot lay A beside B (or, in this novel's case, "alif" beside "baa") in order to create a synthesis if both realities are founded on the insanity of those seeking control over others' lives. In Goytisolo's world all the tales are true—or none.

In *The Garden of Secrets* Goytisolo has given us a beautifully written metaphor for what it means to seek out the truth in a world often dominated by lies.

LOS ANGELES, APRIL 2001

Reprinted from *Los Angeles Times Book Review*, Sunday, April 22, 2001.

The Black Flame: Lies in a World of Truth

PER OLOV ENQUIST **LIVLÄKARENS BESÖK** (STOCK-
HOLM: NORSTEDTS FÖRLAG, 1999), TRANSLATED FROM
THE SWEDISH BY TIINA NUNNALLY AS **THE ROYAL
PHYSICIAN'S VISIT** (NEW YORK: THE OVERLOOK PRESS,
2001)

THE WEB-BASED encyclopedia entries on Christian VII of Denmark each restate that the young king, who came to power at the age of 17 in 1766, "had a winning personality and considerable talent," but was "badly educated," terrorized by his governor, Detlev Reventlow, and "debauched by corrupt pages." He suffered,  so the entries tell us, possibly from schizophrenia. After his marriage to Princess Caroline Matilda (Queen

Caroline Matilda), he "abandoned himself to the worst excesses, especially debauchery," giving himself up to the courtesan Støviete-Cathrine, declaring he could not love Caroline because it was "unfashionable to love one's wife." Thereafter he "sank into a condition of mental stupor" with the symptoms of paranoia, self-mutilation, and hallucinations.

The entries concur that he "became submissive to *upstart* (italics my own) Johann Friedrich Struensee, who rose to power in the late 1760s." The neglected Caroline "drifted into an affair with Struensee. Without explaining the palace coup, the encyclopedias report that the king's marriage to Caroline Matilda was dissolved. Struensee was arrested and executed, Caroline sent, without her children, Frederick VI and Princess Louise Augusta (possibly Struensee's daughter), into exile in Celle. The government continued to be run by Christian "under the pressure" of his grandmother, Juliana Maria of Brunswick-Wolfenbüttel, and the "Danish politician" Ove Høegh-Guldberg until Frederick took over in 1784.

I don't know of the veracity of these recountings (repeated, word for word, on several online encyclopedias, including Wikipedia), but it sounds suspiciously like some official whitewash of events. Nowhere, for example, is there any report of changes in law accomplished by "the upstart" Struensee; indeed, one report

claims no changes were effected. Nothing is said at all about Struensee's own links to, nor the young King's involvement with, Enlightenment figures such as Voltaire and Diderot.

Thank heaven for Swedish writer Per Olov Enquist's new fiction, *The Royal Physician's Visit*, which, whether it is a true story or not (although the historical research Enquist has put into this writing is quite apparent), reads as a far more truthful and, quite frankly, believable and fascinating history than that touted by supposedly learnèd sources. Even if the account I outlined in the first two paragraphs is historically correct, give me Enquist's fictional version of reality; I can better live with that.

For Enquist the tutor Reverdil was a loving and enlightened young teacher dealing with an already mad boy-pupil who, through the tyrannies of the King's father and court ministers, had come to believe that his whole world was, as Shakespeare put it, "a stage," upon which clearly he had not yet properly learned his part. Most of Christian's time, accordingly, was spent in trying to discover how to "play his role." It is clear that this child had no other understanding of "play," and cowered away from the men who were suddenly thrust upon him as his subjects.

Enquist begins his historical fiction by providing us with the report of British Ambassador Robert Murray, written four years after Struensee's death, of attending a dinner where the childlike "mad" King Christian "began wandering around the audience, muttering, his face twitching oddly," under the watchful eye of Guldberg, whose role, according to Murray, seemed to be that of a father with a sick child. Despite the strange behavior of the King, the court basically ignored him, even when he began to grow loud and disruptive. In the middle of a play by the French writer Gresset, Christian "suddenly got up from his seat...staggered up onto the stage, and began behaving as if he were one of the actors.... It was clear that the King was strongly engaged in the play and believed himself to be one of the actors, but Guldberg calmly went up on stage and kindly took the King by the hand. The monarch fell silent at once and allowed himself to be led back to his seat."

The "Danish politician," in Enquist's telling, was a minor court figure who through quiet stealth and insinuation, with the help of the Dowager Queen, negotiated the uprising four years earlier against Struensee, not so much for their own gain as for their hatred of Struensee's Enlightenment policies; part of the old guard, they preferred the religious restrictions which had so long controlled the populace, forcing them into lives of poverty and misery.

Into this mad world had stepped a young doctor from Altona, Johann Friedrich Struensee, whom court advisors, terrified by the young King's behavior, sought out as a kind of mentor-protector for Christian. A quiet man, happy to work as a local doctor, equally treating the rich and the poor alike, Struensee, at first, wanted no part of government involvement, and refused Count Rantzau's entreaties, but gradually was convinced.

As early as Reverdil's tutelage, Christian, in moments of sanity, had read major Enlightenment figures such as Voltaire, and had once written him, to which Voltaire magnanimously had responded. Before Struensee's entry into court, Guldberg and others had exiled a young courtesan, Bottine Cathrine, who, given Christian's inability to sexually engage his young Queen (in Enquist's telling the two engaged in sexual activity, if you can describe it as that, only once), had provided the King with a kind of maternal love. In secret search of that woman, who the mad King described as the "Sovereign of the Universe," Christian, with court members, undertook a European journey during which he met with several Enlightenment figures, Diderot taking Struensee aside to share with him Voltaire's message:

"My friend Voltaire is in the habit of saying that sometimes, by chance, history opens up a unique...aperture to the future."

"Is that so?"

"And then one should step through."

In the years following, Struensee, against his own doubts and fears and because of what he recognized was the "dark flame" of the King, took that momentous step, ordering, with the King's signature, that all court declarations pass through him. Within the short period of his powerful rule, Struensee made hundreds of enlightened changes to Danish law, changes that significantly altered the freedoms of Denmark's masses. The problem is that these uneducated masses had no comprehension of what the changes meant, and Struensee, in turn, had no deep comprehension of the "common folk" for which he was fighting. Agitators such as Guldberg and other court lackeys found it easy, through pamphlets and other methods, to bring suspicion upon most of Struensee's important changes of law.

The young British-born Queen, understandably, was lonely and without sexual satisfaction, and Struensee, at least in Enquist's version, was encouraged by the King to take her off his hands. Perhaps the greatest of Struensee's failures was his inability to perceive how an affair with the Queen might end in his downfall. Yet, the couple, who soon fell in love, were stupidly open about their affair, even after Matilda became pregnant with Struensee's child. That affair, above everything else he did, doomed him in a world were Medieval concepts still held sway over the minds of individuals both outside and within the court.

After a near perfect summer at the King's castle at Hirschholm—a castle that, in the people's retribution for Struensee's and Matilda's relationship would soon be completely destroyed, brick by brick—Struensee and the Queen were arrested. Although the German had long feared just such an end, it was nearly incomprehensible to him, after his "step through the aperture," that the good he was attempting to accomplish, such a determined and often difficult search of the truth, should end in such hatred. What had he done wrong, he queried of himself again and again.

Enquist does not provide an easy answer. Love and truth were simply not what the populace wanted at that very moment. Yet the huge crowds that gathered for his execution left it not as a mob, but, in Enquist's fable, as a citizenry disgusted by what they had just seen. Despite Guldberg's and the Dowager Queen's evil machinations, despite even the "dark flame" that Christian's mind had spread over the kingdom, reason did ultimately prevail. Men and women had recognized in "the Struensee era" what was possible, and with the reign of Christian's son came many of the changes that Guldberg had worked to abolish. In Enquist's engaging retelling of the tale, history could not entirely be silenced, a "truth" I would prefer to believe.

LOS ANGELES, DECEMBER 14, 2009
Reprinted from *Green Integer Blog* (December 2009).

Lies in a World of Lies

ISAK DINESEN **EHRENGARD** (NEW YORK: VINTAGE
BOOKS, 1975)

THE NOTED DANISH storyteller Isak Dinesen's novella *Ehrengard* is a tale of lies. Eager to marry off their son, the Grand Duke and Grand Duchess of Babenhausen arrange, through the artist Geheimrat Wolfgang Cazotte, to have Prince Lothar meet with Princess Ludmilla of the house of Leuchtenstein. As in any such fable—and Dinesen's story has a great deal in common with a fairy-tale romance—the couple immediately fall in love, and are speedily wed. Unfortunately, the Princess suddenly discovers herself pregnant, due with child before the proper time has elapsed after their betrothal.

What to do without causing a scandal?

Upon discovering the predicament, the Grand Duchess arranges for the two to retreat to the country estate, Schloss Rosenbad, where, accompanied by only a few stalwart loyalists, Cazotte among them, the couple will remain until a sufficient time passes after the birth for them to announce the new heir.

Among those joining the Rosenbad (dubbed by the participants as Venusburg) party is the beautiful Ehrengard von Schreckenstein, with whom Cazotte soon falls in love.

A child Prince is born, and the court is overjoyed with the boy's perfection. Indeed the whole fabrication seems to be working wonderfully. Even Cazotte, a wily and seasoned figure, is overjoyed by the beauty of the royal family and the countryside. One night, however, while taking in the rapturously beautiful sunset, he accidentally comes across Ehrengard and her maid swimming nude in a nearby brook. Overwhelmed by her beauty, he is determined to seduce her, not through the usual manly wiles, but by painting her so precisely that when she witnesses the artwork a blush will rise to her face with the recognition of what has occurred, making her, he imagines, his love alone.

So begins Cazotte's dangerous voyeurism, seemingly encouraged by Ehrengard's continued trips to the stream. At one point she even seems to taunt the painter to accomplish his abstract rape:

> My maid tells me," she said, "that you want to paint
> a picture. Out by the east of the house. I wish to
> tell you that I will be there every morning, at six
> o'clock."

Fear and trembling ensue.

Meanwhile, enemies of the court, particularly
Duke Marbod and other intriguers, suspect something
is unusual about the gathering at this castle. Lispbeth, a
woman hired to suckle the new Prince, has a husband,
Matthias, whom she has left behind, who is jealous for
her being taken from him, particularly since she has,
at home, a suckling child of her own, and she has told
him there is no child at the court. Inspecting the castle
grounds, Matthias encounters his wife. She, in turn, is
so fearful of scandal that she reveals that there is a child,
and she will show it to him the next day.

Marbod and the others are delighted to hear from
Matthias the new information, and with him they plot
the abduction of his wife and the baby, determined
to meet up at the Blue Boar, a nearby inn. When the
absence of the child is discovered, both Cazotte and
Ehrengard race toward the inn, discovering the nurse,
Matthias, and others are within. Even more surprisingly Ehrengard encounters there her fiancée, Kurt von

Blittersdorff, who is startled by her looks:

> "Ehrengard!" Kurt von Blittersdorff cried out
> in the highest amazement.
> The girl's cheeks as she tossed back her hair
> were all aflame and her eyes shining. She opened
> her lips as if to cry his own name back, then stiff-
> ened, like a child caught red-handed.

Racing to the room where the child and nurse are imprisoned, Ehrengard ignores Kurt's inquiries. He follows, and upon seeing a child demands to know, "What
child is it?"

At that very moment Cazotte also arrives, just in
time to have two more impossible lies cast into the
comic foray. Ehrengard claims it is *her* child, and when
all demand to know who was the father, she answers:
"Herr Cazotte is the father of my child."

In a stroke of brilliant irony, Dinesen has suddenly
reversed the character roles, as Ehrengard accomplishes
what Cazotte had hoped to impose upon her:

> At these words Herr Cazotte's blood was drawn
> upwards, as from the profoundest wells of his be-
> ing, till it colored him over like a transparent crim-
> son veil. His brow and cheeks, all on their own,
> radiated a divine fire, a celestial, deep rose flame, as
> if they were giving away a long kept secret.

The story of deceit has come to an end, with the first glimmer of truth finally revealed: it is Ehrengard who has seduced the great "Casanova" Cazotte.

It hardly matters that in an epilogue we discover that everything is later straightened out, that Ehrengard is married to Kurt with "the light blue ribbon of the Order of St. Stephan" (an award given to noble ladies for service to the house of Fugger-Babenhausen) pinned upon her white satin frock. For the royal houses of Dinesen's tale have lied only in order to be saved again by her lies. And unable to face the truth of his love, Cazotte escapes to Rome to paint a portrait of the Pope.

NEW YORK, SEPTEMBER 18, 2009
Reprinted from *EXPLORING*fictions (October 2009).

A Double Language

ORSON WELLES (WRITER), BASED ON A NOVEL BY
SHERWOOD KING, WILLIAM CASTLE, CHARLES LEDERER,
AND FLETCHER MARKLE (UNCREDITED WRITERS), OR-
SON WELLES (DIRECTOR) **THE LADY FROM SHANGHAI**
/ 1947

AFTER A VERY pleasant dinner at the Los Angeles
County Museum of Art's Ray's restaurant, and sitting
for an hour transported in time by Christian Maclay's
marvelous *The Clock*, I attended a showing at the Bing
Auditorium of Orson Welles' film noir *The Lady from
Shanghai*.

I had seen this film several times years earlier, particularly when I taught as a teaching assistant in film at
the University of Maryland, where then-professor Joe
Miller included the Welles film in his course. I remember it well for its marvelous images—clearly the reason
why Miller taught it, since he eschewed all talk of story
in favor of camera techniques—but I could never quite

figure out the story, or, at least, the motivations of the characters for their complex maneuvers in trying to outwit and/or destroy one another.

Let me try quickly to get that lumbering beast of burden out of the way, so that I can focus better on the film's achievements and failures.

A somewhat "dumb" Irish seamen, Michael O'Hara (Welles, speaking in a brogue I am sure has never been heard anywhere in Ireland) accidentally encounters a beautiful blonde (the usually red-haired Rita Hayworth, married at the time to Welles) in Central Park. As her coach passes, he is struck by her beauty and is only too pleased to come to her aid a few minutes later when hooligans attempt to overtake her coach.

The woman, Elsa "Rosalie" Bannister, is married to the famous defense attorney, Arthur Bannister (Everett Sloane), a mix of a deformed and bitter old man and a rather witty and world-weary figure. She immediately recognizes the impact of having a young handsome man at her side. How Elsa and Arthur have ever come to marry is unclear, but we suspect her greed—and blackmail, perhaps, on his part—has helped in bringing them together. Her boredom and unhappiness in the relationship are all too apparent.

The Bannisters, newly arrived in New York, are on their way from Shanghai (why they have been in Shanghai is never fully explained) to San Francisco via the Panama Canal. One suspects that the trip was added in Sherwood King's novel, on which this film was based, simply as an exotic element. But, in any event, it serves its purpose when Elsa insists that Michael sign on their yacht as a seaman.

Almost from the moment he signs—an act he does both in reality and symbolically several times in this story—the travelers are joined by Bannister's law partner, George Grisby (Glenn Anders). As Michael goes about his daily duties, he is distracted by the appearance and obvious flirtations of Elsa, and before long the two have fallen for each other—if love in this dark prism of events can be described so romantically. Perhaps it would be more suitable to say they have determined to play out the flirtations, despite the observing eyes of Elsa's husband. As Michael says of himself: "When I start out to make a fool of myself there's very little can stop me."

Obviously, we guess some terrible result will come of their relationship. Yet the story moves in another direction. George Grisby, cornering Michael, proposes that the young seaman "murder" him in a plot wherein he will fake his death to collect the insurance money. He promises Michael $5,000—a sufficient amount for him to run off with Elsa—assuring him that, since he will still be alive and there will be no corpse, Michael cannot be held for murder. The rub is that Michael must sign a confession that he has committed the act.

Although we might find the plot to this point a bit unbelievable, we can still follow its flimsy logic. But here is where we begin to digress, where the story fractures at several points, leading us into cul-de-sacs that seem to trap us in plot. As the yacht reaches San Francisco, we discover that a private investigator, Sydney Broome, has been following Elsa for her husband (remember him?). Broome gets wind of Grisby's plan, realizing that he is actually intending to kill Bannister and to frame Michael for Bannister's murder with the confession in hand. Michael, unaware of these twists, watches Grisby, as planned, take off in a motorboat, and shoots a gun in the air to draw attention to himself. But, in fact, Grisby has discovered that Broome is on to him, shooting the detective and leaving him for dead.

What we don't yet know is that Broome, still surviving, has called Elsa for help, warning her of Grisby's intention to kill her husband. Michael, meanwhile, calls Elsa, startled to find Broome's voice at the other end, warning him, in his last words, of Grisby's plot to implicate him in Bannister's murder.

Michael, who by this time has become a comical aphorist, recognizes that "Everybody is somebody's fool," yet clumsily rushes off to Bannister's office, just in time to see the police removing Grisby's body from the place. Confession in hand, the police arrest Michael as the killer.

Ironically—and clearly perversely—Bannister undertakes the defense for Michael, but can hardly be a fair representative, discovering, as the trial moves forward, just how involved Michael and Elsa had been. He suggests Michael plead justifiable homicide, given all the evidence, although Bannister himself clearly knows who the real murderer is.

Trapped by these absurd situations, Michael, feigning suicide, is able to escape the courtroom with Elsa following, arranging with her Chinese friends for Michael to hide out in a theater in Chinatown. But the friends drug Michael, taking him to an abandoned funhouse, where he awakens to find a gun-toting Elsa within the maze of mirrors and distorting machines of reflection; he gradually perceives that it is she who has killed Grisby, that she and Grisby had been planning to murder Bannister and frame Michael for the crime. As Michael quips, "It's a bright, guilty world."

The film ends in a phantasmagoric shootout in the hall of mirrors, where shot after shot is fired at images of each other, most mistakenly, some hitting home, resulting with the death of both Elsa and her husband.

The surviving seaman trundles off to obscurity again, leaving a trail of further aphorisms in the space behind him: "The only way to stay out of trouble is to grow old, so I guess I'll concentrate on that." "Maybe I'll live so long that I'll forget her. Maybe I'll die trying."

What is obvious even as I was regurgitating the above story is that the twists and turns of the plot are far too complex for the 87 minutes of the film. In fact, when Welles delivered the finished product to Columbia Pictures president Harry Cohn, the executive so detested the film that he offered anyone $1,000 to succinctly explain the story to him. Certainly his editors did not help to clarify the situation by cutting an hour from Welles' original.

Most critics and even admirers, accordingly, have seriously faulted this film—whether they argue it was the director's or the studio's doing—for being narratively incoherent, despite its often wonderful cinematic images. But then, I've never been able to coherently speak about the plot of *The Big Sleep* either. In both

 cases, it seems to me, the directors (Hawks in the *The Big Sleep*) purposely leave their baggy tales full of missing links, distortions, false clues, and outright disjunctions to reiterate the dark, foggy world which their characters inhabit. In such an immoral world as *The Lady from Shanghai*, in which every single character finds some way they can use or abuse the guileless Michael, there can be no straight lines, all is relative.

One by one each of the characters, except Michael, speaks in a kind of double language, in sentences that turn in on each  other, taking meaning, like a snake swallowing its own tail, away from rational comprehension. As Bannister relates to his wife late in the film, "Killing you is killing myself. But, you know, I'm pretty tired of both of us." Or, as he tells Michael early on, "You've been traveling around the world too much to find out anything about it." Or as George Grisby tells Michael as he plots his own death, "This is going to be murder and it's going to

be legal."

Michael might easily claim, as does a witness to Broome's death, "I don't speak their language, see...." As Elsa tells him, "I told you, you know nothing about wickedness."

Welles' strong images merely reiterate this play of language, doubling up hundreds of figures, presenting reality through the distorting positioning of his actors and camera, cutting away so quickly the viewer is not quite sure of what he has just seen, surveying landscapes which one can barely see through (note Michael rushing past the window and the multi-mirrored images above).

Accordingly, while the language of this film (both its spoken words and its cinematic images) very *much* matters, the MacGuffin, as Hitchcock would call it, hardly matters at all, is almost an after-the-fact explanation for the vagaries of the double-crossing characters.

Perfect this movie is not. I might say that there is a sort of lumbering quality to all of Welles' films, even his best. But they are certainly fun to watch.

LOS ANGELES, SEPTEMBER 24, 2011
Reprinted from *World Cinema Review* (September 2011).
Reprinted from *Reading Films: My International Cinema* (2012).

Operating on Words

BOB BROWN **WORDS** (PARIS: HOURS PRESS, 1931);
NEW FACSIMILE EDITION PUBLISHED 2014, WITH AN
INTRODUCTION BY CRAIG SAPER

BOB BROWN, EDITOR AND AUTHOR **GEMS: A
CENSORED ANTHOLOGY** (CAGNES-SUR-MER, FRANCE:
ROVING EYE PRESS, 1931); NEW FACSIMILE EDITION PUB-
LISHED 2014, WITH AN INTRODUCTION BY CRAIG SAPER

BOB BROWN **THE READIES** (BAD EMS, FRANCE: ROV-
ING EYE PRESS, 1930); NEW FACSIMILE EDITION PUB-
LISHED 2014, WITH AN INTRODUCTION BY CRAIG SAPER

IN HIS 1974 ANTHOLOGY *Revolution of the Word: A
New Gathering of American Avant-Garde Poetry 1914-
1945,* Jerome Rothenberg introduced American poet
Bob Brown to those of us of a certain generation, hint-
ing at the wealth of visual poems the man had created
and describing his writing, based mostly on the poet's
1916 collection, *My Marjonary* (announced for publication by my own Green Integer press), as bearing close

kinship with the later New York School writers.

What a marvelous surprise and wealth of information we have now suddenly been provided by Craig Saper, with the facsimile publications of three little-known Bob Brown collections, *words, Gems: A Censored Anthology*, and *The Readies,* that not only take Brown beyond Rothenberg's purview, but reveal the innovative poet had created an entire series of genres not only far ahead of their time, but still quite original today.

words, at first reading, might appear simply to extend the kind of poetic experimentation that Brown was working on in *My Marjonary*. If one simply leafs through this facsimile edition—the original published by Nancy Cunard's important Hours Press in 1931—the poems appear to have a great deal in common, from their witty wordplay and off-the-cuff observations, to the semi-confessional observations of Frank O'Hara and even Ted Berrigan. A poem like "The Passion Play at Royat," for example, might even have been written in a prose version by Gertrude Stein as she wandered through a small French village with her dog Basket, observing the other such animals on her way:

> There is no great gulf between the
> Love life of the
> Dogs in the village street of Royat and

Other dogs or even human beings

Although the slightly more prudish Stein probably would not have made the beast-human connection, and certainly would not have observed, as Brown does later in the poem:

> They bark and bite, snarl and scratch
> Purr and piddle, play ceaselessly at
> Fornicopulation
> Even as talkie actors in gilt ritzyrooms.

Certainly the last two lines are pure Brownisms, representing as they do his love of lively word combinations (fornication and copulation) and his immediate reference to popular culture. I don't remember a single occasion when Stein described herself and Alice sneaking out to the moving pictures.

Like Stein and even Pound, however, Brown is an unapologetic, pure-bred Amur-i-can, employing colloquialisms whenever he gets the chance, even while discussing God's creation:

> It's all right God
> I understand you're an altruist
> Plus God
> I know you had a high purpose &

All that God
In breathing your sensen
Semen-scented breath
Into clay pigeons Chinks Brazies
Yanks Frogs Turks and Limeys
It's a great little old world you made God
But now I'm ready for another eyeful
Mars Heaven Hell &/or
What have you got Gott

So Brown sets up a sort of fallen angel situation, quickly moving on, more like E. E. Cummings than any other
American writer, to a kind of visual wordplay that can
be read down or across.

If I	I would only
O	O
Darling	Sit
O	O
Were marooned on a	Dry-eyed in its center
Little old	Scanning of the seas
Eye of an islette	For you
Dear	Dear

Who else could write a love poem, depending upon
which way you choose to read his columns, that simultaneously sings a song of his imaginary love while wail-
ing out the loneliness of the poor, marooned darling

```
              LA  VIE  AMERICAINE

    8 A. M.            9 A. M.                      12 M.
    Coffee, cereal    Office $$$$$$$$$            Brunch
    cigarettes, eggs        chasing the dollar


      1 P. M.                    5 P. M.              7 P. M.
    Office $$$$$$ ££££         Cocktails            Dinner
         dollar-golf chasing


      8 P. M. _____  1 A. M.
    talkies    chasing the tail              tail-chasing


                           &
```

with her cries of "O O" and "Dear Dear"?

Even more excitingly this poem, titled "La Vie Americaine," begins with a purely visual element that combines time, daily meals, and money, with golf, the talkies, and "tail-chasing," presumably of a young girl such as his later marooned darling.

What is even more amazing about this page of poetry, however, is the little black smudge that appears at the left side at the very bottom of that page. The smudge, in fact, is one of many such poems produced microscopically in the volume so that the reader, if he desires to peruse it, must take up a magnifying glass. I have long had one lying upon my desk, given to me by someone, I presume, who thought, as I aged, it might become necessary. Thankfully, my tired old eyes were restored with what optometrists describe as "second sight," a condition in which I suddenly found myself, after years of resisting bi-focal glasses, able to read very fine print despite the fact that at distances everything remains a blur! But even my magnifying glass was insufficient to read these tiny offerings; fortunately my companion Howard brought out a sharper set of magnifying glasses which he had to better make out the visual images in old-fashioned photographic slides—once a necessary tool for any art curator.

The micro-poem on this page, for example, reads:

I, who am God
Wear lavender pajamas and
Purr poetry
Should I who am God
Dirty my ear on the ground
Striving to catch the
Idiotic waltzing lilt of
Rhyming red-eye dervish
Twirling white pink poet mice
In union suits?

Thus Brown creates a kind of blasphemous commentary about the God he addresses in the other part of the poem, explaining his aversion to the kind of literary conceits usually used in poems addressed to the "All Mighty," a commentary continued in the last stanza of the larger-font poem:

> Fancy in poetry
> Now that aeroplanes
> Anchor to stars
> Is a trifle old-fashioned

In this case, at least, the micro text comments on the larger poetic effort.

In other cases, such as in "To a Wild Montana Mare" (once more, a poem that can be plumbed by reading down its two columns or across), however, the situation is reversed, as the poet ponders the nude Lady Godiva in the larger poem, and merely uses the micro-poem to suggest how little he was moved by Romantic icons such as the Sphinx and Mona Lisa.

Accordingly, the smaller, hidden texts, are not necessarily more outspoken or radical in either their subject or their linguistic usage. And often the "parallel" poems seem to have little relationship to one another, even if the reader is somewhat encouraged to try to discern links between the two.

While we might expect the micro-poems to represent something created to escape the hands of the censors as was Robert Hooke's *Micrographia*—an is-

TO A WILD MONTANA MARE

Lady Godiva
Why
Did you keep me
Awake all night
Last night
Tossing
Lifting white-hot sheets
On my perpendicular tent-pole
A lonely maverick
Making camp in the
Desert of my bed
Gazing through
Gossamer gloom
For glowing glimpses of
Your dimpled
Blank-faced
White Bottom
You siren centaur
Clattering night mare
In the cobbled street
Below my scholarly garret

I am no
Lime-washed
Out-washed
Jet black stallion
To be whinnied at
Neighed at
Nipped
By the vicious mind of a
Flare-eyed
China-toothed
Nipple-dappled
Wide-flanked
Back-biting
Heel-tossing
Hell-fire
Explosive
Back-firing
Pinto pony
Wild-maned
Montana Mare
Like you

Farewell ███ *and Fairies*

(RICHARD CORBET, BISHOP OF OXFORD
AND OF NORWICH)

Farewell, ███ and fairies!
   Good housewives now may ███;
For now foul sluts in dairies
   Do ███ as well as they.
And though they ██████ no less
   Than maids were wont to do
Yet who of late for ███
   Finds sixpence in her ███.

The Old ████ (ELIZA COOK)

I love it—— I love it, and who shall dare
To chide me for loving that old ███!

We Are Seven (WORDSWORTH)

   A simple child
That lightly draws its ███
And feels its life in every limb,
What should it know of ███.
I met a little cottage girl:
   She was eight years old, she said;
Her hair was thick with many a curl
   That clustered round her ███.
She had a rustic, woodland ███,
   And she was wildly ███;
Her ███ were fair, and very ███;
   Her ███ made me glad.
"███ and ████, little maid,
   How many may you ███?"
"How many? Seven in all," she said,
   And wondering looked at me.

sue of much more importance in Brown's anthology of poems from 1931 titled *Gems*—for Brown the nearly unreadable texts, as Saper argues, play the role of something more like "squibs," small jokes and commentary, much like the mistakes from other publications one used to find at the bottom of the columns of *The New Yorker*, a genre in which the poet had had success early in his writing career.

Moreover, the varying sizes of these texts, in their alternation of focus, point to Brown's continued interest in a "writing machine," in which one would be able to adjust the size and speed of texts while reading them.

Finally, the micro-texts suggest, as Saper implies in his useful introduction, other popular genres such as the spy story, with its constant references to hidden texts and disappearing ink, or of mainstream forms of concise writing styles such as stock-quotes, the fine print on food labels, etc., all of which call attention to themselves by their near-impossibility to be deciphered by the uninitiated reader. Certainly, for Brown, his experiment in variable type through his own poetics shares a great deal with Duchamp, a figure who greatly influenced him, and who himself, as Saper reminds us, "tried to sell his optical art-toys like a street vendor in front of his prestigious art exhibits."

In *Gems: A Censored Anthology*, Brown more thoroughly explores the issue of censorship, beginning with a spirited and, at times, quite hilarious send-up of the entire modern history of censored or culturally frowned-upon texts. Like bootlegged liquor, he argues, the more a text is deemed to be unfit for certain readers, the more its value to rare book dealers and, particularly, the young entrepreneurial men and women who bring back texts from overseas and publish, in special editions, what is deemed "obscene" writing. These individuals, whom he jokingly refers to as "book-leggers," can make a good profit if they know where to look, particularly in a time when censors are so busy blocking out passages in great works of art such as James Joyce's *Ulysses*, Djuna Barnes' *Ryder*, and the writings of Havelock Ellis (several others are mentioned). Outlining the major forms of censorship from time immemorial, Brown's introduction alone makes it worth reading the book; and given the continuation of such censorship of books in school libraries and on university reading lists even today, *Gems* is a book worthy of our attention. Along with Norman Douglas' wonderfully obscene collection of *Some Limericks*, originally published in 1928 and reissued in the 1960s by Grove Press, *Gems* demonstrates the poetic liveliness of many popular forms, pulling the poetic away from the whimsical old maids and professorial fuddy-duddies who struggle to deaden poetry and language itself.

As if to outdo Douglas, Brown proposes a much

more radical alternative. Taking absolutely prim and proper poems from Shakespeare to the Victorians, many of the works written particularly for children and young adults, the poet applies to select words the large black censor's stamp, used particularly in wartime to delete sensitive correspondence and to prohibit then-contemporary readers from being sullied by obscene passages. Of course, by using the same tools of the censor to excise words from Keats, Wordsworth, Tennyson, and Shelley, for example, he forces the reader to fill in the missing words, often with alternatives that truly are obscene and blasphemous. On page 184 I reproduce Wordsworth's "We Are Seven," a poetic rendering that I invite any reader to scan without a blush if not a series of outright guffaws—all of his own imagination!

Certainly there is something dilettantish about these poetic renderings, and after a few pages of reading such works, the joke grows thin. If nothing else, however, Brown has certainly proven his point about the censor's ink, and through his use of these utterly boring, mostly Victorian works—the selection itself serving as a satire of anthologists like Francis Turner Palgrave, whose *The Golden Treasury* was long perceived as an uplifting compendium of morally "worthy" poetry—has simultaneously satirized the poetry that used language in the ways he most opposed. Certainly there is not a better example of the manipulation of "found poetry" in existence. And once again, Brown has made good use of popular genres in order to create radical experiments.

Perhaps his most radical experimentation had less to do with the actual texts used as with how that language was presented and disseminated. Through the late 1920s and the 1930s, Brown argued, quite seriously—although many interpreted it as another comic enterprise—for a new Reading Machine, a kind of forerunner of a fiche machine that would run microscopic texts through a viewer which could be sped-up, sloweddown, and enlarged to various degrees. For Brown this machine would make it possible to produce an entire work on the head of a pin, or, as he expressed it in a poem in *words*: "In the reading-machine future / Say by 1950 / All magnum opuses / Will be etched on the / Heads of pins / Not retched into / Three volume classics / By pin heads."

With the intention of showing off his machine, Brown also edited a collection of works by various writers, some rather traditional, others experimental, and many now unheard-of, which he described as "the readies" for his machine. The anthology itself, except for contributions by Stein and a few others, seems not so very interesting. But then, Brown was presenting himself less as an anthologist, than simply selecting texts that might demonstrate the flexibility of his invention.

The ideas behind his reading machine are fascinating, in part because Brown saw it not only as a kind of futurist machine that is not today so very different from the Kindle and other computer-based operations, but argued for a new kind of language to accompany it. Saper and others have, somewhat convincingly, suggested that these linguist-wists (my own combine from **twists** of **linguistic** expressions) parallel the kind of computer-based languages we see today in Twitter, Facebook, and e-mail expressions.

Frankly, I think Brown-talk—what Stein hinted as being a kind of "Bobbed Browning," or, playing his game once more, I'll describe as "Bobs-ledding"—was far more complex and interesting than today's Twitter talk. In *The Readies*, published by his own Roving Eye Press in 1930, Brown posits new combinations of words such as "Verbunions" (Verb, into verbosity plus "I know my onions"), "Shellshallow" (an echo of the Yankee shell game played with a dried pea and three walnut shells), and "Springish sappy" (Bliss Carmen's "Make Me Over," Mother Nature, when the sap begins to stir), doubtlessly the author's undying tribute to the greatest of Canada Dry poets.

But the creation of new words, for Brown, was clearly not enough. As he suggests in his last chapter, "A Story To Be Read on the Reading Machine," it is the combination of these newly-minted words, without all the everyday fillers such as "the," "of," "and," "to," "a," "in," "it," "I," etc. and most forms of punctuation, which he replaced primarily by the hyphen, that truly matters. Four lines will have to do as a sample of his verbal-ized ("verbally energized") writing:

Bermuda-barmaid-season-Harry-could-play-M's---
Spring-Song-flawlessly-without-music-before-
    him—
but-continued-turning-sheets-effectively-Harry---
stood-up-tall-poplar-tree-other-three-sat-down---

The editor of these three volumes has set up a site to show off a version of Brown's Reading Machine. I couldn't quite get it to work on any of the selected texts, but I was able to get the sense of its ongoing motion through a tutorial of the machine. Although one can alternate the speed, stop it, or even go back without seriously intruding, the text itself, moves forward, unfortunately, at its own interminable pace, stealing from the reader the easy possibility or accidental (but sometimes fortuitous) opportunity of repeating, interrupting, or even skipping over passages. The endless scroll from left to right almost scolds the reader not to jump ahead, in and about a text, intentionally slowing down and quickly moving forward again. While this can be accomplished on Brown's machine, it reminds me of using the fiche—a machine I tackled for several years while working of my Djuna Barnes bibliography—trying to tame it from its mad rush forward and leaping moves backward, attempting to adjust its distorting lens into a position between microscopic and giantized. Frankly I would miss all those simple American conjunctions and pronouns, the repetition of which so clearly defines American syntax, as opposed to Brown's hobbled-together word combines.

But no one can deny Brown his rapacious hunger for words or dismiss his endless attempts—as he expresses it in the very first lines of his 1931 collection—to "operate" on words:

> Operating on words—gilding and gelding them
> In a rather special laboratory equipped with
> Micro and with scope—I anesthetize
> Pompous, prolix, sesquipedalian, Johnsonian
> Inflations like *Infundibuliform*
> Only to discover by giving them a swift
> Poke in the bladder they instantly inspissate
> And whortle down the loud-writing funnel.

Like a madly inspired doctor, Brown prods, pushes, and cuts his words into and out of meaning until—I swear—he might even awake T. S. Eliot's etherized patient. If there is, most often, something slightly clumsy about Brown's insistent linguistic embracements, he seldom shied from his commitment, determining to never abandon his love of words, even if he had to create his "Superb swirling compositions / On my back where even I / Cannot see my masterpieces" ("Lament of an Etcher").

We can only forgive Saper if he somewhat overstates the greatness of Brown's poetic achievements, while profusely thanking him for sharing these significant, nearly-forgotten contributions. Knowing Brown makes American poetry profoundly more interesting.

LOS ANGELES, OCTOBER 30, 2014
Reprinted from *Hyperallergic Weekend* (January 3, 2015),
        published as "Language Lessons: The Poetry of Bob Brown."

Secret Lives

JOSEPH ROTH **COLLECTED SHORTER FICTION OF JOSEPH ROTH,** TRANSLATED FROM THE GERMAN BY MICHAEL HOFMANN (LONDON: GRANTA PUBLICATIONS, 2001)

MOST OF THE wonderful stories and novellas collected in this volume represent worlds in which the characters act in ways that seem destined, the figures themselves moving forward in life without seemingly knowing what motivates them and how they might have in any way transformed their own worlds.

This is particularly true of the earliest stories of Roth's as in "The Honors Student," a perfectly terrible portrait of the bourgeoisie mentality epitomized by Anton Wanzl, the overachieving but completely unimaginative son of the local Postmaster. Anton is the perfect student, aping his masters and winning their favor so successfully that honors are heaped upon him:

> His glowing reports, ceremonially folded, were kept in a large brick-red envelope next to the album of specially beautiful stamps....

Yet Anton, moving quietly though his life, is not a happy child, but one "consumed by a burning ambition," we are told, by "An iron desire to shine, to outdo all his comrades...." Beloved by his proud parents, Anton returns no emotion. As Roth tells us, "He lacked heart," and his first relationship with a young woman, Mizzzi Schinagl, is run more like a campaign to win her mother and father's respect than to romance the girl herself. As he moves into the Gymnasium, he easily forgets her and moves on to a relationship with the daughter of a more successful individual, Court Councilor Sabbaeus Kreitmeyr, eventually winning her hand in marriage over the more romantic entreaties of the artist Hans Pauli.

Anton goes on to become a teacher, ultimately requesting to be transferred back to the small town in which he was born and raised. There, instead of seeking for a higher position, he feels fulfilled, eventually becoming the Director of the school where he was educated before his frail sensibility, hitherto subject to his intense ambitions, wins. He dies of pneumonia, highly respected by the locals but without having done anything meaningful in his life.

In a similar way, the mother in the story, "Barbara," sacrifices her life and the love of her lodger Peter Wendelin to make certain that her son is given every opportunity. The child achieves a kind of success, ultimately becoming a student of divinity. But the thick-skinned boy has no ability at feelings, and, as his mother lies dying, he spends his time with her in abstract talk "about the hereafter, and the reward that awaited the faithful in Heaven," rather than expressing his love. As he "stifles a yawn" and goes out for a breathe of air, Barbara lies dying, alone as ever, "stumbling towards Eternity."

In one of the very best tales of this collection, "April," Roth's narrator is a stranger to a small town wherein he notes the comings and goings of the town's figures. He soon is involved with a lusty barkeeper, Anna, and is amused by several other figures, including the local and beloved Postmaster. One man alone he cannot abide, the assistant railwayman.

> I hated the assistant railwayman. He was freckled and unbelievably tall and erect. Every time I saw him, I thought of writing to the Railway Minister. I wanted to suggest he use the ugly as-

sistant railwayman as a telegraph pole somewhere between two little stations....

I couldn't explain my hatred for this official. He was exceptionally tall, but I don't have principled hatred for anything exceptional. It seemed to me that the assistant railwayman had shot up so much on purpose, and riled me. It seemed to me that he had done nothing else since his youth but acquire freckles and grow. On top of everything else, he had red hair.

One day he discovers, while dining in a nearby restaurant, a beautiful woman in the Postmaster's home who completely captures his attention. Another day he nods to her, and every day thereafter they greet one another from a distance, the storyteller imagining that she comprehends what is on his mind. The narrator is told that she is the Postmaster's daughter, who is ill. Soon the narrator discovers himself in love with this beautiful woman, but, unable to communicate with her, he determines that he must leave this small town.

It was so ridiculous, I thought, for me to hang around night after night in front of the windows of a girl who's about to die, and whom I won't ever be able to kiss. I'm not that young any more, I thought. Every day is a task, and each one of my hours was a sin against life.

As he enters the train to leave, he sees the abhorrent assistant railwayman, the beautiful girl in the window trailing after.

> "Stay, won't you!" I heard the railway employee say to her. "I'm almost finished!"
>
> But the girl didn't listen to him. She looked at me. We looked at each other. She stood upright, and she was wearing a white dress, and she was healthy, and not at all lame, and not at all tubercular. Obviously, she was the assistant railwayman's fiancée or his wife.

The irony of the situation sends the story's narrator on a long voyage to New York.

The idyll "Strawberries," told primarily through the voice of Naphtali Kroy, describes the adventures of various figures living in a small Eastern European town where each member of the community, poor or rich, plays nearly equal parts, the poor being fed by the local Count, and the Count depending for his significance on the local folk. Each of these lives, sometimes comically and at other times tragically, are interwoven. But gradually we see the small town changing. The new hotel is constructed, even though there is hardly anyone to inhabit it. To the town square is added a new sculpture dedicated to a local poet, Raphael Stoklos. Finally, an Englishman comes to the city and builds a large new structure without any windows, "a big store, a department store."

The following story, "This Morning, A Letter Arrived...," obviously a follow-up tale in what was presumably to have been a longer fiction, shows the diaspora of that former community, as Naphtali is described in Buenos Aires and, later, Vienna.

The ordinary Stationmaster, Adam Fallmerayer, married to an even more ordinary woman, one day falls madly in love with a Countess he encounters in a train accident some distance from his station. Drafted into war, the Stationmaster teaches himself Russian and, one day, finds himself stationed not far from the Countess' home in the Kiev region. Visiting her, he arranges another meeting and before they know it the two have fallen in love. Fallmerayer's wife writes to say she is leaving him. As the Russian revolutionary forces move toward them, they flee to Monte Carlo, where the Countess becomes pregnant.

By coincidence the Count, who has also been fighting in the war, arrives in Monte Carlo, where he is greeted by the Countess and her lover. But the man Fallmerayer discovers is not at all one with whom he might battle for her love.

Fallmerayer looked at the Count's long, yellow, bony face, with its sharp nose and bright eyes and the thin lips under the drooping black moustache. The Count was wheeled along the platform like one of his many pieces of luggage. His wife followed the wheel chair.

As the wife plumps up one of her husband's pillows, Fallmerayer says good night, never to be seen again. His life, if he were to stay with the Countess, would now mean his own attentive devotion to the old man.

The secret life of Dr. Skovronnek, who in "The Triumph of Beauty" specializes in caring for women at a local spa, is revealed through his incredible story of a friend, a young "upper class" diplomat and a beautiful, but rather stupid English woman, whom the young *galant* marries. While the story portends to be an objective description of how the young man is tricked by a coarse woman (she loves Wagner, he plays Mozart with the Doctor), we soon recognize the tale as a misogynistic fable about women in general who trick and destroy their innocent husbands. What is clear is that the Doctor himself is enamored of the young man and angry at the wife for coming between them. The final flurry of hatred towards women expresses the Doctor's condition quite clearly:

Many, many women passed me in the street, and some of them smiled at me.

Go on, I thought, smile, smile, turn, look over your shoulders, swing your hips, buy yourselves new hats, new stockings, new bits and bobs! Old age will catch up with you! Give it another little year or two! No surgeon will be able to do anything about it, no wigmaker. You will be disfigured, embittered, disappointed, you will sink into your graves and then further, into Hell. But go on, smile, smile!...

The last tale of this marvelous collection, "Leviathan," also is a story of a secret life. In the town of Progrody lives Nizzen Piczenik, a renowned coral merchant, a successful Jewish businessman. Secretly, however, corals are not just the source of Piczenik's income, but represent an obsession, a kind of madness that includes all things connected with the ocean. When a local boy who has joined the navy returns for a visit home, Piczenik takes up with him, questioning him about everything to do with ocean waters, for Nizzen has never himself been to sea. So compelled is the coral merchant with the subject that, when the young man must return to his ship, he accompanies him to Odessa, claiming he is the boy's uncle and joining him for a tour of the vessel and staying on in the city for three days.

With his return to Progrody, Piczenik discovers his business is dwindling and, soon after, another coral merchant opens a shop in a nearby town, selling only synthetic corals at great discount. Against all his principles and his love of the objects he sells (which the merchant perceives as living beings) he begins to mix the synthetic with the real. Sales drop even further, and since he cannot sell only the real ones, he determines to emigrate. On his way to Canada, the boat sinks, Piczenik leaping overboard to join his real corals.

Interestingly enough, in Roth's early stories exceptional-seeming individuals were revealed as absolutely ordinary and boring figures. But in the best of these tales the ordinary men and women he portrays, when their surfaces are slightly scratched, are represented as extraordinarily complex individuals; flawed, yes, but amazing for their secret passions of life.

LOS ANGELES, SEPTEMBER 24, 2009
Reprinted from *EXPLORING*fictions (October 2009).

Bitten by a Snake

INGMAR BERGMAN (WRITER AND DIRECTOR) **VARGTIMMEN (HOUR OF THE WOLF)** / 1968 (THE VIEWING I SAW, IN CONJUNCTION WITH THE MUSEUM'S "KUBRICK AND CO." SERIES OF FILMS, AT THE LOS ANGELES COUNTY MUSEUM'S BING THEATER ON JUNE 21, 2013)

DIRECTLY AFTER HIS experimental, highly artificed, and self-conscious masterpiece of 1966, *Persona*, director Ingmar Bergman, with greater self-confidence, determined to further explore the mental angst of his characters, many of whom had previously been forced to suffer what has been described as a "night journey," a series of psychological tests that can exorcise their inner demons or end, as in in the case of Johan Borg (Max von Sydow), in insanity and death. Except this time round, Bergman clearly no longer felt limited to the kind of psychological realism of works such as *Wild Strawberries* or even the allegorical pantomime of a film such as *The Seventh Seal*, but felt confident enough to link his work to Fellini's *Juliet of the Spirits* (1965), while referencing the early monster films such as Tod Browning's *Dracula* and James Whale's *Frankenstein* and *The Bride of Frankenstein*. The work's structure and some of its tropes, moreover, draw on Mozart's *The Magic Flute*, an opera that would continue to fascinate Bergman throughout his life, leading eventually to a 1974 filming of the work.

With such a broad range of influences, it is no surprise that many critics have described the various symbols and images of *Hour of the Wolf* as simply failing to "coalesce into a coherent pattern" (Dennis DeNitto in *World Film Directors*). Yet, I argue it is this very rich overlay of associations and structures from film and opera history that transforms *Hour of the Wolf* into a work like *Persona*, a film that moves away from psychological realism into a metaphoric depiction of what it is like to gradually go insane as a being falls into ever-deepening fears and doubts.

The story of this film hardly matters: with his wife, Alma (Liv Ullmann), Borg arrives at the small island of Baltrum (Bergman's favorite location to play out psychological crises) where the artist seeks rest. But even more than previously, Borg is approached, like Tanino in Mozart's fable, by strange and inexplicable beings which he can only describe as demons—a Bird-Man, insects, meat-eaters, a schoolmaster—all of whom terrify him and keep him up at night in horror.

His strong and supportive wife determines that she can save him, reading his hidden diary (sometimes directly to the camera) to reveal the horrors Johan is facing. Among the revelations in his "dagbok" is a former love affair with a woman, Veronica Vogler (Ingrid Thulin).

In the final scene of the film, after having lost her husband to insanity, Alma, again addressing the camera, speaks: "Is it true that a woman who lives a long time with a man eventually winds up being like that man? I mean to say, if I had loved him much less, and not bothered so with everything about him, could I have protected him better?" The question is crucial to understanding the film, for, in her determined love, Alma, by staying up through each night to lead him back into morning light (the same pattern of Mozart's opera), she herself also encounters these dark beasts. Approached by Baron von Merkens (Erland Josephson), they are invited to his nearby castle, where the couple endures a surreal dinner party. After dinner, the baron's wife (Gertrud Fridh) invites the couple into her bedroom, revealing a portrait of Veronica by Borg himself, stat-

ing, "It has become like part of my solitary life. I love her." The terrified Borg and Alma leave the castle, with Alma confessing her fear that she may lose her husband to the demons.

During a following long night, Borg admits to his youthful obsession with Veronica and his childhood punishment, where he was locked in a cabinet wherein his parents who had convinced him also lived a small man who fed on children's toes. The most frightening revelation of the night, however, played through a dramatically startling montage of images, is about the day he has returned home to report that he has been bitten by a snake. As Borg fishes, we see a young boy, dressed only in scanty swimming trunks, lying in the sun on a nearby rock, clearly presenting his body up for the man. The boy moves somewhat closer, finally moving to the very rock from which Borg is casting his fishing rod. The tension mounts, culminating in Borg's murder of and drowning of the young child!

We cannot know whether this confession represents another haunting "demon" of Borg's imagination or a real event in his life, but we do comprehend that the incident, real or imagined, demonstrates his sexual confusion: obviously he has killed the child because of his own physical attraction to  him. If the boy is understood as a snake, attempting to lure Borg into sexual activity, the dark forces within the grown man, we perceive that those handmaidens of the evil Queen of the Night rush forward to destroy the snake just as in Mozart's *The Magic Flute*—a puppet version of which has been performed in the baron's castle. Borg is clearly a Tonino, a man who must be further tested in order to make his Panina (Alma) his true wife.

As one of the baron's guests again invites them to the castle, mentioning that Veronica Volger will be among the guests, Borg produces a pistol, supposedly to protect them from what he describes as "small animals"; and when Alma tries to dissuade him from his clear obsession, he shoots her, racing off to the castle.

At the castle, Borg not only meets the "Bird-Man" (Mozart's Papageno obviously), but all the other demons of his dream. His face is painted—lipstick, eyeliner, face powder—as if he were suddenly a figure in drag before entering a room where the seemingly dead Veronica lies under what appears to be a winding-sheet.

When Borg lifts it, he discovers the beautiful Veronica very much alive beneath, but laughing, as he suddenly realizes all of the demonic figures of the castle are voyeuristically watching. Borg's breakdown is nearly inevitable; he cannot consummate the sexual act, his homosexual proclivities coming again into play: "I thank you, the limit has been finally transgressed," he shouts as the demons attempt to devour him, and he races into the underbrush. He has failed the tests.

Although Alma has survived the shooting, and witnesses his final attack, she can no longer help him, as Borg disappears into the woods (the same direction, incidentally, we see Juliet heading at the end of Fellini's film), a world into which Alma cannot/will not follow. "Is it true that a woman who lives a long time with a man eventually winds up being like that man?" The question is the answer.

Bergman's *Hour of the Wolf* is less a story of a couple, one of whom is suffering from psychological angst, than it is an opera unto itself, a wonderfully overwrought series of overlapping images and references from film and opera literature about the inability of a human mind to accept the monsters he perceives within himself.

LOS ANGELES, JUNE 22, 2013
Reprinted from *World Cinema Review* (June 2013).

Truth That Cannot Be Told

GIANNI ROMOLI AND FERZAN OZPETEK (SCREEN-
PLAY), FERZAN OZPETEK (DIRECTOR) **LE FATE IGNO-
RANTI (THE IGNORANT FAIRIES)**, USA A.K.A. *HIS SECRET
LIFE* / 2001, USA 2002

WRITTEN AND FILMED in Italy, Turkish-born director's *Le fate ignoranti* begins with a beautiful woman,
Antonia (Margherita Buy), strolling through a ancient
art exhibit, where she is, so it appears, accosted by a
handsome man, Massimo (Andrea Renzi), who attempts to pick her up. Antonia tells him to go away.
She is waiting for her husband, she proclaims, who is
quite late, to which Massimo reacts with shock that he
should leave such a beautiful wife alone. The two go off
together for what appears to be a night of sex at her
Rome apartment.

In fact, the two are husband and wife, playing a
sort of romantic game, she playfully chiding him for
his lateness, he apologizing in the role of a stranger.

Antonia, we later discover with the help of her mother, is a woman "not very curious about life." Marrying her schoolmate, Massimo, she has given up her post-doctoral ambitions, working instead as a doctor in an AIDS laboratory. Her life in an upper-class villa is a pleasant one, and her marriage seems near perfect.

Massimo is killed by a passing car, however, a day or so later, and Antonia, bereft and in shock, begins to gather up his possessions from his office, painfully trying to piece memories of their life together. In the process she accidentally uncovers on the back of one of his office paintings the following handwritten message:

> To Massimo, for our seven years together, for that part of you that I miss and I will never have, for every time you said I can't, but also for every time you said I'll be back.... Always waiting, can I call my patience love? Your ignorant fairy

What does it mean? Clearly Massimo's wife is in shock, and is desperate to seek out the truth, contacting Massimo's former efficient secretary to determine the source of the art. The secretary reveals an address, to which Antonia drives, attempting to return the painting. Instead she encounters a neighbor who tells her where the lover works and when she will return home.

Antonia tracks down the lover in the market,

presuming it is the beautiful woman standing next to a handsome young man. But when she returns to the apartment, there is no beautiful woman, but only a room of gay, transgender, and other figures, including the young man, Michele, who she has spotted at the market. Bit by bit, the truth comes storming over her uncomprehending mind: Massimo's lover was Michele, another man.

Revealing part of the story to her mother, Antonia tries to gather the strands of remaining reality together; but her mother has seemingly more sympathy for the lover than for her own daughter, revealing that she also spent most of her life loving a married man. The irony is, at first, comic, but also revelatory of just how self-centered Antonia has been. She has never noticed anything unusual about her mother or her husband! If Michele has characterized himself as "the ignorant fairy," it is, in truth, Antonia who has lived in an ignorant fairy-tale world. The small community of Michele's rooftop apartment were completely aware of Antonia's presence, of her robbery of the man they all clearly felt was one of them.

Clearly if she wants to discover all the things she

never knew, she must return to Michele's house, joining in his and his friends' witty lunch- and dinner-time conversations; and gradually she does so, discerning some close connections to her rival. When Michele reports how he and Massimo met, both of them desiring the same rare book by the Turkish poet Nazim Hikmet, she reveals that the book was a gift to her, that Massimo had never heard of Hikmet, quoting an entire poem she has learned by heart. Michele's open and joyful manner, moreover, attracts her. He has even given out a room to a friend, Ernesto, dying of AIDS, to whom Antonia begins to minister. In short, while Massimo's and her relationship had been a cloistered one, Massimo's and Michele's love was shared with a supportive community of outsiders. And in that sense, the film becomes, symbolically speaking, a discussion of insider and outsider love, of truth-telling, and a world in which the truth cannot be spoken. Which is which is often hard to say, but it is clear that Antonia's life has been lived with a deeper sense of separation than Michele's. If Michele has had Massimo only for a few hours each week—a time when Massimo claimed he was attending soccer matches—it has been a far more open proclamation of love than his marriage.

All the more amazing, accordingly, is that Antonia gradually fits into this community, vicariously falling in love with Michele. As Ozpotek reveals in a scene where

Michele publicly and later privately has sex with two other men, it is a love that Antonia cannot truly have, just has she has not truly had all of Massimo's love. Learning to share is perhaps at the heart of this gently witty cinematic work.

Throughout the film, Antonia flits back and forth between her former and new reality as if she were in a sort of fever, never fully breaking through the net in which she has found herself. Finally, however, it dawns on her that something else is happening to her very body: she discovers she is pregnant with Massimo's child. Excited by the news, she buys a bottle of champagne to celebrate the news with Michele and his friends. As she enters the apartment, however, she overhears catty comments about her, freezes, and exits. She determines to leave Rome for an undetermined destination and period.

Her final actions can be read in several ways. In some senses, she has come to realize that she has no real place in this new society, that she will forever remain an outsider, the villain who separated Massimo from his lover and dear friends. Certainly a child can have no place in such a world. But one might also read her exit

as the recognition that, finally, she has a part of Massimo that none of them could ever have: a result of the reproductive possibilities of a heterosexual life. To tell them of that would perhaps emotionally devastate them more than even losing Massimo.

Ozpetek gives us no answers. She may also return with the child, gradually integrating it into her husband's other half of his life. What we do know for certain is that Antonia can never return to the deep incurious ignorance in which she spent so much of her life.

LOS ANGELES, MARCH 31, 2012
Reprinted from *World Cinema Review* (April 2012).

The Time That Has Yet to Exist

JAVIER MARÍAS **DARK BACK OF TIME**, TRANSLATED
FROM THE SPANISH BY ESTHER ALLEN (NEW YORK: NEW
DIRECTIONS, 2001)

ALTHOUGH JAVIER MARÍAS characterizes his own fiction as a "false novel," the work has little to do with the
traditional *roman*, concerned with a hero and his life
(although the author, his characters, and his friends are
featured in the work), choosing instead to focus on the

debris at the edges of
life, the incredible accidents and coincidences
that occur at the borders
of Marías' writing activities.

The book first fo-
cuses on a previous
Marías fiction, pub-
lished in English as *All*

Souls (in Spanish, *Todas las almas*), broadly based upon his tenure as a guest professor at Oxford in 1983-1985. Although Marías goes to some lengths to insist that all but one of the figures of the work were fictional— as with almost all writers, he admits to stealing small characteristics of the people he knew, but argues that he combined them in ways that resembled no one he'd met—many of the professors with whom he worked specifically identify others and themselves as characters in the fiction, determining that his work is a *roman à clef,* and going so far as to rechristen the characters of *All Souls* with the real names of their colleagues.

Marías is quite horrified by that fact, afraid of offending individuals whom he hardly knew (a woman acquaintance is identified by his friends as a character he portrayed as having an affair in his work) and possibly even being sued. Certainly the British publisher, delaying the contract, is quite afraid of slander, and it apparently does not matter in British law that all the characters are fictional, for even if one imagines that he or she is being portrayed a lawsuit is allowed to go forward. At one point in this hilarious conundrum, Marías reiterates the fears of all writers; after the British publisher explains, "All that it would take (for a lawsuit) was for someone's circle of acquaintances...to believe they recognized that person in a character in a novel 'with resultant hatred, disdain, discredit or derision,' and the real individual would be able to file suit against the book's author and publishing house and have the suit accepted for consideration," Marías responds:

> But how can that be avoided when it depends on the way readers read the book and not the way the writer wrote it? Any lunatic can believe anything he wants, can't he? Any paranoid could recognize himself, couldn't he?... How can it ever be known if the arbitrary identification has caused hatred or derision?... It can't be known with any certainty, since that depends, above all, on the perception of the injured party.

In short, almost any writer using fictional figures might possibly—according to British law at least—be liable to a suit. But the problem Marías indentifies is perhaps even more disconcerting than a lawsuit. Since interpreting a fiction or other literary work is also dependent upon the reader, how can any fiction be separated from reality? Or how, to turn the equation on its head, can reality be separated from fiction? How can anyone possibly ever determine the truth, however one might want to define that? And if there is no way to determine "truth," how do we function as a moral society?

The rest of Marías' brilliant work explores that question in various ways, using events and accidents related to his writing of *All Souls* and other works, and employing, in *Dark Back of Time*, presumably "real" histories and facts that seem as fabulous as the events of fiction. One of those figures is John Gawsworth (whose real name is Ian Fytton Armstrong), a poet, who appeared as the only character drawn from life in *All Souls*—although some readers of that book may have felt that the self-proclaimed King of Redonda was too far-fetched to be believed. By chance Marías is named literary executor of Gawsworth and his mentor-friend M. P. Shiel, and so gains the rights to Redonda.

To support his claim of Gawsworth's authenticity, Marías published two photographs of Gawsworth in *All Souls* and reproduces them in *Dark Back of Time*, one representing a handsome younger man, the second a death mask of the poet by someone named Hugh Oloff de Wet (who, so I later discovered, also did busts of British poets Louis McNeice and Dylan Thomas).

Gawsworth, a man connected with a group of writers in early 20th century England, including figures such as Shiel, Arthur Machen, Lawrence Durrell, Richard Middleton and Hubert Crackanthorpe—the last two who committed suicide at an early age—gave them various roles in his uninhabited kingdom of Redonda.

Gawsworth's own literary achievements were devoted primarily to anthologies of "mystery and terror," of which Marías mentions eight volumes between 1932 and 1937, many of them containing writings by his circle and work by younger authors whom Gawsworth promoted, including Wilfrid Herbert Gore Ewart (1892-1922). He attracts Marías' attention, the author going so far as to translate one of Ewart's stories and publish it  in an anthology of rare tales of fear appearing the same year as *All Souls*. Although Marías is able to find names of several books Ewart published, he is unable to locate copies, and knows little about the author except for his "strange" death in Mexico.

Soon after, Marías receives two mysterious letters: one from a Mexican essayist, Sergio González Rodríguez, on the death of Ewart, and another in 1990 from a man named Rafael Muñoz Saldaña, who claims to have tracked down the facts of Ewart's Mexican death. Through a bit of further research, with help from Marías' novelist friend Juan Benet, the author gathers together information on Ewart's service in World War I, his quick rise to literary success, and his breakdown recounted by a close friend of Ewart's, Stephen Graham.

That story takes the character on a voyage from

England to the US and eventually to Mexico, ending in Ewart's "accidental" shooting on New Year's Eve on the balcony of his Mexico City hotel. But the pieces of the tale are stranger even than fiction, and several contradictions arise even in Graham's telling of the story and through other bits of information, including the revelation that the hotel in which Ewart stayed on the fifth floor did not have a balcony at that level. Marías reveals these strange facts with all the eagerness of a great fiction writer and amateur detective. Yet his methods of gathering information are strangely passive. He insists that he only seeks out books through bookdealers and will not move forward unless someone sends him information. Marías claims that he does not use a computer and uses only materials that have "sought him out."

So the plot thickens when Marías receives a book edited by Stephen Graham, the narrator of Ewart's death, signed by John Gawsworth. More significantly, another correspondent writes him that, coincidentally, his first poem was published in a magazine edited by John Gawsworth and that, years later, he met Hugh Oloff de Wet in Madrid and was entertained in a local café for several weeks by de Wet's wonderful stories. Thus the photographer of Gawsworth's death mask and the mysterious poet King Juan I of Redonda are magically brought together as Marías now recounts an equally fabulous tale of de Wet, interweaving the two with various other real figures from Sir Conan Doyle to Ödön von Horvath (the Austria-Hungary writer who spent a life in fear of being struck by lightning and died in Paris of the effects of a lightning bolt) that interconnects the figures he has mentioned with war, their literary activities, their somewhat insane actions, and their deaths, all of which Marías brilliantly reflects back upon his own life and activities.

In a strange way, accordingly, *Dark Back of Time* is almost like a reverse image of a fiction, as if Marías were challenging those Oxford professors who confused imagination with everyday reality; but it is almost certain that many of the characters of this book, who are all real (I found substantial entries for all on the internet, and had previously read works by Machen, Durrell, and von Horvath), will be thought of as imaginary given the outrageousness of their lives wherein events, as the author himself admits, were "random and absurd."

Just as the author learned to write as a child—he is left-handed and learned to write backwards so that his name XAVIER read to others as REIVAX—the strange worlds Marías relates in this fiction are visions of existences where the past is the future, worlds of times that do not yet exist. Thankfully he promises us at least one more future journey to that "Dark Back of Time."

LOS ANGELES, JUNE 7-9, 2009

Marías' approaches to fiction remind me of some of my own methods—perhaps even including the non-fictional fiction of my life in these pages—particularly in my creation of imaginary countries and various pseudonyms. Although I have yet to meet Marías, I do hope I get the opportunity. I also never met Javier Marías' beloved friend, Juan Benet (1927-1993), but Benet did send me, before his death, a small piece titled "Saturday or Sunday Brunch" for my Eating through Literature and Art "cookbook" published in 1994:

> I do not cook. I do not even know how to boil an egg and hardly may I offer a recipe of my own for your book. I only dare to make a suggestion: try every two weeks, on Saturday or Sunday morning, a brunch consisting of Icelandic or Scandinavian marinated herrings, smoked eel, Spanish "salazones" (i.e. mojama, tuna and several other roe), German sweet gerkins, "serrano" ham and lots of Danish beer and Russian vodka. That is all. You will feel great on Saturday or Sunday afternoon.

A wonderful combination to which I will one day treat myself!

I also reviewed Marías' collection of short tales,

When I Was Mortal, *published in English in 2000, which I've included below.*

LOS ANGELES, JUNE 16, 2009
Reprinted from EXPLORING*fictions (April 2012).*

Coincidence and Contradiction

JAVIER MARÍAS **CUANDO FUI MORTAL** (MADRID: ALFAGUARA, 1996), TRANSLATED FROM THE SPANISH BY MARGARET JULL COSTA AS **WHEN I WAS MORTAL** (NEW YORK: NEW DIRECTIONS, 2000)

ALTHOUGH, AS THE AUTHOR makes clear in his brief Foreword, the stories of *When I Was Mortal* were culled from many sources and written often on consignment with specific requirements, there is an odd

continuity between the 12 short works of this book. All but two concern death, and in one of those two in which a death does not occur ("Unfinished Figures"), it is imminent. Seven of the deaths are murders, primarily of spouses and sexual partners. Ghosts haunt two of these works (the title story "When I Was Mortal" and the last tale of the book "No More Loves") and a seeming ghost is central to the best tale of the volume, "Spear Blood." The narrator or onlooker is more or less a voyeur in seven of the tales, and even when the subject of observation is merely a horserace, as in "Broken Binoculars," there is throughout the story a sense of voyeurism as two men at the track share a single pair of binoculars in order to watch the races and the possible entrance of one of the men's employer. Illness stalks the characters of four of these stories, and in two of them ("Everything Bad Comes Back" and "Fewer Scruples") figures central to the story commit suicide. Two of the stories deal with homosexuality. One might simply chalk all these commonalities up to the author's interests, his major themes, his preoccupations. But the continuities between stories—although the works themselves are superficially unlinked—continue. Two tales contain a character named Custardoy, and in two side-by-side tales ("Fewer Scruples" and "Spear Blood") figures visit the same street, Torpedero Tucumán. In two stories central figures are bodyguards, one who plots the death of his employer and the other whose charge manages to kill herself despite his protection. In these same two stories characters wear cowboy hats in connection with sex. And two of the book's characters die at the age of 39. Even within tales, coincidences and continuities abound: in the first story of the book, "The Night Doctor," the narrator leaves a party to accompany a woman to her home, where she is being visited by a late-night Spanish doctor, only to return back to the home of his host, for whom the same doctor later appears. In "The Italian Legacy" two of the narrator's Italian friends living in Paris (a character in the first story was also an Italian friend living in Paris) marry husbands who upon traveling become suddenly ill, recover, and change (or promise to change) into violent personalities.

I mention all of these situations not for any thematic intention on the author's part, but because they lend this assortment of tales a kind of strange magic, a subliminal linking that forces the reader to look more carefully at individuals, events, objects. The story central to the book, expanded from its original form, is, indeed, a kind of detective story which requires exactly this sort of attention to detail that Marías seems to ask of the reader. In "Spear Blood" the narrator's friend from childhood is found dead—the very day after he has dined with him—in his own bed with a spear plunged through his body. Next to him lies a nearly naked South American woman who evidently was speared previous to Dorta, his friend. The weapon was Dorta's, brought back from a trip to Kenya. But the police cannot determine the identity of the other victim nor have they any leads on the murderer himself; they can only presume that the woman was a prostitute brought home by the victim, who was murdered by a jealous husband or pimp. But the narrator, who knows his friend well and, as we gradually discover through the course of the story, has an abiding love for him, cannot believe this version of the murder—primarily because his friend was a confirmed homosexual who eschewed all sexual relations with women. Incredulous as the events seem, the narrator becomes fascinated by the existence of this woman, going so far as to ask the detective for a photograph of her dead body. Without further evidence, the police stick to their version and the case is allowed to be forgotten. One night, however, as the narrator is enjoying an evening at a local restaurant, he spots a woman who appears in every detail to be the same as the one in his photograph—she even smokes the same Indonesian cigarettes as had his dead friend; however, in the photograph he has primarily studied her exposed breasts, and he now realizes he must actually see her breasts to determine if it is the same woman. He follows her and her companion to a bordello. Without giving away the plot, the result—if one has attended to all the small details of the story—is as inevitable as an adventure of Sherlock Holmes.

Not all the tales in this volume are as brilliantly plotted and crafted as "Spear Blood," but all are marvelously mysterious and clouded in suspense. And Marías' suspenseful style of numerous run-on sentences, compounded into ongoing streams of excited phrases marked by commas, comes across in Margaret Jull Costa's excellent translation. One can hardly wait for New Directions to publish, as they have promised, several of this Spaniard's novels.

LOS ANGELES, JULY 8. 2000
Reprinted from *EXPLORING*fictions (April 2001).

On March 7, 2012, I received a letter from Javier Marías concerning his America Award of a couple years earlier, thanking me for that award, his first, he admitted, in the United States. In response, I sent him the following letter:

Dear Javier Marías,

Thank you so much for your kind e-mail. I don't quite recall now why we didn't try harder to get in contact with you previously regarding The America Award. I am also a writer, with a book published by New Directions, and I know Barbara Epler quite well. And, as is obvious, I'm a great admirer of your writing.

I don't know if Barbara told you, but I am the publisher of Sun & Moon Press—a press often spoken of as a smaller New Directions—and, since 2000, the publisher of Green Integer, which specializes in poetry, fiction, drama, and belles-lettres in translation.

Several years ago, at the Frankfurt Book Fair, your earlier publisher (I believe the one you highly criticized in your fiction) gave me a review copy of one of your fictions. Had I only had a good Spanish translator on hand, I might have published your work in the US. But then New Directions has been able to bring most of your books into English in a way that would have been difficult given my finances.

In any event, I have published to date about 300 books on Sun & Moon (including the original City of Glass by Paul Auster, Russell Banks' earlier fictions, and works by numerous US and international writers). And I have published about 200 further books on Green Integer, a list of which you can find at www.greeninteger.com. Among our writers are Julien Gracq, Tomas Tranströmer, Robert Bresson, Luis Buñuel, Osman Lins, Ko Un, Adonis, Norberto Luis Romero, André Breton, etc.

Moreover, I've written, as part of my cultural memoir, My Year_____ (books published annually from 2000 to the present), two essay-reviews on your writing, which I have attached.

I will also send you (if I might ask your address) a more formal statement of The America Award.

Finally, I have an original copy of the first American translation of Odon von Horvath's fiction

The Age of Fish *(Jugend ohne Gott) if you'd be interested.*

My very best regards,

Douglas Messerli, Publisher

At Odds

W. G. SEBALD **VERTIGO**, TRANSLATED FROM THE
GERMAN BY MICHAEL HULSE (NEW YORK: NEW DIREC-
TIONS, 2000)

THE DEATH BY a car accident on December 14 of this year of W. G. Sebald led me to read his first fiction, *Vertigo*, a book, along with his *The Emigrants* and *The Rings of Saturn*, many of my friends have long championed.

In many respects Sebald might remind one of his younger contemporary, Javier Marías. Like Marías, Sebald does not so much tell a single story as observe and seek out a series of coincidental events, historical and personal, which he weaves together through photographs and linguistic images from literature, history, his travels and his own past. All of these aspects, super-ficially similar to Marías' narratives, exist in *Vertigo*, as the narrator moves from Marie Henri Beyle's (better known as Stendhal) terrifying memories of crossing St. Bernard Pass with Napoleon's army to Sebald's own journeys from Venice to Verona, from the journey of Kafka to Riva, near Desenzano, to a recounting of Se-bald's youth in the German village of W.

Through the numerous events in each of the book's four parts, Sebald explores amazing coincidences: for example, a fellow traveler reads Leonardo Sciascia's book *1912+1* soon after a friend reminds Sebald of the journey Kafka took to Riva in 1913, where he may have witnessed the Verona opera festival's first production, *Aïda*. Later, in the town of W., Sebald sees the numbers 1913 over a doorway, and the book ends with a passage from the 1913 version of Samuel Pepys' diary, found in the attic of a building in which he had lived as a child.

Again and again, there is an eerie connection be-tween unrelated things, seeming to present a puzzle for which there is no solution. The various gaps between these events or pieces of information create a sense of dislocation and confusion, as remembered scenes are revealed as false, and what appear as dreams become reality. There is, in short, a sense of dizzying vertigo throughout Sebald's book, as if places, objects, and events have a reality separate from the people who are involved with them.

It is just this sense of vertiginous reality that separates Sebald's literary world from Marías'. Where Sebald actively attempts to connect or at least to understand these "coincidences," Marías often seems just as happy to simply witness and point them out. And there is, accordingly, numerous moments of stupor, of a sickening sense of irreality, in Sebald's work that is fortunately lacking in Marías' writings. One might simply chalk it up to the radically different sensibilities of the Germans and the Spaniards, but there seems to be something else that lies behind the differences which also subtracts from the personal joy I might have expected from reading just such a text.

Perhaps it emanates from the much more academic interest Sebald takes in these strange occurrences. Unlike Marías, who declares that he is often a passive observer of the unusual facts and texts he discovers, at several instances Sebald actively researches the past, visiting libraries and friends with special information with whom he attempts to make sense of these puzzles. The fact that no coherent truth is ever possible, however, appears to take on disorienting aspects, almost haunting his life. Marías is far more like a kind of amateur sleuth who will gladly take on his adventures, but is more often just has happy to find no apparent answer.

In short, there is a sense of *angst* to Sebald's world, and the writers he features, Stendhal and Kafka, share his feelings of displacement. It is as if Sebald were a high modernist who has discovered himself in a postmodern world, and he is not at all happy about that fact. He often seems to be working at odds to his own tales, as if all the disconnections, accidental photographs, and odd peregrinations he recounts were an expression of his failure to create a more coherent whole.

Yet, there is another perspective about this; for at several points, particularly in recounting his child-hood, we know of or at least suppose a coherent real-ity to explain away the strangeness. But he cannot or will not speak out to those around him or even attempt to explain the story to himself. One of the best exam-ples of this is his witnessing the beautiful barmaid at the Alderwirt, Romona, having sex in the back of the building with an isolate former hunter, Schlag. The next morning he discovers the bar's owner has utterly destroyed everything in the place, and later in the day, Schlag's body is found at the foot of an icy cliff, where, so it is believed, he inexplicably (he is a seasoned hiker in this territory) has fallen to his death. Sebald recounts these events just as if they were as oddly coincidental as all the others he relates. But we suppose, at least, that here there is a connection, that somehow the Alderwirt landlord, Sallaba, also discovered the sexual act, reacting with rage against the old sinner. In this and other cases, accordingly, it feels as if the author is purposely withholding information, refusing to reveal any logic in a world where he has painfully determined to be utterly mystifying.

It is this desperate search for coherence under conditions where memory and significance are so vague, I believe, that draws so many readers to Sebald's books. Like Sebald, they feel utterly ill-at-ease, even sickly, when they face the inexplicably dangerous terrain standing before them. I simply do not share this great dis-ease, and was somewhat irritated for having to endure it.

LOS ANGELES, JULY 15, 2009
Reprinted from *Green Integer Blog* (July 2009).

Out of a Dream

JAY DRATLER, SAMUEL HOFFENSTEIN, AND BETTY
REINHARDT (SCREENPLAY, BASED ON THE NOVEL BY
VERA CASPARY), OTTO PREMINGER (DIRECTOR) **LAURA**
/ 1944

DESPITE ITS NEAR universal acclaim—the film has received almost a 100% rating on the internet's Rotten
Tomatoes and was chosen for inclusion in The National
Film Registry—I've always felt that Otto Preminger's
1944 movie *Laura* was a kind of creaky, if slick melodrama with an almost sickly romantic theme song, repeated over and over again until any discriminating audience member develops a headache. Each time I watch
this film, I am forced to hum its sweeping/weeping
strains for days on end, and for that very reason alone
I have tried to steer my viewing habits away from it for
years, encountering it only by accident again the other
day, after watching a Turner Classics Movie reprise of
Hitchcock's *North by Northwest*.

Speaking of Hitchcock, for a far better version of

Laura, its lead equally mesmerized by a dead woman who after haunting him comes back to life, you might watch *Vertigo*. Much like Laura, Judy Barton / Madeline Elster  is stunningly made over by the men in her life, which ends in not only a loss of identity but in her death, both symbolical and actual—the only major difference being that Laura survives her "death." Or does she?

Perhaps *Laura* is a film that, like the fine bottles of wine that Waldo Lydecker (Clifton Webb) impeccably chooses, improves with age. For what I had dismissed for most of my life, I admired this time round, at the age of 54. As a youngster, I might hazard a guess, I could not have recognized just how "creepy"—as the enthusiastic but seldom well-spoken Drew Barrymore characterized some of the film's major figures in a chat with *The Essentials* host Robert Osborne—the Kentucky-born gigolo Shelby Carpenter (Vincent Price) and his wealthy would-be mistress Ann Treadwell (the marvelous Judith Anderson) truly are. As Treadwell makes clear to Laura Hunt (Gene Tierney), Shelby, like herself, is no good—surely not the right person for the glamorous advertising executive.

Treadwell needn't really worry, for by that time Laura has already perceived that Shelby, the man who "before her death" she had planned to marry, is not Mr. Right. Besides, from the very moment she encounters the handsome, tough-talking cop, Mark McPherson  (Dana Andrews), she is attracted to him; and he is equally determined to win her away from the bad lot with whom she has involved herself (as McPherson tells her: "I must say, for a charming, intelligent girl, you certainly surrounded yourself with a remarkable collection of dopes"). One might even say that, somewhat like Scottie Ferguson in Hitchcock's *Vertigo*, his own neurotic, voyeuristic and necrophiliac-inspired love has called her into being again.

The film certainly suggests that possibility as, virtually camping out in Laura's empty apartment and after having read her personal diaries and letters—let alone enduring the ambient theme music every time his eye (or the camera's eye) catches a glimpse of the kitschy painted-over photograph of the high-toned dame—he falls into a kind of cheap scotch-induced sleep. At that very moment the door opens and a suddenly resurrected Laura enters her apartment!

All right, there is still a great amount of action to be played out after that. And Laura explains her absence: she has been at her country house, thinking things out. The dead woman, the plot reveals, was not Laura, but a fellow employee, Diane Redfern. Finally, McPherson hasn't yet solved the murder!

But let us imagine that in his poor confused mind, he solves the crime not in real time, but in dream time: that he has called up a seemingly real-life dame in order to get to the bottom of things, and that the rest of the film is simply a dreamscape which resolves what logically—particularly given the dozens of abandoned clues and dead-ends that are never resolved—cannot otherwise be sorted out. The film even clues us into that possibility when, as Laura Hunt enters the door, suddenly back from the dead, McPherson rises and rubs his eyes as if to reassure himself that he isn't dreaming. But, obviously, the visual clue reasserts that very possibility, as does Lydecker's own final radio broadcast, suggesting that love "reaches beyond the dark shadow of death."

Surely that would explain why the man who appears the most likely to have committed the crime, Shelby Carpenter—who not only illicitly meets with Redfern in Laura's apartment, but sends her off, by insisting she answer the door, to her death—later attempts to cover up the use of Laura's rifle, simultaneously implicating

Laura herself. Likely perceiving that his relationship with the unattainable Laura is finished, he has the most reason to want to kill her—yet McPherson and the plot suddenly leave him off the "hook."

Although Ann Treadwell has a motive, she appears to be too wrapped up in herself to have plotted out such a murder—although, as she admits, she has certainly imagined it!

No, the man who most irritates McPherson is the nasty, spiteful, effeminate, class-conscious snob, Waldo Lydeck-  er, who abuses the young policeman every chance he gets, even to the point of diagnosing McPherson's "disease," suggesting that he should seek out a psychiatrist's help:

> You'd better watch out, McPherson, or you'll finish up in a psychiatric ward. I doubt they've ever had a patient who fell in love with a corpse.

Beginning with the insertion of his naked body in the very first scene (demeaning McPherson even more by demanding that the cop hand him his towel and robe, as if he were a personal dresser), Lydecker has pushed

his way into the cop's life as if *he,* the journalist, were stalking the cop, rather than the other way around. Given Lydecker's recognition of McPherson's slim, attractive body (qualities which he accuses Laura of having been smitten by), it almost appears that Lydecker, himself, rather than Laura, is on the "hunt"; that despite Lydecker's obsession with his Pygmalion-like creation Laura, it is McPherson who takes him over the edge.

The game of BB baseball that McPherson plays throughout is the only way he can steady his nerves around so many—just as Barrymore characterized them—creeps! And Lydecker, the biggest creep of them all, fits nicely into McPherson's private solution of his Laura-come-alive-again fantasy. Just as Lydecker has previously turned Laura against all her previous suitors, so now does McPherson successfully turn Laura against Lydecker, as she finally cuts off her relationship with the often priggish slanderer ("I don't use a pen. I write with a goose quill dipped in venom," he quips).

Since the savior-policeman has defeated time, like Orpheus freeing his Eurydice from death, it is utterly necessary for McPherson to destroy all remnants of present time that remain, including Lydecker's two beloved matching grandfather clocks. He kicks in Lydecker's home clock in search for the missing "weapon," and, discovering the hidden entry to the lower parts of the second clock in Laura's apartment, he ultimately uncovers the murder weapon, oddly returning it to its hiding place so that he might, inexplicably, pick it up again in the morning. Like so many of his actions throughout the film, his explanation further represents his illogical behavior—the behavior of dream-time rather than sober daily police sleuthing. And in the final shootout with Lydecker that clock also is revealed as having been destroyed.

It is almost as if he expects Lydecker's return, much like Lydecker himself, who anticipates the cop's return, so that they might have the symbolic "appointment" for which they were destined from the very beginning. Predictably, the shootout ends neither in Laura's nor in McPherson's death, but with Lydecker being killed; it is, after all, McPherson's dream fantasy, the movie closing with the beautiful Laura clinging to him for what apparently will be for the rest of his life.

Whether or not she truly exists hardly matters. Having fought for her, the "dumb" cop has won, and Laura is now his (for eternity if the reality is one of his own imagination). She is now able to transform him— a change he seems utterly willing to embrace—into a more civilized and sophisticated human being. Indeed, underlying the entire film and the Vera Caspary novel upon which it was based, is a struggle for self-improvement, class mobility, and social improvement.

If my version of this otherwise unconvincing film seems too far-fetched, it certainly seems more plausible than studio head Darryl F. Zanuck's revision of the film's ending, in which the entire story was revealed to have been a product of Lydecker's imagination. Even the savvy columnist Walter Winchell admittedly could not comprehend that scenario, insisting to Zanuck that he had to change it.

For me, it's just as difficult to believe that Preminger's ending represents a kind a realist playing out of events. At least, if it's McPherson's imaginative recreation of reality, things work out better for everyone, even if Laura simply represents the fantastical illusion of a cop who's gone over the edge—the same position, after all, in which *Vertigo*'s cop, Scottie discovers himself in the later Hitchcock masterwork.

LOS ANGELES, SEPTEMBER 29, 2001
Reprinted from *World Cinema Review* (November 2014).

Into the Frame

DANIEL MAINWARING (SCREENPLAY, BASED ON THE NOVEL *BUILD MY GALLOWS HIGH* BY JAMES M. CAIN, WITH UNCREDITED WRITING BY CAIN AND FRANK FENTON), JACQUES TOURNEUR (DIRECTOR) **OUT OF THE PAST** / 1947

IT'S INTERESTING THAT in the vast majority of American *film noirs*, it is the women who betray the heroes, usually world-weary gumshoes or seedy punks who are taken advantage of by wealthy crooks or society figures; the women surrounding them lie and murder, leaving the male figures very much "framed" and in the lurch. Never has this fact been more apparent than in Jacques Tourneur's masterful 1947 film *Out of the Past*.

The "hero" of the film, Jeff Bailey (Robert Mitchum), has, in fact, attempted to escape his shady past with a move to the small paradisiacal town of Bridgeport, California, where he now runs a gas station, fishes in the nearby pristine creeks and rivers with a young

 boy who can neither hear nor speak (Dickie Moore)—the perfect fishing partner, one might argue—and has fallen in love with a local girl, Ann Miller (Virginia Huston). In this prelapserian world, he has almost been able to create a new life; but before the film can even begin, we are introduced to the hulking figure of Joe Stephanos (Paul Valentine), a well-dressed stranger on the prowl for Jeff, whose past, we quickly perceive, has suddenly caught up.

The rest of the film is swallowed up in the story of that past and its continuing consequences, which, as in nearly all such films, ends, through the fewer and fewer choices available to its central figures, in death. A great part of Jeff's (whose last name, as he tells Ann, is really Markham) story is presented as a kind of confession to Ann, revealing how he was hired by Whit Sterling (Kirk Douglas) to track down Sterling's girlfriend, after she attempted to kill him (shooting him four times) and stole $40,000 of his money.

Not really wanting the job, but unable to turn down such a large payment, detective Markham tracks down Sterling's girl, Kathie Moffat (Jane Greer), in

Acapulco, where, under a more brutal sunlit landscape, Jeff is forced to spend his days drinking as he waits to encounter Whit's woman friend. When he does finally meet her, it is almost love at first sight—at least for him—as Kathie slowly tells her side of the story, insisting that although she had tried to kill Whit, she has stolen no money:

> KATHIE: But I didn't take anything. I didn't, Jeff.
>   Don't you believe me?
> JEFF: Baby, I don't care.

Together, the two plan their escape back to the States, but at the same moment Jeff encounters Whit and his henchman in Acapulco, checking up on him. Again, Jeff asks to be released from the case, but Whit refuses. Insisting that Kathie has slipped past him on a steamer heading south, he hurries off with Kathie to San Francisco.

The San Francisco in which this couple hides out is not the brightly lit city of Northern California but a dark, hidden world where the two attempt to escape notice. When they temporarily let their guard down, they are spotted at a race track by Jeff's old detective partner, Fisher, who was to share 50% of whatever Jeff got for bringing back Kathie. The two break up, taking different routes to a rural cabin in order to get Fisher off their

track. But when Jeff turns up to the cabin wherein Kathie waits, Fisher is already there. As the two men begin a fistfight, Kathie picks up a gun and shoots Fisher dead, and Jeff suddenly realizes that she has not only lied to him about stealing Whit's money but has now framed him for Fisher's death.

So Ann and Jeff arrive, back in the "present," to the dark gate of Whit's country estate, the grille of the gate itself reminding one of the long act of confession we have just experienced. At Whit's house, Jeff finds, unexpectedly, Kathie once again living with her former boyfriend. She has made the convenient choice once again.

This time Whit is in trouble with the Federal government for failing to report taxes, and his crooked lawyer, Leonard Eels, is blackmailing Whit for more money. Again Jeff attempts to escape his fate, but realizes that if he does not help he will be accused of having killed Fisher.

This time the world-weary Jeff perceives it as another frame-up, and back in an even darker San Francisco tries to warn Eels of the danger he is in. Another woman, Eels' secretary, Meta Carson (Rhonda Fleming), is involved this time around. Like Kathie, she is willing to kill her boyfriend, and does, as Jeff slips back into Eels' apartment to find him dead. Hiding the  body elsewhere, he slips into a nightclub where Whit's documents are kept—along with an affidavit that Kathie has signed insisting that Jeff has killed Fisher.

Again on the run, Jeff returns to the nearby Bridgeport streams, joined by his friend, the Kid. But unknown to him, Kathie has ordered Stephanos to trail the Kid, who leads him to the river where Jeff is fishing. Stephanos, about to shoot Jeff, is spotted by the Kid, who sends the tackle and hook of his fishing rod up to the rock where Stephanos stands, about to shoot, causing Kathie's henchman to fall to his death.

Back at Whit's, Jeff attempts to convince Whit of Kathie's double cross, while insisting that she also murdered Fisher. But when he returns again to Whit's Lake Tahoe house, he discovers that Kathie has killed Whit, and that she is now in charge. Either Jeff joins her or she will accuse him of all three murders! Finally, Jeff has no escape left—except to secretly call the police and warn them of their route.

Suddenly observing the roadblock ahead, Kathie realizes that she has been betrayed, and shoots Jeff dead. The police kill her. Beside her a large cache of money has fallen from her purse.

After Jeff's funeral, Ann attempts to make sense of these events, while her boyhood lover, Jim, tries to convince her to turn her attentions back to him. Asking the deaf Kid whether Jeff was truly running away with Kathie at the time of his death, Ann eagerly awaits his response. The Kid sheepishly nods his head "yes," and she turns back to the town and her ordinary life there. The Kid looks up at the gas station sign declaring Jeff's name—the same sign that drew Stephanos there in the first place—and salutes it, as if, through his act, he has done Jeff's bidding by allowing Ann to go on without regret and grief.

The plot of *Out of the Past*, if not exactly opaque or clear, at least makes reasonable sense, especially when compared with works such as *The Big Sleep, Laura*, as just described above, or Welles' *The Lady from Shanghai*. But the important structures of this dark work are the film's movement from light, to a more oppressive light, and into the black of the final scenes. For the haunted characters, moreover, the work functions almost as a puzzle-box in which door after door closes for each of them, until they are all trapped within each other's fates. If even one of them had been able to say "no," or to truly escape—as Jeff has so nobly attempted—all or at least some of them might have been saved. But the events of the past, in this film, are like steel bonds of fate, drawing the characters again and again closer to each other until they destroy every individual in their claustrophobic circle. Only with the Kid's final gesture is the past finally over and done with, freeing Ann to remain out of its grasp, even while it dooms the true hero to a kind of eternal damnation in the minds of those remaining in the still unfallen world. The only link between those worlds is a young boy who *cannot* and will not speak the truth. Yet in receiving and hearing Jeff's confession, Ann has, unknowingly, forgiven him, even if she cannot save him from his past acts; and so too, in attending to this sad tale, has the viewer.

LOS ANGELES, SEPTEMBER 14, 2001
Reprinted from *World Cinema Review* (February 2013).

A Way Out

GEORGE ABBOTT AND DOUGLASS WALLOP (WRIT-
ERS, BASED ON THE NOVEL *THE YEAR THE YANKEES LOST
THE PENNANT* BY DOUGLASS WALLOP), RICHARD ADLER
AND JERRY ROSS (MUSIC AND LYRICS) **DAMN YANKEES** /
NEW YORK, 46TH STREET THEATRE, MAY 5, 1955
  GEORGE ABBOTT AND DOUGLASS WALLOP (WRIT-
ERS, BASED ON THE NOVEL BY DOUGLASS WALLOP),
RICHARD ADLER AND JERRY ROSS (MUSIC AND LYRICS),
GEORGE ABBOTT AND STANLEY DONEN (DIRECTORS)
DAMN YANKEES [FILM VERSION] / 1958
  GEORGE ABBOTT AND DOUGLASS WALLOP (WRIT-
ERS, BASED ON THE NOVEL BY DOUGLASS WALLOP),
RICHARD ADLER AND JERRY ROSS (MUSIC AND LYR-
ICS) **DAMN YANKEES** / NEW YORK, MARQUIS THEATRE,
MARCH 3, 1994 / THE PERFORMANCE I SAW WAS IN 1995

ABOUT TWICE EVERY SUMMER, Howard and I watch
the 1958 movie version of the American hit musical
Damn Yankees. In 1995, moreover, we saw the Broad-
way revival of that musical with Bebe Neuwirth as Lola

 and Jerry Lewis as Mr. Applegate.

It was only the other night, however, that I realized that this work—which I believe I first witnessed at a community theater production as a child in Cedar Rapids, Iowa—metaphorically expresses the tribulations of those I have described throughout these critical memoirs as the American boy-men: adult males who, through their obsession with their memories of childhood activities, particularly sports, appear unable to cope when faced with their older selves.

I am sure women also have a parallel phenomenon (perhaps in the form of the eternal "beauty queen"), but I have particularly noticed this painful condition in American males when they reach what is generally described as a "mid-life crisis," which the character at the center of *Damn Yankees*, Joe Boyd, "the most devoted fan of the Washington Senators," is surely suffering from. Six months out of every year, he literally abandons his wife as his attention turns to sports, particularly baseball. But this year, more than ever, he is furious with the Yankees, and is willing to sell his soul for "one long ball hitter."

Suddenly the devil appears in the form of Mr. Applegate (played on stage and in the film by Ray Walton, who died on New Year's Day this year), whom passing friends of his wife cannot even see. To them Joe appears to be aging, muttering to himself. No matter; as fast as you can say Hannibal, Mo., Joe signs away his life, and, transformed into a much younger man (played in the movie, somewhat ironically given his gay sexuality, by Tab Hunter), leaves his wife a short note that explains that, while he'll miss his "old girl," he must be off.

Although we recognize that in the movie the separation will likely be only temporarily (after all Joe has insisted upon an escape clause), metaphorically speaking his disappearance stands for the thousands of American boy-men who at middle age suddenly seek out women other than their wives and/or are convinced they must escape the "confines" of their marriages (we've seen public examples of that behavior in all walks of life, including our Presidents, and I have personally observed such behavior by several of my relatives and friends).

Like many such males, Joe, without his marital ties, feels like (and in terms of the play's device, *actually is*) a younger man. But we all know that youth, after one has lost it, can never be regained "as it was." Joe can suddenly hit the ball out of the ballpark, but he is clearly unprepared for his transformation—he literally cannot fit into his shoes—and as he explores his new-found youth, he is as shy and bashful as a virgin.

In his newly discovered role as a handsome young man, he can barely tolerate the advances of Applegate's minion, Lola, a sexy bombshell (brilliantly played in the original production and the movie by Gwen Verdon) who climbs around, over, and across his body in her attempt to seduce him ("Whatever Lola Wants"). Tab Hunter's obvious discomfort in the role is absolutely perfect, for whatever new-found power and freedom Joe now feels, he is quite unable to consummate a new relationship, and, consequently, seeks out a way to return secretly to his abandoned wife.

But then Joe has the advantage of looking unlike his previous self, and it is likely that, having him rent a room in her house, Joe's wife, Meg, feels some vague sexual excitement herself.

The joy of this work is in our observation of the mad machinations of the Devil in disguise, Applegate, as he attempts to cheat Joe out of the agreement and send him on his way to eternal damnation—which in the 1950s was what some folks deemed as the natural punishment for such behavior. And ultimately, Joe feels as lost in his new identity as Lola is in hers—having been centuries ago transformed from the ugliest woman in Provincetown, Rhode Island to the beauty she is now. Ross and Adler's lovely lament of their condition, "Two Lost Souls"—

> Two lost sheep, in the wilds of the hills
> Far from the other Jacks and Jills, we wandered
>   away and went astray
> But we ain't fussin'
> Cuz we've got "us'n"
>
> We're two lost souls on the highway of life
> And there's no one with
> whom we would ruther
> Say, "Ain't it just great, ain't it just grand?"
> We've got each other!

—speaks of their estrangement from life. Enraged by Lola's betrayal, Applegate transforms Lola back into an ugly hag, and, as Joe reaches for a catch at the end of the final game, changes him back into the middle-aged misfit he was at the beginning of the movie. Suddenly, they do not even have that lamentable friendship.

Despite Applegate's fury, however, Joe does catch the ball, saving the day and dashing off to return to his marriage with Meg.

As the Devil attempts to convince Joe to return,

Joe begs Meg to hold him tightly as he sings of his failed attempt to solve the fears and frustrations of old age:

A man doesn't know what he has until he loses it,
When a man has the love of a woman he abuses it,
I didn't know what I had when I had my old love,
I didn't know what I had 'til I said, "Goodbye, old
    love!"
Yes, a man doesn't know what he has 'til it is no
    longer around
But the happy thought is
Whatever it is he's lost, may some day once again
    be found!

So ends Douglass Wallop's and George Abbott's fable about mid-life male infidelity in the "Age of Anxiety." Would that all such suffering men could so clearly perceive their inevitable fates.

LOS ANGELES, AUGUST 16, 2008
Reprinted from *American Cultural Treasures* (January 2010).

City for Failed Acrobats

VÍTĚZSLAV NEZVAL **ANTILYRIK**, TRANSLATED FROM
THE CZECH BY JEROME ROTHENBERG AND MILOS SOVAK
(LOS ANGELES: GREEN INTEGER, 2001)

AFTER A COUPLE of years in
pre-production, my Green Integer press finally published
in July 2001 Jerome Rothenberg's and Milos Sovak's excellent translation, *Antilyrik,* a
selection of poems by the forgotten (almost unknown, at
least in the US) Czech experimentalist, Vítězslav Nezval.

Nezval, born in the village of Šamikovice in Southern Moravia, studied philosophy at Charles University
in Prague at the very time when Czechoslovakia was
the "first real and socially oriented democracy in central Europe" (Rothenberg and Sovak), and like most

Czech intellectuals of the time aligned himself with the Communist Party. The artistic counterpart of the political revolutionary spirit of the day was, for Nezval, an alliance with what was called the "Nine Powers" (*Devetsil*), a poet's and artist's collective that included some of the major figures of Czech experimentalism, including Jindrich Styrsky, Jaroslav Seifert, Karel Teige, Frantisek Halas, and Toyen (Marie Germinova). One of his first publications with this group was his long poem *The Remarkable Magician*, published at the age of 21.

From 1923 on Nezval presented his own program of poetics described as "Poetism," which set itself against "literary poetry" and proposed "a new art which will cease to be art." This movement would later ally itself with the Surrealists of Paris, particularly after Nezval's meeting with André Breton in 1932. Over the next 35 years Nezval would continue to publish, despite periods in which his art was banned and described as "degenerate," dozens of audacious works of poetry and fiction, as well as works of drama and art.

Our collection was only the third selection of his work to appear in English, and included several remarkable poems, including "City of Towers," where Nezval mesmerizingly repeats the word "fingers" to celebrate that human tool that helped him bring his Prague to life:

o hundred-towered Prague
city with fingers of all the saints
with fingers made for swearing falsely
with fingers from the fire & hail
with a musician's fingers
with shining fingers of a woman lying on her back
....
with fingers of asparagus
with fingers with fevers of 105 degrees
with fingers of frozen forest & with fingers
    without gloves
with fingers on which a bee has landed
with fingers of blue spruces
....
with fingers disfigured by arthritis
with fingers of strawberries
with spring water fingers & with fingers of
    bamboo

"The Dark City" presents a dream-like ghoulish world, a city like a carousel, houses like accordions, streets composed of beds from which the citizens come out like "giant worms" or "A pack of dogs that leaped out of a mirror." As the narrator escapes this nightmare world, the city crumbles into ruins and is left as only a pile of earth and ash.

A similar nightmare world is experienced in "The

Seventh Chant" from *The Remarkable Magician*, in which the sights and sounds of the city are linked to European history:

> I heard the secrets in a kiss
> the words around it circling like a line of colored
>   butterflies
> saw thousands of bacteria
> in a sick man's body
> & every one of them looked like a spiky chestnut
> like a cosmos making war
> with a skin of scaly armor
>
> I saw a human break free from his dying comrades
> in the pit of history that has no bottom

"Fireworks 1924" consists of 82 directions which Nezval defines as a "cinemagenic poem."

"Diabolo: A Poem for Night" is a longer more narrative work that recounts the movements of a sexually attractive but also vampire-like woman as she removes her clothing and ultimately "her breasts & rests them on the nightstand / then slips out thru the monastery crypt to take confession." Like the poem that follows, the woman's courtier is represented at times as being an "acrobat," a man caught upon the wire "between his wife's bed / & another woman's." The "nite vaudeville" Nezval describes becomes a story of equilibration, a "marriage halfway station for failed acrobats," presumably fallen beings from the wires connecting the city's many spires (Prague is commonly  known as the city of a hundred spires).

In his 1927 poem "Akrobat," Prague is seen as a meeting place of all Europeans where the acrobat, both a marvelous shape-shifter and a fallen fool, reveals the pleasures and tortures of modern life. Like a fairytale, the poem, Nezval argues, "redeems our happiness," to which, by the end of the poem, Nezval bids "farewell": "I leave you now so I can keep returning."

 Jerry Rothenberg is a long-time friend of whom I have written elsewhere. Milos Sovak, who was formerly a physician and now heads up a medical research company in San Diego, also has homes in Paris and Prague, where he grew up. I visited his Paris home on Rue Jacob in 1997, having a beautiful luncheon with him, his wife Dietland Antreter, and Diane and Jerry Rothenberg. When I told him where I

was staying, the Hotel Notre Dame, he claimed he had always stayed there before buying his Paris apartment. On this occasion Sovak also displayed several of the beautiful books of  poetry he had published by friends such as Cees Nooteboom and Manuel Ulacia, each accompanied by original artworks by noted painters.

In 1999 I visited Milos in Prague.

Milos, who comes from an illustrious Prague family, spent a couple of days touring me through the city, the first night taking me to the Švejk restaurant, whose walls carry the drawings by Joseph Lada and George Grosz for famed Czech novelist Jaroslav Hašek's *The Good Soldier Švejk*.

The next day Milos was kind enough to take me on a long walking tour of the old town and other parts of the city. At one point he showed me a large building where, during the final days of Nazi control, his father had worked as head doctor. As the German tanks were leaving the city in the early days of May 1945, one gun tank was conspicuously pointed at the hospital; it was clear that the Germans were determined to destroy the

 hospital (the only one that would accept Jewish patients) as they left. Those at work in the building, including Milos' father, were horrified by their imminent destruction. Meanwhile, as Milos describes it, an elderly woman who worked as the head secretary, sitting at her window and witnessing the scene, carefully took out her pistol from the drawer of her desk and aimed it at the operator of the tank, shooting him directly in the head. The tank careened around the square for several minutes before finally coming to rest.

That afternoon, Milos and I visited Argo publishers, where I met the publisher and his assistant, who some days later joined me in Frankfurt (in attendance at the Frankfurt Bookfair) for a Japanese dinner.

Back in Prague, Milos took me out to a splendid dinner at a lovely restaurant. I believe I ordered boar. On our way back home we walked across the Vltava River, stopping in a small park along the way where he pointed across to the home (more like a lit-up mansion, it appeared to me) in which he had grown up. "What a beautiful city," I sighed.

Prague was in near-complete renovation when I

visited. Nearly all of the buildings were enjoying new coats of the bright colors that now identify the Prague skyline. Milos scoffed, somewhat jokingly I presume, at all the renovation. "I somehow got used to and now prefer the old gray city Prague was for so many years under Soviet rule. Everything now seems so artificially bright!"

A few years later, Milos introduced me in Los Angeles to the beloved Mexican poet Manuel Ulacia, with whom Horácio Costa had lived for several years before I met him on my first trip to Brazil. Ulacia drowned while swimming in the ocean this year. A good swimmer, he was swept out to sea by undercurrents and was unable to return to shore.

LOS ANGELES, OCTOBER 17, 2009

In 2002 Milos and Jerry won the PEN Center USA award for their translation of Nezval's Antilyrik.

On January 26, 2009 Sovak died in San Diego, after a prolonged illness, at the age of 67.

LOS ANGELES, OCTOBER 18, 2009
Reprinted from Green Integer Blog *(October 2009).*

Broadcasting Silence

LARRY EIGNER **WATCHING/HOW OR WHY** (NEW ROCHELLE, NEW YORK: THE ELIZABETH PRESS, 1977)
LARRY EIGNER **THE WORLD AND ITS STREETS, PLACES** (SANTA BARBARA, CALIFORNIA: BLACK SPARROW PRESS, 1977)

FEW AMERICAN poets have sustained the consistency of voice, style, and poetic integrity that Larry Eigner has. After 22 collections of poetry and the publication of hundreds of as yet uncollected poems in little magazines, Eigner's two most recent books, *watching/how or why* and *The World and Its Streets, Places*, still present a world of people and things as fresh and revealing as his earliest works.

This is even more remarkable considering the seeming narrowness of Eigner's poetic range. Too much has been made of his cerebral palsy and his primarily house-bound life, yet the fact cannot be ignored that Eigner's subject and focus is almost entirely centered around the natural images viewed from the glassed-in front porch of his Massachusetts home. And in vocabulary alone, for example, Eigner's poetry is limited in scope. Words such as "sky," "tree," "squirrel," "street," "bird," and "sun" are key words in poem after poem. His poetry, accordingly, is without many of the effects—the Surrealist juxtapositions, the discontinuous narrative, the exotic images and vocabulary—that are so predominant in contemporary American poetry. Yet for all this, Eigner's work has continued to attract readers of "experimental" poetry and experimentalists themselves. From the Objectivist experiments of the early 1950s to the present-day linguistic experiments of the New York- and California-based "Language" poets, Eigner and his work have continued to exert an important influence.

But it is difficult to describe what it is about an Eigner poem that makes for such an impact. In the first place, Eigner would probably decry any such attempt. Like many poets writing since the 1950s, Eigner eschews intellectual analysis of his poems or poetics. And, secondly, the typical Eigner poem breathes simplicity:

ominous

sinister

the rain

smiles

(*TWAISP*, p. 11)

Poems such as this, in their naive-like use of pathetic fal-
lacy, carry with them an illusion of primitivism, an illusion Eigner himself often perpetuates. Writing recently
in a letter to the magazine *Là-bas*, Eigner remarked of
his poetics: "I myself go on serendipity.... I'm another
H. Rousseau if not Grandma Moses."

However, while some of his weaker poems never
transcend this primitivist impression of landscape,
Eigner's best poems—of which there are many in these
two volumes—reveal a personal involvement with
"things" that is as intellectually sophisticated as the
poetry of William Carlos Williams and Ezra Pound.
Indeed, it is to the Pound-Williams tradition that
Eigner is most often linked. As Samuel Charters, in his
introduction to Eigner's *Selected Poems* of 1972, has
perceived,

It [Eigner's work] is a poetry that accepts implicitly
the point of language and image that Williams had
honed out of the Rutherford, New Jersey, doctor's
office windows....

Eigner's poetry, like Williams', is of things rather than ideas; as Eigner wrote very recently in
$L=A=N=G=U=A=G=E$, "behind words and whatever language comes about are things...things and
people...." And Eigner's image is something akin to
Pound's "radiant node or cluster...through which, and
into which ideas are constantly rushing." Thus, while
Eigner's images are often grounded in the visual and the
aural, the poems, like Pound's and Williams', are dependent upon his engagement with the landscapes he presents. If meaning, as Eigner suggests in *The World and
Its Streets, Places*, "depends on your eyes" (p. 78), it also
depends upon the poet's and, ultimately, the reader's
participation in this world of things.

> thunder
> planes
>   I sneeze
>   a lot
>   of
>   things
>   slow
>   to take

<pre>
      slipped
         look
higher than itself
         some second ago
              the dam
                     broke
</pre>

(*w/how*, p. 36)

In this poem, the thunder, the sound of the plane and the poet's sneeze, are bound in a sequential relationship that results in both the natural and emotional releases expressed in the metaphoric "breaking of the dam" (in rainfall and psychological relief).

Yet here we also see where Eigner's poetry is radically different from Williams' more tightly controlled "machine of words." What is most important in the Eigner poem is not syntax or even line break, but the relation of words through their placement on the page. Superficially, this appears to have a great deal in common with Olson's theories expressed in his "Projective Verse," but as Eigner has explained, while Olson saw the poem as a field of energy, he (Eigner) thinks of the poem as "spatial quantity" (Charters, quoting Eigner in *Selected Poems*, p. xiii). This is a crucial distinction. Whereas Olson's kineticism demands that the poem be structured around a connective flow of ideation (as

Olson wrote in "Projective Verse," "One perception must immediately and directly lead to A FURTHER PERCEPTION."), Eigner's use of space tends to break connections, to sever ideational flow, to isolate and dissociate words and phrases.

The effect of this, of course, is to put stress on the word, the syllable and phonemic relationships, which, in turn, forces the reader to examine the word or syllable and to reevaluate it. Even in a poem that is primarily thematic we can see this at work.

        what a
         uniform is
       one thing

              yellow yellow yellow
                         star

                    (allowed publicly not to wear)
                    Sol Rossi   Mantua
                         composer   court musician
                    18th cent. syn
                         agog   sound   special
                           mark

....

(*TWAISP*, p. 173)

In the fragment printed above, Eigner obviously is writing about the uniform that Jews were forced to wear in persecution, and the rest of the poem deals with other uniforms which are forced upon people at the expense of their freedom and individual identity. But just as important as what this is *about* is how the poem breaks up thematic continuity. The repetition of "yellow yellow yellow," for example, pounds yellow into the reader's mind, so saturating it with the color that the word almost loses meaning and becomes a yell of frustration instead. It is only in the next line, with the word "star," that the obsession with the color and that resulting frustration make sense. A few lines later Eigner even takes apart words, as in "18th cent. syn / agog sound special." The abbreviation of century and the separation of the syllables "syn" and "agog" here allow for all sorts of new linguistic possibilities (including the concept of "sin," and the intense excitement of being associated with that "sin"; the Sol Rossi to whom Eigner refers was a Jewish musician, Salamone Rossi, court musician to the Gonzoga Dukes of Mantua in the Renaissance), as meaning is derived from prefix and suffix and attached by the reader to the words surrounding it.

In less thematically oriented poems, moreover, this process is carried even further.

Depth

a tree
   inches   felt
            distance

   a phonepole the sky slants

Leaves crying death, death, the wind
   in the sun
            rises

(*TWAISP*, p. 102)

Here, except for the possible continuous flow of meaning between "a tree" and "inches," the reader is presented with only fragments. Even more than in the other
poem above, the reader must focus on the phrase, the
word, or as in "D e p t h," on the letter, rather than the
continuous flow of ideas. The language itself, then, its
sounds, its rhythms, its denotative meaning wrenched
from associative context, is almost all the reader has to
go on. It is no wonder that the "Language" poets are so
attracted to his work.

    Just as significantly, however, the emphasis on
word and partial phrase draws the reader's attention
to what is *not* on the page, to what is missing, to the
space which surrounds the isolate fragments. And it is

there, as much as in the language, where Eigner's poems grow into meaning. In an Eigner poem it is as if most of the words have been erased, and the few that are left are merely clues to a complex mental process. The reader must be as attentive to space, to what happens between lines or between words, as he has been previously to the words themselves. In the poem above, for example, everything hinges upon what the reader makes of the space between "distance" and "a phonepole the sky slants." This forces the reader to participate, to search beyond the linguistic surface in an attempt to make meaning. In this process, paradoxically, Eigner's "things"—his "sky," "sun," "tree," "phonepole"—although originally grounded in specificity—become for the reader abstractions, universals which permit him his own specificity in confronting and resolving the void of Eigner's space.

Eigner poetically expresses this paradox as "broadcasting silence" ("the broadcast silence / like the sky," *TWAISP*, p. 94), a phrase which recognizes, it seems to me, the separateness of each individual; what for the reader is meaning can only be expressed by the author as silence, and vice versa. The shards of Eigner's language, then, serve as touchstones to the reader's discovery of his own life.

On the other hand, this does not mean Eigner's poems work primarily through association, that they serve the reader as a sort of Rorschach blot. In his best poems, reader and poet work together to make the world around them startlingly new. And there is something serendipitous about this process. One example will have to serve as illustration:

> noise absorbed
>   in the air
>
>   happiness
>   is quiet
>
>   have fun,   they say
>
>   the birds lean on bark
>   and sing
>   to our ears

(*TWAISP*, p. 110)

After the thousands of years and thousands of poems containing bird imagery, there is something truly wondrous about Eigner's birds leaning on that bark, upon the noise of their own singing.

COLLEGE PARK, MARYLAND, 1977
Reprinted from *PIP (The Project for Innovative Poetry) Blog* (June 2013).

Beginning as early as 1976 and lasting through the early 1980s, Larry Eigner sent me several typed letters and new poems for publication in my "second" magazine, Là-bas, a mimeographed monthly named after Huysman's famed novel. Those letters, typed from the very top to the very bottom, from the far left edge to the right on both front and back, seemed, at first glance, impossible to read. But with a great deal of attention it was possible to make one's way through this forest of words, and the journey was always a rewarding one. Below is a short sample:

Snday May 1st

The ephemeral nothing to sneeze at, any more, maybe, than the eternal, even if eternity shd exist. As I've forgotten at times, been frgetting. Ahh! And the long-ru cd never be without short terms, as in fact long stretch are made up of short ones. And after hearing, recently, Paul Whrich on thr radio sat he'd give it all up, judy retire and do nothing or hust abt naught if

he weren't a little optimistic, around the umpteeth environmentalist (ecolofosy I've hrd sat rgat, it finally dawbed [dawned?] on me - whereas 13 yrs vck Iwrote the forest// ytrrs.. toget-

ger. kow) that if something is big and-or
c, licated [complicate] engh, seeing or
trying utywyleo [?] is pretty mch a spe-
cialty, you're not getting enough of the
details to really be realistic.......

*Suffering from cerebral palsy, confined to a wheel-
chair, Eigner could not always clearly express what he was
thinking, but for anyone who cared, the ideas he proffered
in these thorny word woods, given an empathetic reading,
brought wonderment and joy. I consider these letters one
of my great treasures.*

*In 1995 Larry wrote me, asking if I'd be interested in
printing a new collection of his poems,* readiness / enough
/ depends / on. *I wrote him on July 10th saying that I
loved the manuscript and couldn't wait to publish it. We
began work on the book, but poet-friend Bob Grenier, who
was editing it, was insistent that each poem be presented
on one page (a difficult task given the standard Green Integer or Sun & Moon format) and that it be printed in
a typestyle close to that of the typewriter, Courier type, a
style I detest. Bob also wanted all letters to align precisely
as they did in Larry's typewritten poems, an almost impossible thing to accomplish in any other typestyle.*

*I visited Bob in Berkeley where we discussed several
alternatives. I changed the format to 6 x 9, and found a
typestyle that suggested typewriting but was somewhat*

more sophisticated. The editing process continued over the next four years.

On February 3rd of 1996, Larry Eigner died of pneumonia at the age of 68.

The Green Integer publication finally appeared in 2000.

The review above was written for Parnassus, but the editor seemed diffident about Eigner, demanding numerous changes, and I withdrew it.

LOS ANGELES, SEPTEMBER 20, 2009

Two Films by Hiroshi Teshigahara

A House at Sea

KŌBŌ ABE (SCREENPLAY, BASED ON HIS NOVEL),
HIROSHI TESHIGAHARA (DIRECTOR) **SUNA NO ONNA**
(**WOMAN OF THE DUNES**) /1964

THE DEATH OF Hiroshi Teshigahara on April 14th of 2001, led me to review this film, which I last saw, I believe, while in college. Having remembered little of my previous viewing, I was delighted to rediscover/discover this masterpiece.

Although critics of the Sixties (and some today) made a great deal of Abe's existentialist concerns, I think today the film points us less to its

philosophical (and thematic) issues, and reveals more its closer relationship to the Absurdists of the 1950s and early 1960s such as Eugène Ionesco and Samuel Beckett. While clearly having a relationship with Sartre's and Camus' ideas, the film has less to do with moral action than it does with indeterminate purposelessness, and its metaphors continually point to the absurdity of the major characters' situations.

Like many of the film's beautiful images, the plot is nearly an abstraction and can be easily summarized: an entomologist, Niki Jumpei, visits an isolated island consisting mainly of sand dunes, home to the beetle he is researching. He plans three days on this desolate island, returning to civilization each afternoon by bus. When he misses the bus, some local villagers, actually wily town elders, suggest that he stay in a local house. The houses, however, all appear to be located in deep ravines of sand, with access only through rope ladders.

Niki, a true innocent, descends to the house assigned to him, and enjoys a pleasant meal, despite the continuing intrusion of sand, with the woman living there, a widow whose husband and daughter have been buried in a sandstorm.

At first, the widow seems highly uneducated, explaining that her house is also subject to rot because of the moisture in the sand, an idea which the scientist, Niki, ridicules: we all know sand is dry. Other such sentiments have led some critics to describe her as ignorant, but we later learn that she is far wiser than her "guest."

The widow spends the night, oddly to Niki's way of thought, digging out the sand from around her ramshackle house, depositing it in containers which the locals hoist up and spirit away (for illegal use, we later

learn, in construction; sand with such a heavy salt content is good for making concrete). She explains that it's easier to work at night, and the sand must be taken away if

her and her neighbors' houses are to survive. Despite the continual rain of the fine grains of sand, Niki eventually falls to sleep, awakening to observe his now-naked host lying upon her futon.

Dressing, Niki arranges his knapsack and bugs, preparing to leave; but when he seeks out the ladder, he discovers it has been pulled up. Desperately, he tries to climb the walls of sand on either side of the house, producing merely small avalanches of more sand that result in him falling back to where he has started from.

Querying his host, the terrified Niki demands an explanation for what she answers "he already knows."

He has been duped by the locals, and is now trapped like an animal in this hell of a sandpit. The island gets few visitors, and like others before him, he has been "kidnapped" to help in the village's activities.

The rest of the film is a study in Niki's reactions, as, at first remaining determined to escape, he refuses to help shovel the sand, later turning to violence, gagging and tying up the woman. When he finally takes the towel from her mouth, she explains that the drink and food they have are rationed, and they will not deliver any new water until he begins to work.

As the two endure the never-ending rain of sand in their horrific thirst, Niki finally surrenders, and water is delivered. In a beautifully filmed scene of high eroticism, the two carefully brush and wash the sand from each other's bodies, the woman—who obviously has been starving for the touch of a human hand—gasping in the simple pleasure of the act.

Niki later binds together enough rope to temporarily escape, but when he attempts to outrun the local posse, he falls into quicksand; they dig him out only to return him to his internment. Pleading for just an hour each day at the ocean, Niki is hopeful that the local leaders may decide in his favor. They will grant him his wish, they report, only if he has sex with the woman while the entire village looks on, evidently their only form of entertainment. In a violent scene in which he attempts to force her to join him in the act, Niki loses out to the woman who is determined to keep her moral ground.

Niki, it is apparent, must come to terms with the absurd conditions of his existence. At one point, he asks the obvious existential question: "Do you shovel to survive, or survive to shovel?" Yet a far more important interchange reveals the miraculous salvation of their lives; referring to the endless sand about them, the man observes: "It's like building a house in the water when ships exist. Why insist on a house?" The wiser woman provides the simplest of answers in such an absurd world: "You want to go home too."

The home Teshigahara builds for the film viewer is an ever-shifting reality that is simultaneously breathtakingly beautiful and horrific. For this couple not only must live in a world in which no values are permanent, but endure an ever-changing landscape that reminds them every moment of their own mortality. Whereas, at the beginning of the movie, Niki checks his watch often, by the end of the film his new Eve reports that she has no idea of the time.

What ultimately comes to matter most is the relationship forged between the two. When the woman becomes pregnant and the villagers are forced to lower a ladder to take her away, they forget to pull it up, and Niki cautiously follows them into a possible escape.

Yet in the next scene we see him leaning against the house in the pit of sand. He cannot leave her. Besides he has made a new discovery: he has found a way to draw water out of sand just as she has maintained a house on a sea of sand. The absurd has been transformed into reality.

LOS ANGELES, MAY 4, 2009
Reprinted from *Green Integer Blog* (May 2009).
Reprinted from *Reading Films: My International Cinema* (2012).

Living in Vain

GENPEI AKASEGAWA AND HIROSHI TESHIGAHARA
(WRITERS, BASED ON A FICTION BY YAEKO NOGAMI),
HIROSHI TESHIGAHARA (DIRECTOR) **RIKYŪ** / 1989

THE GREAT 16th century master of the tea ceremony
and aesthetician Sen no Rikyū carefully fills the pot
with water in preparation for the highly ritualized tea
ceremony. Upon choosing a single flower from a bush
for a floral arrangement, he commands that all the others in bloom be cut away. The ceremony itself, the tea
prepared as part of Rikyū's lessons for his master, Toyo-
tomi Hideyoshi, is a slow one, filmed by Teshigahara in
dark tones, with only the red bowl (Hideyoshi will not
permit black bowls, although they too are described as
"venerable") that will eventually contain the tea glowing against the rest of the screen.

   In a sense, this one scene is the essence of Teshigahara's 1989 film: the pace of this scene, the quietness
of tone, and the fraught relationship of master teacher

to his master warrior alters little throughout the rest of the movie. Like the ceremony itself, everything in *Rikyū* lies in the subtle details of movement and verbal expression.

Hideyoshi is most appreciative of Rikyū's (the great Japanese actor Rentaro Mikuni) lessons, and it is clear that the master would like to become as cultured a man of aesthetics as his teacher, and that he seeks the graciousness and ceremony of the traditions. Yet he is a crude version of his own desires, at heart a brutal warrior, who, as the movie proceeds, grows into an increasingly blundering ox. It is clear from the beginning that, ultimately, the two men, Rikyū and Hideyoshi, cannot coexist.

One of Hideyoshi's first great joys is his invitation to serve tea to the emperor himself, an honor that might overwhelm anyone. Teshigahara's subtle direction shows us an unsure server who begins with shaking hands; yet he does succeed, and this, in turn, leads him to award his tea room with a surface of gold. A new pot, cast especially for him, is rejected since it has turned black.

In the hands of a broader director, we would immediately perceive Rikyū's displeasure in the changes taking place in his master's house. Indeed, some of Rikyū's friends, Soji in particular, are surprised by the teacher's placid acceptance of these changes. Although remaining true to himself, Rikyū admits, however, his own love of the gold-covered walls which make the room seem almost "infinite."

Like numerous artists before him, Rikyū clearly attempts to remain apart from the political world stirring around him. But when Hideyoshi declares his decision to go to war against both China and Korea, Rikyū recognizes the folly of the acts. Hideyoshi has already demanded the death of his own brother for daring to doubt his intentions, and commands Rikyū to poison the brother in the tea ceremony.

As the two men, Rikyū and Lord Hidenaga, dine together we are still uncertain of the outcome. But when Rikyū joins him in the drink, we realize that he will disobey his orders and that he can no longer remain neutral in the inevitable war between the moral

values of the past and the expedient demands of the present. But Teshigahara also suggests, through Rikyū's passivity, that there may, in fact, be no gap between the two. As we all know, the worship of past values and the aggressive brutality of the present may actually represent different aspects of the same thing. One need only remember Hitler's adoration of Wagner to comprehend this fact. The gift of a globe to Hideyoshi might be read almost as a reference to Chaplin's comic portrayal of Hitler in *The Great Dictator*, particularly in the context of Chaplin's own neutrality in World War II.

Even though he has disobeyed his master, Rikyū still refuses, despite Soji's and his brother-in-law's pleas, to save himself and his family. Yet the showdown between the two is inevitable, as Hideyoshi's visits Rikyū, presumably seeking advice. Rikyū advises against his master's attacks on China, which results in the removal of all statues of Rikyū and his being banished to Kyoto. For his insolence he is later ordered to kill himself.

Finally, it seems, Rikyū has realized that art cannot substitute for a life nor protect one from it. As he leaves, he discusses his actions: "I do not want to die, but I do not want to have lived in vain." The film ends with the terrifying vision of a father and daughter playing with the globe, followed by the facts that help us to realize, in the context of this dark and brooding dialogue between action and aesthetics, that all life is fleeting: Rikyū died in 1591. The shogun died six years later in Korea.

LOS ANGELES, MAY 30, 2009
Both pieces reprinted from *Nth Position* [England] (June 2009).
Reprinted from *Reading Films: My International Cinema* (2012).

The Smell of Death

ORHAN PAMUK **MY NAME IS RED**, TRANSLATED
FROM THE TURKISH BY ERDAĞ M. GÖKNAR (NEW YORK:
ALFRED A. KNOPF, 2001)

 ORHAN PAMUK'S 1998 NOVEL,
My Name Is Red, first published
in English translation in 2001,
is both a history about art in the
Arab world, and a story of a culture's erasing of that very histo-
ry. Set in late 16th and early 17th
century Turkey, Pamuk's work is
also a love story embedded in a
mystery. Before the book is over
two important Ottoman Court painters are killed, and
the murderer decapitated. And, at the same time, the
spiritual and intellectual struggles behind these events
bring an end to the long tradition of miniaturist book
illumination, jewels in Islamic art.

Pamuk's great gift of storytelling allows him to write a story that explains and admires the long tradition, while still questioning it. Simultaneously, through the multiple perspectives of his fiction, he reveals both the great love (often homosexual) between the miniaturists and the leaders of the court studios, while exploring the often brutal treatment of the younger miniaturists and their own struggles and plots to outshine one another and win over the adoration of their master.

Further, this complex tapestry of Turkish history is centered in a love story between a "potential" widow, Shekure—her husband has failed to return from the warfront—and a former painter, Black, who has just returned from battle. Black, who for years worked with Shekure's father, Enishte Effendi, has long been in love with Shekure. But her marriage to another, resulting in her two children, has made it difficult for him to express that love.

Traditionally, Shekure would have stayed with her husband's family until her husband's body was found or officially declared dead. In this case, however, Shekure's brother-in-law is determined to marry her, and, confused by that situation, she returns to her father's home.

Earlier in the book, another of the painters, Master Elegant Effendi, has been killed. Now suddenly, as Black and Shekure vow their love for one another, Enishte Effendi, Shekure's father, is found dead. Black, we know, is innocent. Who among Enishte's group is guilty: Olive, Buttterfly, or Stork?

The couple quickly hold a funeral for Enishte. Finding a preacher who will declare Shekure's husband dead, the two marry soon after. But their troubles have just begun. The former husband's family insists she must return to them, and the authorities, who suspect Black, are determined to torture all the painters until one confesses. In Shekure's house and elsewhere there is an overpowering smell of death.

Joining forces with the great Master Osman, head of the Sultan's studio, Black studies the Sultan's great library of manuscripts in search of a painting style—in this case the flared, open nostrils of a horse learned by one of the miniaturists at an early point in his studies— that reveals the identity of the criminal. What they discover remains vague; in some respects Master Osman cannot truly believe the murderer could be any of his beloved students. Yet what they witness in these books is the entire history of Islamic painting: pictures that, unlike those of Western artists (which the characters

refer to as "Frankish influences"), utilize stylized scenes and figures based on the earliest of the masters, with only slight shifts in form and line over the thousands of years.

While pondering these great books, Master Osman blinds himself in the tradition of the numerous masters who in their dedication to their art have gone blind. And Black is basically left alone to uncover the culprit.

All of this is made even more complicated by the outcries of several religious groups in the city against the work of the illuminators, and, in particular, against the painters secretly gathered by Enishte Effendi, who himself has seen the Frankish artists and, purportedly, has been influenced by them—which is most evident, so it is believed, in his last picture, stolen by the murderer himself.

I have often been accused in these volumes of revealing the entire stories of the books I discuss (their plots are seldom what motivates my reading and love of these works), but, in this one case, I will leave the discovery of that murderer to future readers of *My Name Is Red*. It hardly matters, moreover. Although Shekure's and Black's marriage survives, the incidents described in this book have brought an end to the miniaturist tradition, at least in Turkey. The Western styles of art have won out against the traditions expressed in these manuscripts. Sultan Ahmet I, who follows the beneficent Sultan of this work, is opposed to any work of art, even destroying a large clock with statuary sent to him by Queen Elizabeth I. The beautifully artful expressions of the Koran and folktales described in Pamuk's fiction are suddenly doomed to be forgotten, some are destroyed.

Even more importantly, a whole way of seeing the world has been altered. The abstractions of the miniaturists have been replaced by self-expression; art in subservience to belief is exchanged for an art that expresses the artist and his subjects.

LOS ANGELES, MAY 15, 2009
Reprinted from *EXPLORING*fictions (May 2009).

The Hidden Self

OSCAR WILDE **THE PICTURE OF DORIAN GRAY**
(NEW YORK: THE MODERN LIBRARY, N.D.)
ALBERT E. LEWIN (SCREENPLAY AND DIRECTOR,
BASED ON THE NOVEL BY OSCAR WILDE) **THE PICTURE
OF DORIAN GRAY** / 1945

IT MAY AT FIRST seem strange that Oscar Wilde's 1891 novel *The Picture of Dorian Gray* should center around a work of art that quickly begins to reflect the inner self of its subject, Dorian Gray, particularly given Wilde's insistence on the separation and difference between life and art. As Wilde insisted in the preface to this book, "All art is quite useless," and he admonished elsewhere that it should be admired just for that reason, because it is not life but something finer and of more importance than the real.

Yet Dorian Gray finds Basil Hallward's painting of him extremely useful in that it hides his true inner self from the world, at least if he can keep the portrait out of sight. Any physical evidence of his aging and his increasingly treacherous acts, indeed, has been subsumed by art in this fiction; and by hiding away that reality in his boyhood study, Dorian can cheat the world, despite the rumors surrounding him.

The metaphor here, of course, is not only about his villainous actions—Gray's corruption of friends and lovers, his use of drugs, and other devious transgressions—but concerns his own relationship with Lord Henry Wotton, a relationship that might remind one of Wilde's "friendship" with Lord Alfred Douglas.

In one of the earliest scenes between the two men, Lord Henry comes close to Dorian and "puts his hand on his shoulder," and the scene that follows is as close to a love scene—one in which the startled Dorian finds "his finely-chiselled nostrils" aquiver as "some hidden nerve shook the scarlet of his lips and left them trembling"—as the age might permit. A few moments later Lord Henry praises Dorian's beauty: "...You are the most marvellous youth, and youth is the one thing worth having." Soon after Lord Henry finds himself in near complete control over Gray's aesthetics through his introduction to the young man of what is obviously Huysman's *Against Nature*, a work that soon after determines Gray's collecting and reading activities. Later in the novel, moreover, we discover that Lord Henry and Gray have been sharing not only evenings at dinners and plays, but a vacation house. Gray's hidden portrait, accordingly, is a clear metaphor of an entirely closeted self, a hidden self that is not only ashamed of the consequences of his behavior, the suicide of Sibyl Vance and the ruination of several friends, but of its own sexuality.

It is no coincidence, therefore, that Dorian feels compelled to reveal to the artist himself the miracle of his painting, a work which Hallward has described as being rendered with his soul. And the murder of the artist is almost inevitable, given the fact that he has created a monster, an artwork that actually has an effect on life. Had Hallward heeded Lord Henry's (and Wilde's) own statements and created merely a work of great beauty, Dorian might have been spared, simply because his face would have revealed his criminal acts as his own beauty decayed. But Hallward has been so successful in his realism, that, as in a fairytale, he has turned the painting into a kind of fetish that connects it to being itself. Such a transgression, in Lord Henry's critical terms, is necessarily punishable by death. And just as Dorian has "lost" his real body to the painting, so too does he arrange to chemically dispose of Hallward's corpse; after Alan Campbell's "dreadful work," nothing is left of the body.

The consequences also of hiding one's own essence—one's actions and behavior—from the world has long been understood to result in self-loathing, evidenced in this fiction in Dorian's final days, as he, like the thousands of other closeted individuals before and after him, seeks to cleanse himself of his past. But given his hidden sexuality, it is no wonder that Lord Henry scoffs at his contrite act of breaking off a relationship with a young country woman; and there is something delightfully humorous in that act. It is also predictable, perhaps, that Gray must attempt to destroy "the evidence," so to speak, to wipe away any trace of his own condition, obviously, which ends in the self-destruction he has all too often been played out in real life. Only through an attack upon the painting can life be restored to its proper vessel, the human body.

Wilde uses the story of Dorian Gray, accordingly, almost as a moral lesson for the dangers of mimeticism. Art, he argues, must remain in its own sphere, in the world of the ideal. An art that attempts to mimic life can only diminish the trials and tribulations of the living.

LOS ANGELES, MARCH 21, 2001
Reprinted from *Green Integer Blog* (March 2001).

Hiding Out

DON DELILLO **THE BODY ARTIST** (NEW YORK: SCRIBNER, 2001)

WE FIRST GLIMPSE Lauren Hartke and her husband Rey Robles at breakfast in the seaside New England house they have rented. Like any couple, they go through the mechanics of eating, side by side, with little conversation, he awaiting the toast 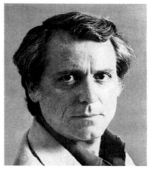 which must go through two cycles of toasting, she mostly staring into her bowl of soya, cereal, and fruit which she is about to eat. They meet only at the edges of life to discuss a hair she has found in the juice, the birds darting across their window, and a strange noise in the house they have both heard. In their silence, however, we not only recognize the normal patterns of a married couple, but the fact that they are also resisting something—trying to hide something from themselves not only about their relationship, but to escape living. Both, we later discover, are performers of sorts: Lauren, a body artist, a woman who performs less with language than her entire body, transforming herself into other figures; Rey, a film director who has apparently spent his life entertaining others in order to transform himself from a Spanish "war baby" into a Hollywood figure, uses his gifts of language and sex to obtain his version of the American Dream.

That same morning, we discover later in the book, Rey disappears on a long drive, ultimately arriving in the New York City apartment of his ex-wife, where he puts a gun to his head and commits suicide. DeLillo makes no attempt to explain these actions, nor does he give us much evidence through which to psychologically analyze their obviously failed relationship. Indeed the author almost seems to hide any possible information which might help us understand their acts.

Why, for instance, after the death, does Lauren remain at the isolated summer house, despite the pleas of her friends to return to New York? Far more importantly, why does she allow the man she discovers hiding out in that house—the source, perhaps, of the noise they have both heard—to remain there? Although she ruminates that she should be contacting mental institutions, old people's homes, and other places from which the strange man living in her house may have escaped, she passively accepts his entry into her life, even going so far as to bathe and shave him.

One obviously suspects that this being, whom she calls Mr. Tuttle, a person unable to speak coherent sentences, may be a figment of her imagination, a replacement for the missing Rey. It is tempting to see him as a kind of ghost-like figure created by her imagination to help alleviate the loneliness she must now endure. Indeed DeLillo, in several vaguely suggestive passages, presents this stranger as just such a transformative figure:

> He moved uneasily in space, indoors or out, as if the air had bends and warps. She watched him sidle into the house, walking with a slight shuffle. He feared levitation maybe.

At another point, after Mr. Tuttle attempts to explain her situation ("I know how much." He said, "I know how much this house. Alone by the sea."), Lauren attempts to fill in the spaces of his conversation:

> He looked not pleased exactly but otherwise satisfied, technically satisfied to have managed the last

cluster of words. And it was in fact, coming from Mr. Tuttle, a formulation she heard in its echoing depths. Four words only. But he'd placed her in a set of counter-surroundings, of simultaneous insides and outsides. The house, the sea-planet outside it, and how the word *alone* referred to her and to the house and how the word *sea* reinforced the idea of solitude but suggested a vigorous release as well, a means of escape from the book-walled limits of self.

When Mr. Tuttle does speak at greater length, she realizes that the words coming from his mouth are not his own, but fragments of conversations between herself and Rey, remnants from the lives of two beings as hidden from reality as Mr. Tuttle has been from them.

In short, *The Body Artist* is less about the performance of living (although the situations Lauren experiences are later *performed* by her in New York) than about the traces of lives. It is as if DeLillo were creating characters by drawing his fingers across a mirror or a window, revealing them momentarily as the light, air, and flickering movements of nature just as quickly shift our attention away, so that we discover, upon refocusing on the sketches, they have all but disappeared. The author, accordingly, seems less interested in the humans populating his work than in the fragmentary images of their body parts:

> She was looking at the backs of her hands, fingers
> stretched, looking and thinking, recalling mo-
> ments with Rey, not moments exactly but times, or
> moments flowing into composite time, an erotic of
> see and touch, and she curled one hand over and
> into the other, missing him in her body and feel-
> ing sexually and abysmally alone and staring at the
> points where her knuckles shone bloodless from
> the pressure of her grip.

In other words, DeLillo presents this work less in old-
fashioned literary terms than in snippets of images, as
in film. Moreover, we gradually come to see that it is a
filmy, hazy world, a fabrication of reality, in which Lauren and Rey have lived.

By the work's end, we can only wonder whether
or not Lauren will give into her hidden world, inhabit
the vision of a sexual hysteric, or step out into the "real"
world with which she has seldom engaged. Even she
is uncertain, as she expects to enter a room where *he*
(Rey, Mr. Tuttle, whoever he is) sits smoking. Instead,
she enters the room to find no one there, only her own
imprint on the side of the bed where she has slept:

> The room was empty when she looked. No
> one was there. The light was so vibrant she could

see the true colors of the walls and floor. She'd never seen the walls before....

She walked into the room and went to the window. She opened it. She threw the window open. She didn't know why she did this. Then she knew. She wanted to feel the sea tang on her face and the flow of time in her body, to tell her who she was.

From the fragmentary images of a life, a hidden life, Lauren has seemingly emerged as a real being, a person with a true identity. But then, as we all know, just as the pretense of fiction depends upon the words detailed into pattern, the pretense of film depends upon light.

LOS ANGELES, DECEMBER 3, 2001
Reprinted from *American Cultural Treasures* (January 2002).

The Thing Itself and Not

YOEL HOFFMANN **THE HEART IS KATMANDU**,
TRANSLATED FROM THE HEBREW BY PETER COLE (NEW
YORK: NEW DIRECTIONS, 2001)

YOEL HOFFMANN's 1999 fiction *Lev hu Katmandu*,
translated this year by Peter Cole, is a fiction consisting
of 237 small chapters made up of dream-like imagery,
profane observations, and religious iconography somewhat like tiny linguistic equivalents of Chagall's paintings. Many of these almost seem fey in their surreal-like
metaphors:

20

Like the water cow that lowers its head and sees, for
a moment, the murky green, he asks himself:
   What *else* do I have to do? Inquire about
something in a shop? Write to a certain office?

His thighbone is weak, and his left foot will go (he

knows) somewhere else. Chinese ladies holding delicate fans waft a breeze over their faces and, with gentle voices, ask the foot: Wong Way?

The ears are directed toward the large grass-hoppers, standing there motionless, and the right hand (a sign, as it were, of life) agrees to die because what...

Suddenly he's thinking about soccer fans ("jerks...").

And after reading 20 or 30 of these short sections one has a sensation of having too many sweet confections, almost as if having consumed that same number of jelly beans.

That is not to say that all of these miniature comments and observations contain only pleasant images. Often, particularly early on in the book, the major character, Yehoahim, sees the world with a kind of vague dismay that accompanies an unacknowledged sorrow.

Now he is thinking:
    I had a dog and the dog died.
    I had a woman and she went away.

I have seen cadavers. The empty shell of a man, and I have heard the terrible sound lying beneath the world.

Others of these condensed fictions seem to be almost out of a Fellini film such as *Juliet of the Spirits*:

> The voices whisper to him: Open the umbrella! Open the umbrella! But his hands are frozen with fear.

Overall, there is such a gentleness in Hoffmann's tone that occasionally one feels that he is writing the book with rose-colored glasses.

Indeed his story of *The Heart Is Katmandu* is a kind of love tale, a story of the "innermost streets" of the heart that wind through the mazes of the mind. Having lost his wife and being lost in his own life, an older man Yehoahim asks a local woman like his wife, Batya, for a date, and, despite Batya's Mongolian baby (whose father she refuses to name) and the existence of

a current boyfriend, Robert, the two quickly fall in love. That love, in turn, lets loose a world of new possibilities and questions, which the fiction ponders in these compressed poetic passages.

To say that Hoffmann's short sections are "compressed" is almost an understatement, for the author (who is also Professor of Eastern Philosophy at the University of Haifa) creates, at his best, black holes of intellectual energy to give voice to his everyday characters. While neither Yehoahim nor Batya are brilliant thinkers, in their imaginations and emotional make-up they encompass both the sensuous world around them and profound revelations:

> Yehoahim rises like a foot at half past seven, wraps his body in a bathrobe, and sits down to write:
>
> Dear Berman,
> In your last letter you argued that Quantum Theory involves an inconceivable logic according to which a thing is both itself and not itself. Last night I understood that such a logic is in fact quite feasible.
>
> How is the horse you take out of the drawer each morning?

In the end, accordingly, Hoffmann's sometimes-sweet poetic passages are anything but simple, for they explore a world in which what things appear to be are in fact just that—and yet are not. By fiction's close what was once a world made up of a lonely man and an unhappy woman with a Mongolian baby becomes a family:

...and the baby's name is Jonathan, and Yehoahim receives his name, and Batya hers, in the way a general pins a medal to the chest of an outstanding soldier. The caption "this is a family" flashes across the ceiling, as though being drawn by a small airplane. Everything has its name, and the name has one as well.

The untold story has at last been revealed.

LOS ANGELES, JULY 15, 2001
Reprinted from *Green Integer Blog* (July 2001).

FOUR LONG NIGHTS

A Romantic Paradise

ARMYAN BERNSTEIN AND FRANCIS FORD COPPOLA
(SCREENPLAY, WITH ADDITIONAL DIALOGUE BY LUANA
ANDERS), FRANCIS FORD COPPOLA (DIRECTOR) **ONE
FROM THE HEART** / 1982

I SUSPECT MANY critics and moviego-ers disliked Coppola's absolutely charming *One from the Heart* for its lack of realism, something they may  have felt was essential to his great *Godfather* films. In ac-tuality, however, Coppola has always been a romantic, with a greater interest in the theatricality of film than in its realist perspectives. Any filmmaker who might undertake to direct the absurdly ridiculous (but loveable) fantasy of *Finian's Rainbow* has to be possessed of an inflatable heart, ready to expand at the slightest of yearnings. Equally incredible is Coppola's huge remake of Conrad's *Heart of Darkness*, a murky tale in the first

place, but even darker and more inscrutable in Coppola's *Apocalypse Now*, a film that nearly killed everyone in its making. I think any slightly perceptive viewer realized the *Godfather* films were romantically inspired—if nothing else Nino Rota's and Carmine Coppola's musical scores make that evident—yet many felt that the New York and Italian settings lent these films a deep sense of realist sensibility. Looking back on *Godfather* and *Godfather II* we can now see just how both films are romantic *noirs* at heart, bigger and more audacious than any "slice of life" movie might possibly have been able to achieve.

In *One from the Heart*, however, Coppola seemed determined from the beginning to attempt to outdo Douglas Sirk and Nicholas Ray, to make it clear to his admirers just how deeply his work was embedded in theatricality and melodrama. Instead of shooting on location, the entire film, including Las Vegas' McCar-

 ran Airport, was shot at his Zoetrope studios—that is, except for the most theatrical scene of all, shot on the back lot of a "Las Vegas junkyard" set. The lighting is pure hokum, everything awash in stage lights throughout, while the minimal dialogue is elucidated through the music of Tom Waits, as if the work were a homegrown opera. Those who know my writings will immediately recognize that, while Coppola might have disappointed American audiences (the film cost more than 26 million dollars, while netting only $636,796, bankrupting his studio), the director gave me much of what I wanted to see.

That is not to say that *One from the Heart* is an entirely successful work of art. The story is so simple that it is difficult to describe it as plot. Hank (with the sad-sack look of Frederic Forrest) and Frannie (the very much "egg-shaped" [as she is described by Hank] Teri Garr) are about to celebrate their fifth anniversary. But during the minimal celebrations Frannie announces she is leaving him. Long desiring to get away from her travel-agent job—with an intense desire to go anywhere or do anything out of the ordinary—she runs into the arms of the sleazy romancer Ray (Raúl Juliá), who, on the night she visits the club in which he has told her he sings and plays the piano, is actually working as a waiter. He quits on the spot, impressing the desirous Frannie with his spontaneity, if nothing else. During two long nights, the couple make love and plot to escape to Bora Bora, often described in tourist books as "the center of the romantic universe." Both Frannie and Ray live life less in the moment than in a sort of idealized future, just like the world Coppola has whipped up through his designers and lighting artists.

If Hank is less imaginative and slow to catch on, with the help of his "friend" Moe (a role well acted by Harry Dean Stanton), he goes on his own romantic spree,  picking up a circus artist, Lelia (Nastassja Kinski), along the way, and spending at least one long night with her wandering through the magical junkyard set I described above, where everything seems to proclaim the possibility of romantic apotheosis.

Yet, "the little boy blue," Hank is not thoroughly satisfied with his new romance, and unthinkingly tracks down Frannie and Ray in a motel room, carrying her away like a naked trophy; she is, in fact, undressed, and must redress herself during their quick voyage home.

This time, Frannie is determined to leave forever, and, apparently, is off to Bora Bora with her new lover. Desperately, Hank—the romantic urge rising up in him—rushes off to the airport to bring her home once more. Frannie turns to see him as the airplane door is about to close.

Having previously pleaded:

If I could sing, I'd sing. I can't sing, Frannie!

Hank now bleats out "You Are My Sunshine." But it is too late.

Hank returns to their house in despair, followed shortly after by a repentant Frannie.

As one can observe in my brief recounting of the film's "story," there's not much there to keep one interested, and the acting—although certainly competent—is equally vague, since the chorus of Chrystal Gayle and Tom Waits far outweighs the lines given to the cast. As Janet Maslin complained in her *New York Times* review, "the sets are invariably more interesting than the people who inhabit them." This is simply neither a character nor a dramatic piece, but, like much of opera, is based on the composer's skills and the director's ability to bring out the epic wonderment of an often slender tale.

If you think that the real Las Vegas, with the

bright lights of its architectural absurdities, would be sufficient as a theatrical backdrop, Coppola obviously disagrees, providing a far more lurid desert town with the kind of lit-up dizziness of Las Vegas in its early days combined with the ruins of that one-time world. The way Coppola portrays it, Las Vegas is far more romantic, even paradisiacal, than any Tahitian island could possibly have been.

LOS ANGELES, SEPTEMBER 21, 2011
Reprinted from *Reading Films: My International Cinema* (2012).

Gamblers

MUCH LIKE *One from the Heart*, Rudolph's movie of two years later begins with music and, in this case, dance. Teddy Pendergrass' song "Choose Me" ("Come on, choose me, baby / Ooh, choose me, baby") serves as a kind of overture, both structurally and literally, for Rudolph's own operatic-like story. One by one, as Eve's bar closes and people enter the street to be tempted by each other and the seemingly ever-present prostitutes on this small cul-de-sac, we meet some of the major players—all desperate for love, but unable to find the right partners. Each poses, dances, momentarily flirts, but each also leaves alone.

Like Coppola's film, *Choose Me* is filled with garish colors and theatrically-lit sets that reference theater far more than American film history, with the exceptions, once more, of Sirk and Ray. Rudolph, accordingly, makes it clear from the beginning that what we will be witnessing is not a realistic portrayal of down-and-out Los Angeles life, but a comic romance with dark tones and narrative possibilities.

Finally, Rudolph tips his hat to Coppola again (instead of to his mentor, Robert Altman) by heavily employing music throughout, music by Phil Woods, Luther Vandross and Pendergrass, that comments on the feelings of the film's characters and its events.

Yet Rudolph's film is much less "sweet." The dialogue, unlike *One from the Heart*, is highly witty, and the film's thematic implications are far more reaching. In one of the very first scenes we witness what is clearly a Veterans Hospital where one of the directors is trying to explain to a family member that she will have to take back into her care a mental patient, Mickey (Keith Carradine), whom they are about to release. Even though his previous violence is mentioned, it is clear that they need the room for more seriously ill patients. But the relative is obviously reluctant, and while the two are speaking, Mickey walks off, reappearing soon after at Eve's bar, over which Eve (Lesley Ann Warren), as owner, superintends. This Eve, however, is not the Eve for whom Mickey is looking, the one who has apparently killed herself. But this fact hardly seems to matter as Mickey quickly appears to be smitten with the new Eve, staring intensely at her as he drinks (vodka and a beer with "two inches of head"), a habit to which he later readily admits.

> PEARL ANTOINE: God, you love to stare at women.
> MICKEY: Old habit.

The implications of his behavior are obvious: he is either a Satan, a snake ready to tempt any Eve he encounters, or an Adam seeking love. We never do discover which being he is, but before the first of these long nights has ended, he asks Eve to marry him.

A regular in this bar, Pearl Antoine (Rae Dawn Chong) is a silly rich woman with pretensions of being a poet. Her poetry might remind some of Gilbert Sorrentino's hilarious satire of poetic aspirations in his fiction *Mulligan Stew*:

> No matter who I'm with,
> They want to know if I'm still sleeping with you.
> I say that you sleep while I die a little
> But I'm not afraid of death.
> At least you get laid in your coffin.

Mickey's lack of response results in Pearl Antoine's up-braiding of him, and his comeback is worthy of a Sor-rentino character:

PEARL ANTOINE: You weren't even listening.
MICKEY: You want to get laid.
PEARL ANTOINE: It was just a poem.
MICKEY: Just a thought.

In fact, Mickey soon reveals that he once taught poetry at Yale, the first of many seemingly "fish tales" he tells, making us  suspect that he is still quite insane. Later he suggests that he has been an international spy and a commercial photographer, as well as working as a machinist. He has also, so he reports, killed another man over a woman. But whatever his fascinating past, Mickey spends the first night of this tale, sleeping on a bus station bench.

Later we discover that Pearl Antoine visits the bar just to keep an eye on Eve, who is having an affair with Pearl Antoine's seedy ex-husband, Zack. Jealousy and revenge are already in the air, and when Mickey walks away with Pearl Antoine, we witness the look of hurt and suffering in Eve's face. Both Satan and Adam have evidently forsaken her.

In her pain, she telephones the radio doctor, Dr. Love, who goes by the name of Nancy (Geneviève Bujold), a hilariously portrayed radio host who spouts psychological jargon about men, women, and love but who herself is nearing a mental breakdown and is apparently still a virgin ("I've never loved anyone. I don't think I can."). When Dr. Love fails to help, Eve calls up her slightly creepy bartender, Bill Ace (John Larroquette), for sexual fulfillment.

Mickey has joined Pearl Antoine not for sex, it turns out, but because she will take him to a special location where men, including Zack, are gambling. Mickey is desperate for the cash that might take him

 by bus to Las Vegas so that he can collect the possessions and money he left there. Luck is with him this time around, as he bests Zack.

The marvelous thing about *Choose Me* is its clever relationships to 19th century French Boulevard comedies. Once the major characters are introduced, one by one Mickey sexually encounters them—first Nancy, who coincidentally has just moved into Eve's house as a roommate. Much like Terence Stamp in Pasolini's film

Teorema, each character finds something that excites and enchants them about Mickey's personality and appearance. Nancy is quickly released from her sexual inhibitions, bringing a newfound excitement and wisdom to her radio commentaries, somewhat shocking yet thrilling to her colleagues, particularly her boss, Ralph Chomsky (a reference to the linguist Noam Chomsky?) (played by artist Ed Ruscha).

We also begin to realize through this incident that Mickey may be speaking truthfully when he claims he never lies. In his suitcase Nancy discovers a *Yale Review*, original photographs of major celebrities, international passports, and articles from the German magazine *Stern* about Mickey's arrest in the Soviet Union.

Yet we still can only imagine that Mickey is pathological when he suddenly asks Nancy to marry him.

> NANCY: Mickey, Mickey. You can't go around ask-
>   ing every woman you kiss to marry you.
> MICKEY: Why not?
> NANCY: Why not....
> MICKEY: I only kiss women I'd marry.

Pearl Antoine is equally sexually gratified by Mickey, and, for a few moments, it appears that she may finally free herself of Zack—that is until he enters her apartment at the very moment when Mickey is snapping her almost nude photograph. A fight ensues, Zack becoming the victor, relieving Mickey of his gambling winnings, and socking his ex-wife in the eye.

Coincidences in this film abound. Earlier Zack had called Eve, with Nancy answering the phone, providing him (she has little else to offer) with sexual advice. When he determines to pay Nancy a visit after being scorned by Eve, he discovers Mickey in the house, who has come to talk to Eve. Another fight between the two men breaks out, this time Mickey grabbing a gun and demanding his money back!

Eve, with whom Rudolph's quirky story has begun, is the only one who has not yet been the recipient of Mickey's sexual charms. Their encounter in the final scenes begins with potential violence—perhaps a repeat of the past—as Eve threatens suicide with a gun. Mickey fails to dissuade her, until he too pulls his gun, threatening his own life.

The two collapse into each other's arms, admitting that their guns were unloaded: in short, that it has all been in demonstration. In the final scene they are on the bus to Las Vegas after, apparently, quickly marrying. Mickey grins like a Cheshire Cat, having won the love of Eve. Eve, finally somewhat content, smiles. A brief conversation with another passenger, who asks if they're going to Las Vegas to gamble, however, troubles her. She replies, "You could call it that," her commentary bringing fear into her face. Is Mickey a true lunatic? "That's why you chose me," he reassures. She smiles, looks troubled again. Mickey remains frozen in his grin.

All of the characters have gambled everything over the three long nights of *Choose Me* in the hopes of gaining love and meaning in their lives. We cannot—perhaps no one can—know if they have chosen right. For there is no one "truth" when it comes to love.

LOS ANGELES, OCTOBER 13, 2011
Reprinted from *Reading Films: My International Cinema* (2012).

Oz

JOSEPH MINION (SCREENPLAY, BASED, IN PART, ON A
RADIO MONOLOGUE BY JOE FRANK), MARTIN SCORSESE
(DIRECTOR) **AFTER HOURS** / 1985

MARTIN SCORSESE's 1985 film *After Hours* begins as a
kind of romantic comedy in league with the two I have
already discussed. Scorsese's standard use of city lights
and rain-reflected surfaces, moreover, bares a great deal
of resemblance to Coppola's and Rudolph's Sirkian settings.

But after the first opening scenes, in which computer programmer Paul Hackett (the likeable Griffin
Dunne) meets Marcy Franklin (Rosanna Arquette) at

a local cafe, deciding
to call her—osten-
sibly about his de-
sire to purchase her
friend's papier-mâché
sculptures of bagels—

and agreeing to meet her in a SoHo loft, things begin to happen that are darker even than the edges of Rudolph's film. While *After Hours* flirts with the romantic comedy genre, its tone is far closer to Kafka (a scene mentioning him occurs later when Hackett encounters a nightclub bouncer). And while both *One from the Heart* and *Choose Me* have quite preposterous plots, *After Hours* presents us with a pure fantasy.

Early in the film Marcy tells Paul of her sexual experiences with her former husband, who was obsessed with *The Wizard of Oz* and could not help himself from shouting, upon orgasm, "Surrender, Dorothy!"

> MARCY: Instead of saying something normal like, "Oh, God," or something normal like that, I mean, it was pretty creepy! And I told him I thought so, but he just, he just couldn't stop, he just, he just couldn't stop, he just...couldn't stop.

Without being too literal in its connections, in fact, *After Hours* might be said to be an updated version of that great American fantasy, wherein Hackett becomes a desperate Dorothy after a whirlwind taxi ride that ends with his landing in a strange new place where everything he knows is turned upside down. In Minion's somewhat perverted and misogynist retelling of the tale, the witches are closer to man-eating S&M harridans (Kiki Bridges [Linda Fiorentino] and Gail [Catherine O'Hara]), with their flying monkeys represented by the SoHo vigilante mobs in search of a victim.

The Scarecrow without a brain, the Tin Woodman without a heart, and the Lion without any courage are perhaps encapsulated in the  central figure, Paul, rather than split into parts. But the images of fire, air, and water which dominate *The Wizard* are all here, in the mysterious references to burn victims by Marcy and Kiki the miserable rain-storm which Paul must endure and in the overflow of the bartender Tom's toilet and in the air-headed desperation of waitress Julie (Teri Garr) and the mad Mister Softee truck driver, Gail.

Like Dorothy, all Paul wants to do, as he explains over and over, is "to go home." But having lost a $20 bill—his only cash—and having not even enough change to pay for the fare (hiked at midnight) for the subway, he is unable to escape, and is forced to remain in this world that seems, as Marcy has put it, "unable to stop." No one sleeps in this Oz.

If, in fact, the original Baum story is an allegory

against the Gold Standard and the greed of the Wall Street millionaires, we recognize that Scorsese's story is also centered on the haves and the have-nots. The robberies taking place throughout this SoHo neighborhood are being committed by an unlikely pair, Pepe and Neil (Cheech Marin and Tommy Chong), who are clearly just attempting to survive—although in Minion's satiric version, even they, like nearly all the citizens of this neighborhood, are mostly seeking art:

PEPE: Art sure is ugly.
NEIL: Shows how much you know about art. The uglier the art, the more it's worth.
PEPE: This must be worth a fortune, man.

If art is money in this world, it appears that it is only through "art," in a creative re-envisioning of the world, that one can find a way "out," the way to survive. The trouble with Paul is that he has no imagination—in short no brains, no heart or empathy, and no moral courage—although, as in the original, he eventually proves that he has all these qualities. His ridiculous attempt to find an easy "lay" ends up in her death and his own entrapment. The SoHo figures may look ridiculous, but in their S&M outfits, their 1960s hairdos, their absurd Mohawk haircuts, they are at least attempting to remake themselves into something else; they are creating a kind of kitsch— or, we might say, populist—art. In this world, Paul is nothing; like his almost empty apartment, is too bland to survive.

If there is a Glinda the Good Witch in this tale, it is the near-invisible June (Verna Bloom), who sits each night drinking in the raucous noise and filth of the Club Berlin, and lives in a basement apartment beneath it. Touched by Paul's kindness, she takes him into her cavern, transforming him from a human being into an artwork that looks similar to Kiki's Edvard Munch-like image of *The Scream*. Of course, Paul, entombed by these layers of papier-mâché, *is* screaming out for help, but can no longer be heard. The robbers snap him up the moment June has left the room, Neil proclaiming the absurd truism of this world: "a television is just a television; art is art!"

Undergoing another cyclonic voyage, Paul, now as an artwork, falls from the truck precisely where he has begun his voyage, at the front gate of the company where he works. Like a mummy come to life, he cracks open his shell, marching to his desk to be greeted, like a friend, by his computer: "Good morning, Paul!" Surely he must ask, after what has had to have been the longest night of his life, and as Peggy Lee has in her song played in the film only a few moments earlier: "Is That All There Is?"

LOS ANGELES, OCTOBER 16, 2011
Reprinted from *World Cinema Review* (October 2011).
Reprinted from *Reading Films: My International Cinema* (2012).

Out of Control

RON KOSLOW (WRITER), JOHN LANDIS (DIRECTOR)
INTO THE NIGHT / 1985

IN THE SAME YEAR as Scorsese's *After Hours*, director John Landis filmed his *Into the Night*, both works sharing numerous similarities, notably the portrayal of their heroes as nebbish-like failures, cast out into a world they could not possibly have imagined and are not able to comprehend.

Ed Okin (Jeff Goldblum) is having trouble sleeping, and, as he admits to his friend and co-worker Herb (Dan Aykroyd), something is wrong with his home life. His wife leaves him each morning with a purposeless kiss, wishing him "a nice day" the way a bank teller might speak to her customer. His insomnia is beginning to interfere with his work (he has missed the fact that the engineering group with whom works has announced the application of a different set up of frequencies weeks earlier). A trip back home in the middle of the day reveals that his wife is having an affair with a co-worker. Although he is dismissive of Herb's coarse advice to fly out to Las Vegas—"There's a girl there who do 'anything you want' for 50 dollars an hour." "Will she bring me a pony?"—he suddenly finds himself at the Los Angeles airport without any real destination.

By accident Ed witnesses the brutal murder of a handsome young Iranian, Hasi, and an attempt on the life of Hasi's companion, Diana (Michelle Pfeiffer), by SAVAK (Iranian secret police controlled by the evil Shaheen Parvici [Irene Papas]). Many of the minor characters of Landis' film are played by fellow film directors, including Landis serving as one of the SAVAK bunglers. Throughout, these figures are presented as racial stereotypes, foolish and incompetent; but given the number of murders they and others actually accomplish by the end of the film, they are definitely dangerous fools, despite Okin's often casual disdain for all that happens around him.

The moment he drives Diana to temporary safety, he is trapped in a nightmare scenario where the SAVAK agents track them throughout the city; a Frenchman, Melville (Roger Vadim), and his henchman (David Bowie) try to kill them; while Diana's brother, a gay Elvis imitator, is completely indifferent to their survival. Landis somehow balances all the blood-letting with wit and humor as Ed and Diana incredibly manage to outwit and outrun the evil forces attempting to destroy them.

Diana has been unwittingly involved with the appropriation of some valuable jewels which the Shaheen is determined to retrieve so that she can make escrow on a property. The obvious and ridiculous greediness of this underground world makes for some comic-book moments as Ed meets challenge after challenge with a wry sense of humor. Even Melville's man, Colin (in one of the best scenes of the film), marvels at Ed's nonchalant style:

> COLIN MORRIS: [*ED is waiting outside the Tiffany store for DIANA*] You're very good. You're really very good. I'm amazed we've not met before.
> ED: I beg your pardon?
> COLIN MORRIS: I've been watching you ever since

you left Caper's yacht. Very impressive.

ED: Oh yeah?

COLIN MORRIS: You can stop performing now, Ed. If that's your name.

ED: Heh, I don't know, what are you talking about?

COLIN MORRIS: Okay. I represent Monsieur Melville, and I can assure you that he will be far more reasonable than the SAVAK.

ED: The SAVAK?

COLIN MORRIS: The Shah's secret police. Death squad. Iranian gestapo. Shaheen's boys.

ED: Shaheen's boys....

COLIN MORRIS: Heh, heh, I like you Ed. I do like you. You're very good.

[*Draws pistol, puts it in* ED'S *mouth.*]

COLIN MORRIS: The stones.

ED: What?

COLIN MORRIS: Where are the stones?

ED: I can't help you.

COLIN MORRIS: [*Cocks pistol*] We do understand each other, don't we?

ED: Uh, I don't know.

COLIN MORRIS: [*Sees police car approaching, puts pistol away*] Very good. Very impressive. I'm sure we'll chat again.

Much like early film comedians such as Buster Keaton and Charlie Chaplin, there is a complete innocence, almost an idiocy about Ed that both saves

 him (and Diana) and gradually transforms him into a kind of loveable fool.

The character Diana, on the other hand, ultimately, is one of the most merciless manipulators possible. Although Landis attempts to make her also a near-innocent, unaware of any of the larger effects of her relationships with men like Hasi and the wealthy Jack Caper (Richard Farnsworth), she is anything but uninvolved. With no vacillation she uses her friend, a wannabe actress, to hide her jewels within a secret pocket of her coat, which later results in the woman's brutal murder by the SAVAK. Nonetheless, Diana breezily returns to the house after the attack to pick up the coat, using a passing policeman as a way to escape Melville.

Just by showing up at the apartment of Hasi, she causes his murder and that of most of his family and servants. Everywhere she goes, including a short visit to her brother, mayhem and murder follow. If Ed previously has fretfully found life uneventful, in the two nights he spends with Diana (one of them in a dark culvert) he encounters a whirlwind of destruction far deeper and more perverse than Scorsese's computer nerd, Paul, encounters on his long outing.

"She is a woman who will go with anyone," Shaheen tells Ed; but this time, it appears, she has no one else left who might save her. Ed is her only hope.

In a final attempt to contact Caper, her former lover, she breaks into his house, only to discover that he is gravely ill and his wife has returned to claim his estate upon his death. Caper suggests yet another "caper," a meeting between Ed and Shaheen to make a deal for the return of the stones.

Again, Ed's oddball lack of consequence saves the day, as he convinces the mad Medea-like villain that she has no choice but to go along with their plan: Diana has hidden the jewels within dozens of bouquets of roses at the flower market under the name of Parvici, allowing the couple time to escape.

But the trip to Mexico is delayed, as the captain explains: the plane is malfunctioning, and the couple has no choice but once again to face the murderous forces of Melville, SAVAK, and, this time, government police, brought in presumably by Caper. A standoff results, and suddenly the humor that has been partner to the film's horror turns sour. Ed, once more with a gun pointed at his head, begins with his usual banter: "This is ridiculous. Big shot, huh? You got a gun. Now what? Shithead, you. Huh?"

His next word, however, says it all. The possibility of the "real" world has dropped away. The man he

faces is a "maniac." And suddenly we recognize the level of despair in which Ed has survived these horrific days and nights: "Let me ask you something. Maybe you can help me. What's wrong with my life? Why is my wife sleeping with someone else? Why can't I sleep?"

His very personal plea resonates even with the maniac, who turns the gun upon himself and shoots out his brains.

Before Ed and Diana have even had time to recover from these new circumstances, FBI men whisk them away, as the couple fear another kind of arrestment. Landis returns to humor as the FBI agent dumps a suitcase of money before them upon the bed: it's all theirs. Which, in the director's cynical view, is slightly contradicted as the agent picks up several packages of bills, stuffing them into his own pocket. "Who's gonna tell?"

For the first time in this pummeling, pulsing movie, the "lovers" are left to themselves. But instead of falling into an embrace and sex, Diana luxuriously cleans her blood-stained body, while Ed finally falls into a profoundly deep sleep.

A sharp bang declares a new day, actually the afternoon of the following day. Diana has disappeared—just as we might have expected. Only this time, things are different. Perhaps she has turned a new corner, cleaned up not just her body but her life. She comes bearing gifts: the suitcase, tickets for a Mexican escape. It is hard to say whether this couple will fall in love or simply experience further lunatic adventures. But perhaps Ed, at least, can finally sleep at night. And nobody will ever again be able to tell him, "Have a nice day."

LOS ANGELES, NOVEMBER 15, 2011
Reprinted from *World Cinema Review* (November 2011).
Reprinted from *Reading Films: My International Cinema* (2012).

Nine Nearly Forgotten Nights in Our Nation's Capital: The 1ˢᵗ Night (Tallulah's Magnolia)

AFTER MY COMPANION Howard and I moved from the University of Wisconsin to Washington, D.C. so that he could work on his PhD. at the University of Maryland, I went looking for jobs; we could not afford to pay the admission for me to finish my B.A.

The first job for which I applied was a position as editor at The Carnegie Institute. They were interested in hiring me and called me back for a second interview, but in the end they decided against it, a decision which pained me at the time.

I contacted an employment agency who sent me to all sorts of incompatible job interviews. Finally, one morning, when I reported at the designated address only to find it was a McDonald's, I decided to take my chances, once again, at a university. The employment office at American University sent me to the library, where I was immediately hired as a shelver! Clearly this was little better than serving up burgers, but at least it was in a pleasant location where I would be surrounded by my favorite things—books.

The head of the library was Frank Schork, a somewhat elderly gay man (I say this, knowing that at the time Frank must have been only in his late 50s), who took an immediate interest in me. By the second day I was working on Reserve books at the front desk, and within one week I was promoted to Head of Circulation and Reserves!

Soon after, Schork began inviting Howard and me to dinner, and since we both lived in the same neighborhood—we were renting an apartment in the Adams-Morgan district and his row house was located near the adjacent Dupont Circle—his invitations became a regular thing.

Frank was a somewhat embittered but witty, knowledgeable man, highly conservative, but also surprisingly tolerant (he also served as the Librarian for the Middle East Institute). Since Howard and I were fairly intelligent and witty ourselves, I am certain our regular visitations to his home helped to keep a lonely man occupied.

Most of our evenings were spent with Frank talking about university gossip and his queries about the sexuality of his other male employees, many of the younger ones of whom he had evidently hired on the basis of their attractiveness. From what I witnessed during that year, he seemed to like young men who were perhaps unsure of their own sexuality, but who would ultimately marry the opposite sex.

The house was a narrow three-storey-high brick building, with a living room and kitchen on the first floor, a bedroom and bath on the second, and a small-study/library on the third. The place was furnished with very little furniture, Schork decorating the rooms in the Japanese manner. Like the man himself, the house was elegantly stark.

The most pleasant aspect of the place, and the location of our unforgettable late-afternoon drinks and hors d'oeuvres, was a beautiful back garden graced with numerous pots of flowers and a fabulously large magnolia tree; Frank insisted that it was the most beautiful magnolia in the city, and I believe he was probably correct in that assessment.

The home had been previously owned by William Brockman Bankhead, a man who had served in the House of Representatives from 1917 to his death in 1940, and who was the Speaker of the House for the last four years of his life. His daughter was the legendary actress Tallulah Bankhead, and along with Schork, Howard and I often tried to imagine her, on visits to her father, lounging upon a chair as she languidly smoked a cigarette, where we now sat, under that giant magnolia, her husky-voiced laughter rising to its highest boughs. After a while that grand magnolia—with its heavily perfumed flowers—came to be Tallulah's magnolia in my mind.

While Schork became a friend of sorts to Howard and me, he was not at all liked by several of his employees, particularly the librarians of the opposite sex. And about halfway through the year I could see that his position was most untenable. Evidently some of these employees had complained to higher-ups, and Schork's job was in jeopardy.

While I was finally making a salary that allowed Howard and me to move to a College Park apartment which we filled with newly purchased furniture (some of which still sits in our condominium today), Schork was planning an escape, which finally came his way in an offer from the United Nations in Geneva, Switzerland, where he had been hired as a librarian.

Needing to sell his place rather quickly, he offered it to us—at the unimaginably low price, Howard reminds me, of $50,000. In 1970, however, that relatively small amount of money might have been the several million dollars which it likely would fetch today. I suggested we take a loan from his father, but Howard couldn't bring himself to ask. And so that beautiful Washington, D.C. townhouse so splendidly shaded by Tallulah's smoky

magnolia slipped from our hands into the world of pleasant memories.

And Schork? He returned to Washington, D.C. on a couple of visits, and over dinners described his new home, a former stable, located in the woods outside of Geneva. The boys, evidently, were even more lovely and more unapproachable in Switzerland than they had been in Washington, D.C.

LOS ANGELES, JULY 30, 2008
Reprinted from *Green Integer Blog* (August 2008)

One of the major problems in writing any autobiographical work is that when one begins discussing events that include other people one is in danger of representing both in a biased manner—representing points of view which may be at odds with how friends see themselves or remember the incidents. I like most of the people I describe in the pages of My Year, *and even those I am not particularly fond of I find interesting nonetheless. So I determined from the beginning that when I had finished a piece about a friend, I would send it out for his or her own comments before publishing it. Indeed, this has stood me well, help-ing to correct some misconceptions, allowing others to cor-roborate my "facts," and, most importantly, permitting me to maintain the friendships.*

When I finished the above piece, I went looking through the internet to find the current address of Frank Schork, discovering only a photograph of him with The American Friends of Versailles at the Salon d'Hercule. Not much to go on. After waiting a few weeks, I posted my piece on my Green Integer Blog.

A few days after, I heard from a young man in Los Angeles, Brandon Howe, reporting that he enjoyed the piece, having himself once met Frank in Europe on a train.

A couple of weeks later came an email from Frank himself, simply saying, "Douglas, can you be so kind as to call me at my Paris telephone number?" I immediately did.

Frank was "flabbergasted, simply flabbergasted," that I would write such a thing! I laughed—suddenly remind-ed of his love for exaggerated speech—assuring him that it was meant as a friendly portrait, although I granted there were a few things I'd said that perhaps he hadn't wanted to advertise.

"I just can't imagine why you wrote about me!" he repeated.

For a moment or two, I also wondered why I'd both-ered.

I attempted to explain what I was trying to do in My Year, *and that the piece was not just about him, but about Washington, D.C., his beautiful house, and the grand magnolia in the backyard. And he had been, like it or not, one of my first adult employers.*

"Well, you absolutely ruined my Christmas," he laughed, "not that I ever enjoy Christmas—or even care about it for that matter. I don't even have a computer or know how to operate one. But one of my friends decided to go online and look me up, and, finding your article, read it aloud to a raptly attentive group of celebrating acquaintances."

I apologized, but reminded him that I had no address so that I might warn him.

"Well, will you please be so kind as to take it off your blog?"

I assured him I would, but again tried to determine why he found it so offensive.

"Well, you must know that I hate any kind of statement about me anywhere. I always have. That's just the way I am. I live in anonymity."

I repeated that I would remove it from the internet, but reminded him that it was part of a book of my cul-

tural memoirs for 2001.

Before long, we were both inquiring about each other and our activities in the years since we'd last spoken. He now lived on rue Jacob in Paris. "Do you know rue Jacob?" he queried.

"Yes, of course I do," I answered. "Djuna Barnes lived

there when she was in Paris. And a friend of mine, Milos Sovak, has an apartment, which I once visited, on your street (oddly enough I heard news of Milos' death only a few days later).

"Well I am now, of course, retired. I'm 88! But I am quite joyfully busy. For a price of $3,000 each I take people on private tours of Versailles. I have my own key, and tour them at times when the palace and its buildings are closed, so they can see areas the public never gets to visit. I give all the money back to the Versailles foundation, so they love me, and allow me to go in and out as I please! I have a beautiful apartment with a garden and the same red chair you used to sit upon by that grand magnolia tree."

I told him a few of the changes in my own life.

"You sound exactly as you always did. How wonderful to hear your voice," he chuckled familiarly. "If nothing *else, this occasion has, at least, brought us back together. Please let us stay in touch. I don't have a computer, so call or write!"*

After hanging up, I deleted the essay from the blog. Now, except for the small photograph on the page devoted to The Friends of Versailles, nothing of Schork remains on the internet. It amused me that he announced his desire for such concealment in the volume I had already titled "Keeping History a Secret."

LOS ANGELES, FEBRUARY 8, 2009

Nine Nearly Forgotten Nights in Our Nation's Capital: The 2ⁿᵈ Night (An Invitation)

AS I NOTED in *My Year 2007* in my piece on our neighbor Bob Orr, when we first moved to Washington, D.C. in the early 1970s and, soon after, the suburbs of Maryland, Howard and I were quite active in the kitchen, trying our culinary skills with all sorts of recipes of the day, particularly those in books in the popular *Time-Life* series of "Foods of the World," Julia Child's *The French Chef Cookbook*, Craig Claiborne's *The New York Times Cookbook*, Paula Wolfert's *Mediterranean Cooking*, and, later, Diana Kennedy's *The Cuisines of Mexico*.

In our new high-rise apartment on the uneuphonious Mezerott Road, we had recently purchased new furniture in the Scandinavian style, a long, low teakwood coffee table (which we still have today), a light green corduroy-covered couch, and elegantly simple hanging lamps, into which we put amber bulbs. Over the summer we had fashioned a dining table, based on Howard's father's crafted doors, out of various kinds and colors of metal decoratively nailed together in a patchwork-quilt-like manner and topped with a raised pane of transparent glass. Howard's mother had sewn up loosely transparent curtains in orange and light yellow and had used some of the left-over material to cover throw pillows for our couch. Along with our retro 1950-ish Butterfly sling chairs (still in perfect condition), and a few other pieces of furniture, our apartment seemed, in those days, to imbue a sense of stylish modernity; and, as we began to invite our fellow graduate students over, it became a rather popular dining spot. As we both joke today, "We lived better as graduate students, with hardly any salary, than we do as somewhat elderly adults."

Howard cooked the Portuguese dish "Rojões Caminho," braised pork with cumin, coriander, and lemon; I, the "Arroz con Pollo," chicken with saffron rice and peas. Howard whipped up our Scandinavian favorite, "Frikadeller" (Danish meat patties, a delicate dish that, when Howard tried to cook it, for acquaintances Hugo and Robin—a couple of experienced chefs who even made their own stocks—completely crumbled into mush), while I tried my hand at the "Dillkött på Lamm," Swedish lamb in dill sauce with "Agurkesalat," pickled cucumber salad. Imagining our-

selves in the provinces of France, Howard served up "Gigot d'Agneau Rôti," a roast leg of lamb seasoned with lemon, salt, and pepper, while I whipped up a "Blanquette de Veau à l'Ancienne," old-fashioned veal stew with cream sauce. Both of us eschewed the complex dishes of classic French cooking, but I did once try "Poulet poché aux aromates," chicken simmered in white wine and vegetables. I helped Howard roll lamb into rinsed and dried grape leaves, while he fried up the oil-laden eggplants into which I folded layers of seasoned ground lamb topped with Béchamel sauce for a delicious "Moussaka." Howard was a whiz with "Osso Buco." I found it easy to cook "Scaloppine al Limone," sautéed veal scallops with lemon. We both loved our "Farsu Magru," stuffed beef roll. Later, Howard became a somewhat accomplished home-bound chef for several Chinese dishes, spending all day in the kitchen to serve our friends "Five-Flavored Egg with Tea," "Stir-Fried Shredded Pork with Chili," "Pork Ribs in Brown Sauce," and other delicacies. On the day of New Year's Eve Howard would spend the whole day in the kitchen producing plates and plates of hors d'oeuvres—so many that we would invite friends over on New Year's Day just to finish them.

Over a short period—before Howard grew tired of my chaotic employment of all the pans and utensils in our kitchen, and banned me from cooking forever—we grew popular among our peers at the University of Maryland.

One day, I was called into the office of the English Department Chair, Shirley Kenny, a former professor of Restoration and 18th-century literature and, later, Provost at the University of Maryland of Arts and Humanities before becoming the first female President of Stony Brook University in New York.

"I hear from several sources that you have been inviting your fellow graduate assistants to lavish dinners," she announced in what seemed to be an accusatory tone.

I was somewhat confused. Were our dinners against some unknown departmental policy, a secret infraction of an ancient English Department protocol? "Yes, we do like to cook."

"I hear you have a lovely apartment too," she added, as if totaling up our offenses.

"We're happy with it," I meekly responded.

"And you have these excellent dinners nearly every weekend I have been told."

"Pretty often," I responded, wondering whether

she was about to criticize our culinary activities as interfering, perhaps, with our studies.

She looked somewhat fiercely across her desk: "Why haven't *I* been invited?" she exploded with a short, sharp laugh.

"Next week?" I smiled, standing to begin my escape. Then I turned back. "Saturday night, 7:30. Will you be there?"

"Bet your boots," said the Texas-born administrator.

LOS ANGELES, AUGUST 1, 2008
Reprinted from *Green Integer Blog* (August 2008).

Nine Nearly Forgotten Nights in Our Nation's Capital: The 3rd Night (Casual Dress)

WHEN MY COMPANION Howard began working as a curator at the Hirshhorn Museum and Sculpture Garden in Washington, D.C., he quickly became friends with Sidney Lawrence, then Head of the Publicity Department at that institution. Sidney, a native Californian of a noted family, a branch of the famed Ghirradellis of San Francisco, has what I might describe as an outrageous sense of humor that delighted both Howard and me; and over the years Sidney (now a painter), his companion Tom Birch (a lobbyist on Capitol Hill), and we have remained good friends.

When we first met Sidney, he was married to a woman, but some time after his divorce he announced that he was gay. A few months later, in part to celebrate his own sexual outing, he mailed out numerous invitations for a late-afternoon cocktail party which, aside

from the usual announcement of time and place, added *casual dress*.

For most readers today, it may seem strange that I would even mention the attire, and even odder that I might have chosen to put such words in italics. But in the 1970s, when this event occurred, Washington, D.C. was a city, with regard to dress, unlike any other. We had long ago recognized that *casual dress* did not mean the same thing in that city that it did everywhere else.

When we arrived at this party, the place was already filled nearly to capacity, and before long, it was almost impossible to weave one's way into the kitchen for a drink. There Howard and I were among what seemed like more than one hundred guests, mostly young men, standing back to back or front to front, depending upon who was included in one's conversation, packed into Sidney's small apartment on K Street like sardines. Washington, D.C., built as it was upon swampland, is extremely hot and humid in the summer, and, accordingly, all of us—the whole room, each young man dressed in a suit and tie (one, on his way to a later event, was dressed in a tuxedo), the definition of *casual dress* in the nation's capital—suffered sweat rolling down our faces which, hidden beneath our shirts and coats, raced equally on down our backs.

Suddenly the doorbell rang. It was quite impossible for Sidney to move toward the door—it was nearly impossible for anyone to move—so the person nearest the entrance cautiously opened it, as all eyes turned toward the possibility of fresh air and escape. There stood two young boys dressed in T-shirts and shorts.

As these two looked into the room packed with so many besuited males, their mouths fell open in apparent shock. "We're from Wisconsin," one of them said, in a suitable Wisconsin accent, "and we were told to meet our friend here, at the party. But..." he paused, looking down at his bare legs, "perhaps we should apologize; on the invitation it said *casual dress.*"

For an instant the room quieted as if to meet the startlement registered upon their faces, and, just as suddenly, a boom of raucous laughter broke like a roll of thunder across the space. "Come in, come in," we all cried in near hysteria for the absurdity of being there, so very properly dressed.

LOS ANGELES, AUGUST 15, 2008
Reprinted from *Green Integer Blog* (August 2008).

Nine Nearly Forgotten Nights in Our Nation's Capital: The 4th Night (One's Enemies)

THROUGHOUT OUR YEARS in Washington, D.C., Howard and I—primarily through his role as an art curator—were invited to numerous embassy parties. At some point in the early 1970s, for example, we were invited to several events at the Australian and New Zealand embassies. Occasionally those invitations were even extended to the personal residences of the ambassadors of those countries.

The Aussies, I remember, were somewhat like American frontiersmen, a bit fearful of "high cultural" events. At one particular occasion, the evening began with a concert, whereat the wives of the various embassy officials sat dutifully attentive, while the men rambled about in an adjoining room, drinks in hand, impatiently awaiting the concert's completion.

The New Zealanders, on the other hand, although

completely unpretentious, were highly interested in culture. I recall a long discussion with the Ambassador's wife one evening about the writer Janet Frame, whom she described as a "dear friend." The food, which consisted of platters of slightly greasy lamb chops, may have been somewhat unsophisticated, but the conversation was another thing.

I don't recall to which ambassadorial home we had been invited in December 1974 to a Christmas party, but it was one of those Washington, D.C. townhouses where such parties were celebrated downstairs, in what normally might be described as a basement, but had been so redecorated that no one could hardly think of it as such.

There I met the representative of the Federated States of Micronesia and another Oceania leader. Howard and I spoke with both gentlemen for some time.

But gradually, as one does at such events, we broke off into other groups: I noticed a gathering of individuals standing around a plain-looking but friendly woman and joined them, listening in upon the conversation. Clearly, this woman had just received some high accolade, and the women surrounding her were curious about how she had reached this position. Gradually, I began to understand that she was somehow involved with religion, and a few seconds later I realized who she was. At that very moment, Howard came up to the group, standing next to me, hoping, I presume, for an introduction.

The woman continued to speak intensely about how she achieved her position, using, over and over again, terms such as "those against change" and "one's enemies." At one point, she began a short diatribe against "one's enemies," chastising those, apparently, who refused to accept change.

Howard is a born diplomat, a careful but easy conversationalist, unlikely to say anything that might offend. But perhaps because he had still to be introduced to this slightly garrulous individual, or just out of an uncontrollable urge, he suddenly blurted out: "One's enemies can go straight to Hell." Suddenly all faces turned to him in apparent shock, and he quickly recognized that he had said something out of turn. He smiled and quickly fled the little clique, as its members turned back to continue their discussion.

I gradually shifted away from the group, cornering Howard alone. "What was that all about?" he innocently asked.

I began to laugh. "Well, Howard, I don't think you could have chosen a more ill-suited phrase! Do you know who that is?"

"No."

"It's Alison Cheek, the Anglican priest, the first woman to celebrate communion in an Episcopal church." In January 1975, *Time* magazine chose her as the Person of the Year.

At the party, we returned to the conversations about Melanesia, Micronesia, and Polynesia, safer ground on which to talk.

LOS ANGELES, SEPTEMBER 27, 2008
Reprinted from *Green Integer Blog* (November 2008).

Nine Nearly Forgotten Nights in Our Nation's Capital: The 5ᵗʰ Night (Lasagne)

ONE DAY, in 1976 I believe, I inexplicably donned a plastic mask we had been given by friends that resembled Groucho Marx—a mask most people have seen, consisting of heavy eyebrows set over a pair of glasses, underneath which lay an extravagantly large nose and an enormously black, plastic mustache.  The mask was the perfect size for my face, and completely transformed me, changing me, despite its clearly male characteristics and my own moustache and beard underneath, into someone looking like a Commedia dell'arte figure. To that I added my long, white-and green-striped cotton bathrobe and, on a whim, I topped it off upon my head with a pair of white jockey underpants. The combination, when I glanced into the mirror, immediately suggested to me a kind of maddened artiste or chef.

Although I seldom enjoy costumes, I immediately entered our living room, displaying my transformed self to Howard. As quickly, I became this artiste-chef, putting on an exaggerated French-Italian accent and describing myself as "Lasagne!"

Howard broke into laughter, quite loving my new manifestation. Accordingly, when a few months later we were invited to a Halloween party given by some of his Hirshhorn Museum friends, he suggested I should come dressed as Lasagne.

By the time we reached the house near Dupont Circle where the event took place, its rooms were filled with quite extravagantly dressed celebrants. One I remember, a flasher, wore a long black overcoat which, when opened for the flash, revealed a fully dressed body except for his penis, framed in a kind of plastic-covered window. "Just look, don't touch," Howard jested.

My costume, by comparison with the others, seemed to me to be quite simple, and I presumed it would draw little attention. I was surprised, accordingly, when many of the more cleverly dressed individuals pointed me out to each other. Even more strangely, to my way of thinking, few of them seemed to recognize who I was underneath my "disguise."

I spotted our friend Phyllis Rosenzweig, a museum curator who shared an office with Howard, across the room and quickly joined her, speaking to her in the voice of Lasagne. Phyllis, who is quite shy when it comes to overbearing individuals—and Lasagne was overtly large in his gestures and linguistic tropes—almost panicked. As I came toward her, she quickly backed away. "Ahhh, but my dear little one," I responded in my obviously fake French-Italian accent, "you are so terrified of me, but, I assure you, I am one with whom you must be so well acquainted." As she backed further into the corner, I pulled a bit away, calling over to her: "You really don't know who I am, do you?" She shook her head emphatically, "No, I don't!"

I laughed as only the French can laugh. "Oulala, my dear. I shall have to leave you alone and come back later when you have thought about who I might possibly have been."

In short, my simply conceived costume was a great success. I seemed to have become the mystery guest of the evening.

A year or two after that event, we were invited to attend an opening at the Corcoran Museum of Art, a museum, for those acquainted with Washington, D.C., located across the street from the White House. The dress for this occasion, so the announcement proclaimed, was either black tie or Halloween costume.

Howard is not the kind of person to wear anything that might hide his true identity. I believe at that previous costume party, he had come dressed as himself.

He has several times described how, when he was a child, his mother had designed and sewn a frog costume for him. As the night approached, she slipped him into the costume and zipped it up. "Come look in the mirror," she implored. "You look great!"

Little Howard cautiously approached the extended mirror, peering out through the eye-slits of his green-colored frog suit, and burst into tears! "I thought that I *was* the frog," he explains, "that I had become a frog, and I was horrified!"

It thoroughly surprised me, therefore, when he suggested that we both go in costume.

"You, in costume?" I queried.

"I thought I might go as Jane Livingston."

Jane was a friend of ours, and curator at the Corcoran. Several years later, in 1989, she curated the legendary Robert Mapplethorpe show, which, because of its sexual and homoerotic images, and presumably fearing that they might never again receive NEA support, her museum cancelled two weeks before its opening; at that time Associate Director of the Corcoran, Livingston promptly resigned.

I could not imagine that Howard was serious about his intent, until, a day before the opening, he came home with a fright wig and a pair of hot pants! I was astounded. Was he truly going through with it? I had, of course, decided on Lasagne as my persona.

Suddenly, there we were, parked on the ellipse, Howard looking absolutely ridiculous and not at all like Jane Livingston, and I trying desperately to get into the character of Lasagne, about to cross Constitution Avenue. "How do I look?" Howard asked, for what must have been the 10th time.

I giggled. "Absolutely beautiful!"

I moved to open the car door. "I don't think I can do it," he suddenly announced. "You go first, look the place over and tell me if it's okay."

"What to you mean, me first!" I protested. "Either we both go or neither of us goes."

"No, just check it out. I'm afraid to go in looking like I do."

I knew there was no convincing him otherwise. And I knew, once I had opened the car door, there was no turning back. With all the self-inflated ego I could gather, I began my walk across one of the most noted avenues in the world. Cars came to a standstill, some tourists spilling from their vehicles just to wave. I waved back. People began to gather at the corners, their faces filled with wonderment, awe, and outright disbelief. Today, I am certain, I would have been immediately arrested!

But then, like an actor determined to play the role larger than even the character might bear, I insistently walked up the several steps of the museum and into the large atrium which greets Corcoran visitors. Flanked by two great banquet tables serving food and wine stood small groups of the numerous guests, all of them in costume, but of a different sort—gowns and tuxedos only.

Like Andersen's emperor dressed in an invisible robe, Lasagne strutted around the entire perimeter of the large hall, nodding at the discreet pairings of well-dressed attendees and, on occasion, when he began to notice laughter springing to their faces, even waving.

He was a great success!

Having swirled across the entire space, I exited and descended, as royally as I could, the Corcoran's stairs, once more crossing Constitution Avenue while waving to my loyal admirers before escaping into our awaiting car.

"No, Howard," I nearly exploded in laughter. "I think you should not go into the party. I think we should now go home."

Howard, who had observed my street-side sensation, broke into a hoot of laughter, and drove away. By this time we had become near lunatics in our recognition of our audacity and my public performances. But Howard had also now become somewhat nervous. He was, after all, still dressed in a woman's blouse and hot pants, having pulled the fright wig off and thrown it into the back. I had removed my mask and even my white toque of underpants, but was still fully robed. And just as suddenly, we were caught at a stoplight in the all-Black neighborhood through which we had necessarily to pass on our way home.

Fortunately, it was getting dark. Howard suggested that we quickly leave the well-lit street and pull into an alley, where, presumably, we could change into our everyday clothes. As soon as we turned into the alley, however, a car followed. We quickly swerved into another alley, the car still behind us, and into another and another—traveling through a virtual maze of back-street alleys until we finally lost our pursuers. As quickly as he could, Howard opened his door, pulling off his blouse, bra, and hot pants as he attempted to pull on his own slacks.

Suddenly, as we stood beside the auto, we realized our pursuers had rediscovered us. They pulled up behind us, as we jumped back into our car and drove off!

Our howls of laughter, tinged by our inner fears of terror, probably could be heard by all who passed us as we sped out of the city and into The Old Line State.

LOS ANGELES, SEPTEMBER 6, 2008
Reprinted from *Green Integer Blog* (September 2008).

Nine Nearly Forgotten Nights in Our Nation's Capital: The 6th Night (Pat Nixon's Cloth Coat)

IN 1980, the year I began to teach at Temple University in Philadelphia, I was invited for the first time to read my poetry at the Washington, D.C. Public Library. After 10 somewhat frustrating years of living in Washington—where, as I have commented elsewhere (see, for example, *My Year 2007: To the Dogs*, "Reading on the Hill"), the poetry community was particularly conservative—I was surprised by the invitation, particularly since it came in the same year that Ronald Reagan had been elected President.

The city had almost immediately changed. I remember attending a party in Chevy Chase at the home of a wealthy collector early that year. The collector, whose name I do not recall, had invited a rather large contingent of artists—something one seldom observed in the nation's capital—along with numerous political friends. The afternoon began well enough; drinks were poured, appetizers served, and the conversation, if not exactly scintillating, was intelligent. Suddenly small groups of men and women began to arrive—all dressed in black from head to toe. These individuals, it soon became apparent, were California Republicans, almost all of whom had recently moved to the city because of the election. Suddenly, before we knew it, the room had become divided in two, the artists on one side, the politicos on the other. During the previous administration, particularly with Joan Mondale's involvement with the arts, such a gap between the groups had seldom been witnessed.

Some of us on the artists' side determined to enter the conversations of the others. As I have mentioned elsewhere, Washington society generally obeys social protocols, particularly when it comes to party conversations. Generally, a person standing near a group in conversation is, at an appropriate pause, invited into the conversation, perhaps even introduced by a member of the group. Howard and I both attempted this timeworn pattern, without any encouragement. At one point, I tried to introduce myself as the group moved off. In another instance, they closed up into a small circle, like threatened bison, excluding any possible "intruders." This became the pattern not only that afternoon but for years to come. Civility had suddenly

disappeared.

The library invitation, accordingly, was quite unexpected. And I was happy to be joined by two poet friends, Tina Darragh and Jim Wine, sitting among this so highly politicized audience. I read first, beginning as I often did in those days with some brief comments on my writing, necessitated, I felt, by the recognition that to this audience my poems, without narrative impetus, might sound strange. As I read the poems themselves, I felt a bit as if I had been stranded on some weather-beaten boat in the middle of the ocean, an ocean of disinterested and sometimes frowning faces. With relief, I finished and sat.

The second reader, whose name I cannot remember, stood and imperiously walked to the podium. She was clearly a local favorite.

"Unlike *some* people," she began, "I do not feel that poetry needs explanation. And I do not intend to describe any of my motives or methods...." She continued in this vein for at least another five minutes, thoroughly excoriating what she described as "intellectual writing." When I looked over at Tina, I could see her desperately trying to control her laughter. This poet had now gone on about something *other* than poetry far longer than I had spoken about my techniques. And small titters of laughter had begun to break out around the auditorium. Finally, she finished her lecture on my failures and proceeded to her unmemorable work. I truly recall nothing else about her or her poetry.

When she finished, and polite questions and answers had been fielded—very few in my direction—the three of us quickly escaped.

Nearby was a famous bar, a popular gathering place for the political set—the Old Ebbit Grill, Tina recently reminded me—and I suggested we go there for dinner.

Since it was still early we quickly cornered a table, and threw our coats on nearby chairs, ordering up three beers. As we took our first sips, we all simultaneously began to laugh at what we had just experienced. Jim said: "Well, that will go to show you. Don't ever talk *about* poetry again!"

Tina—a truly joyous person who reminds me of a down-to-earth Irish-American woman of the plains—asked: "Whatever did you *do* to her? She truly hated you."

"I guess," I laughed. "What was her name?"

We had grown tipsy from our amusement rather than the alcohol, and a waiter came over to us to ask if we wanted something to eat. "We probably do," I answered, "but first, another round of drinks!"

The waiter brought another round, and we began to tell imaginary stories of outraged readers! "Words are what they *say*," Tina concluded, "not what they *mean*."

"And what I say is apparent to any ninny willing to sit and hear me spout," added Jim.

Before long we began to notice that the place was filling up with its usual well-dressed clientele. The three of us looked a bit like street-urchins in comparison, and our conversation quickly turned to our inappropriateness in such a setting. The jokes came faster, and we laughed a bit louder.

The waiter quickly came back: "Are you ready to order now?"

"Soon," Jim responded.

"May we ask you to be just a little quieter?" the waiter scolded.

"Sorry, we will try to be quieter."

But just as quickly, as we attempted to hold in our laughter, it rolled out in waves of hilarity.

At the neighboring table, a serious-minded man and woman impatiently accosted us: "Do you mind removing your coats?"

"Yes, we do mind," answered Tina, "but we will move them anyway."

"But what's wrong with my coat?" she turned to me, asking in a louder voice. "It's a good, respectable,

Republican cloth coat. I may not have a *mink* coat, but...."

"You look good in anything, Tina!" I came back.

"Yes. So I've been told."

The waiter threatened to return to our table again, but I quickly signaled for the check, and he turned his searing eyes away as he quickly wrote it up. We paid, and left, joyfully laughing our way to our cars.

LOS ANGELES, OCTOBER 5, 2008
Reprinted from *Green Integer Blog* (October 2008).

Jim Wine was a student of mine at the University of Maryland.

For several semesters as a graduate assistant, I taught a very popular course titled "Avant-Garde Fictions," in which I discussed works by Djuna Barnes, Flannery O'Connor, John Hawkes, Paul Bowles, and several others. Certainly, I wouldn't describe the work as "avant-garde" these days, and I am not sure that I would put O'Connor and Barnes together with Hawkes and Bowles, but I was clearly exploring what I would later describe as "Non-Modernist fictions."

Jim, whose father was an ambassador, had grown up with his identical twin brother Charlie in several inter-national locations, including Switzerland, so both were fluent in other languages. The course had attracted some of the brightest of Maryland students, and Jim was one of the best. For his final report, he asked to do an essay on Francis Ponge, the noted French writer. I assured him that it would be an appropriate subject for the course, but warned him that very little had yet been translated into English—in fact I probably knew less about Ponge in those days than he did.

After that course, we became good friends, Jim inviting me a couple of times to his Georgetown home. On one occasion I traveled with Jim to New York City, introducing him to Mac Wellman, the two of them engaging over dinner at Mac's house in a shouting match concerning various literary theories. Jim has always been passionate about life and ideas.

A short while later, Jim announced that he had fallen in love with a young Swedish woman, Eva. The only problem was that she was in the United States on a limited visa, and even his father could not effect a stay. What should he do? he asked me. Of course, his father wanted him to stay in the country and finish his education. But would Eva and his relationship survive their impending separation?

The son of an educator, I was (and am) an ardent believer in education. Yet, I advised him that he could always get an education, but he may never find another woman like the one whom he had described.

As he reminds me, Jim took my advice and traveled to Sweden, but he returned, graduating summa cum laude *in a double major of International Relations and Literature. He also took another of my courses in the German Department on modern Scandinavian fiction, where I taught books by Hamsun, Strindberg, and others.*

After graduating, Jim returned to Sweden and married Eva. He lives there still today.

One day in 1980 Jim's mother, much beloved by both sons, suddenly became ill and, a few days later, died. I was at work on my second book of poetry, Some Distance, *and dedicated one of my favorite poems, a poem about death, to him. I read that same poem, "Harrowing," at the funeral service for Howard's mother, Rose.*

In the late 1990s the two brothers moved to Virginia, where their father was living in a large country house near Front Royal. Jim lived there with Eva, and Charlie with his fiancée, whom he ultimately married. Howard and I visited them in the country on several occasions, enjoying its peace and quiet, combined with the musical and literary discussions of the two brothers.

While Charlie composed music, Jim began to write poetry. I published his first and only book to date, Longwalks, *as one of my earliest books of Sun & Moon Press. I recently reread the poetry, and joyfully realized that it had been a work of real talent—despite my memory that, when it was first published, fellow professor Alan Wilde* and his friend Jack Undank had dismissed it as "simply bad writing."

Charlie took some of the poems and put them to music, which the two recorded and attempted to get distributed internationally.

My friend Joe Ross, a student of mine from Temple University a few years later, befriended the Wines and moved out with his wife to Virginia near them, creating for a while what I liked to joke of as a kind of "ex-Messerli student cabal" of artists there.

In 1990 their father died.

In the years that followed, Charlie's and Jim's wives began having differences, ultimately resulting in Jim and Eva moving back to Sweden, where they became neighbors and dear friends with the great Swedish poet Tomas Tranströmer and his wife Monica, a friendship that remains today.

In late 1996, I held a meeting in the Sun & Moon offices with the presses who had received Mellon Foundation grants over the past few years; we were attempting to begin a loosely-constructed organization that might work together for information and, perhaps, even for some fundraising purposes. Suddenly at my front door, I saw two figures attempting to enter my space. The door being locked, they began to pound on it. I tried to signal them to go away, gesturing to the table of meeting participants, but they refused. As I came forward to tell them to leave us alone, I suddenly recognized Jim and Charlie, wildly waving greetings. "My God, you guys! What are you doing here? Come back tonight when we're planning a big party"—which they did. It was wonderful to see them again! And it was the last time I would see them together.

In 2003, Charlie had a stroke. For the next several years, the brothers spoke by phone almost every day. During a 2005 visit to the farm, Jim watched his brother undergo a second stroke, which forced him to spend three months in the hospital. In 2008 the doctors diagnosed liver failure as a result of that second stroke, and Jim and Eva flew back to be with Charlie, unsure whether he would still be living by the time they arrived.

Jim spent the next night with Charlie in the hospital at Front Royal, and by morning the patient amazingly had improved. For the next several weeks, his condition went up and down, but in general he improved enough that Jim got tested for a liver transplant that he would donate to his brother. As they were ready to take Charlie off the respirator, he suddenly came down with a highly resistant hospital virus, and died quickly after.

The brothers were very close, at one point even warning their wives that their brotherly bond was deeper than their own marriages. With Charlie's death, Jim was inconsolable for over a year.

Upon hearing of Charlie's death, I sent the poem below to Jim.

Here
        for Charlie Wine

Here
divides
a life
from the fold of your voice
the cross-cut of memory
fantasy, fluctuation...one plumbs to protect
oneself from...really nothing
but not quite, so it seams
sinking us both
into line. Did I mean time?
Our detonation digests the brink,
eyes ogling reflection as a sun
can strike eventually
everything it desires. Just turn your head,
time slips
that fast!
The silence is the real diagnosis
of the ongoing portrait
existence defines.

LOS ANGELES, FEBRUARY I, 2009

I first met Tina, indirectly, through New York poet Bruce Andrews. Talking about the new issue of Roof *for which* he was editing a "Washington, D.C. forum" for publisher James Sherry, Andrews mentioned that, besides my own poem—"Dinner on the Lawn," which I considered my first successful work of poetry—there would be new pieces by several other Washington, D.C. writers, including Lynne Dreyer, Bernard Welt, Diane Ward, Peter Inman, and Tina Darragh, the last whom he described as a "diehard experimentalist." This group of poets and others would later become the heart of a poetry reading group that I have described in the pages of My Year 2005 and elsewhere. But in 1976 or 1977, when this conversation occurred, I had met none of these figures. In 1976 I had begun my own journal, Sun & Moon: A Journal of Literature & Art, which coincided, more or less, with my own poetic beginnings.

Sometime during that year, perhaps in connection with poetry readings at Doug Lang's series held near Dupont Circle, I met most of these writers and others. Tina Darragh appeared much younger than I expected for someone described as "diehard," and, sharing this piece of information, we hit it off immediately. I equally liked her husband, Peter Inman, a quieter, almost shy man who worked for most of the time I knew him at the Library of Congress. Peter and Tina also lived, as Howard and I did, in the Maryland suburbs, so we felt less of the intense group aesthetic than many of the poets living near Dupont Circle, some of whom also shared a house. It did not mean that we saw each other more often, but it seemed there was a kind of linked experience; if nothing else, our involvement with the D.C. reading group meant a long trip downtown and back each week, a commitment that the others did not have to make.

Howard and I did have Tina and Peter over for dinner, and I believe that once we visited their house. And a kind of friendly intimacy was built up between the four of us. One of the first books I published on the press that emanated from my Sun & Moon journal was Peter's Platin—a side-stapled, Xeroxed book—in 1979. Tina's on the corner to off the corner, the first book of Sun & Moon Press to be printed in our 5 x 7½ size, was published in 1981.

During this period, Tina and Peter had a son, who they named, after Tina's family name, Darragh. As Darragh grew older, however, he began to complain of such an unusual moniker, and his parents told him he could rename himself, but he had only one choice of a substitute: Darragh chose Jack, and as Jack he grew up.

Over the years, I have seen the family seldom, the last time, I believe was at a Modern Language Association reading years ago in D.C. But somehow I have the sensation that they share the same close feelings I have for them.

LOS ANGELES, FEBRUARY 21, 2009

Nine Nearly Forgotten Nights in Our Nation's Capital: The 7th Night (Free Tickets)

IN THE GRADUATE STUDENT BULLPEN I shared with others at the University of Maryland, a large basement room crammed full of desks, I became friends with Donald Duncan. Duncan had been in a couple of seminars I'd taken, and he was interested in theater and opera. Moreover, he worked regularly as an usher at the Opera House of the Kennedy Center.

Some time into our friendship, Duncan suggested

 that Howard and I come one night to the Kennedy Center to meet the head usher, Pat, since she often was able to find free seats for those recommended to her.

Howard and I had attended a number of events at the Center, but on our teaching assistant salaries we could simply not afford to go to the theater, opera, etc. very often. Pat took us to her hearts the very first time we met her, and over the following months we were able to see numerous plays and performances—including productions of *Elektra*, *Cat on a Hot Tin Roof*, The Bolshoi Opera's *Eugene Onegin*, *A Moon for the Misbegotten*, and others—for free.

Despite Pat's great friendliness and seeming affection, however, both Howard and I felt somewhat guilty for the pleasures she offered us, and we alternated the free events with ones for which we had paid. In fact, we probably spent more money on drama and opera than we could afford.

Moreover, when we did attend, we were often asked to join Pat and Don with cast members at nearby bars and restaurants after the performances. Although these were generally enjoyable events—I recall a long conversation after *Cat on a Hot Tin Roof* with actress Elizabeth Ashley, who we had also seen in Wilder's *The Skin of Our Teeth*—everyone had to wait for rather long periods for the actors to remove their makeup and for the closing down of the theater before we could begin our group treks to the selected locations. And once there, Howard and I felt beholden to pay since, after all, we had been given "free tickets." Accordingly, we often spent more money on these after-theater celebrations than had we simply paid for the tickets in the first place.

There is no question that there was something exciting about these seemingly covert acts; we were always seated or positioned at the very last moment before the curtain rose, one time taking over the President's box in the balcony, at the Bolshoi production standing behind the last row of the orchestra seats until it became clear that there were two empty seats in the house into which we were clandestinely moved. Yet this very sense of undercover theater-going also made us uncomfortable. Was there danger should the management discover our secret? Probably not; I am certain most theaters have such arrangements, if for no other reason than to fill the house.

But with the often added cost of food and liquor, the late hour of our returning home, and this sense of discomfort, we began to take less and less advantage of this gracious arrangement. And over the period of about a year we stopped going, feeling somewhat guilty, given the generousness of Pat and her staff, for even attending as paying members of the audience. Were we rejecting the kindnesses they so readily offered us?*

So, I recall, it happened that we began attending more theater at Washington, D.C.'s famed Arena Stage and the theater at Catholic University than at the renowned Kennedy Center.

---

*These circumstances become a theme in my play "Intentional Coincidence," Act II, collected in my (Kier Peters') *A Dog Tries to Kiss the Sky* (Los Angeles: Green Integer, 2003).

LOS ANGELES, NOVEMBER 11, 2008

Nine Nearly Forgotten Nights in Our Nation's Capital: The 8th Night (Roger)

I HAD KNOWN Fluxus poet Dick Higgins for four years, meeting him several times at small press book fairs, where he showed books published by his renowned Something Else press (which published Gertrude Stein, Marshall McLuhan, Emmett Williams, Claes Oldenburg,  George Brecht, Ray Johnson, among others). I also published a story by Higgins, "The Truth about Sadie Mee," in the fiction/narrative issue of *Sun & Moon: A Journal of Literature & Art*, 6/7 (1978-79). But I did not know Dick well, and our correspondence over the years had not been extensive.

I did know that early on in his career, Higgins had studied with John Cage, and in 1960 he'd married Alison Knowles, with whom he later taught at CalArts near Los Angeles. Yet I hadn't followed his writing or performances over the years. Recently he had sent me a gay story that rather startled me with its porno-like content. I wrote saying that I felt it wouldn't work for *Sun & Moon*. Dick wrote, explaining that he had recently realized that he was gay!

Later that same year in 1980 someone at the Folger Shakespeare Library—a noted D.C. institution, recognized for its remarkable Shakespeare collection and productions of his plays—called to ask if I might introduce Dick Higgins at his reading there in a few months. At first I was simply surprised to hear that such an august and orthodox institution had invited a figure such as Higgins to perform; my first reaction was to explain that I was not well-acquainted with the author or his work. Yet I quickly comprehended that the Library was perhaps finding it difficult in Washington to even come up with someone who knew his name! Ultimately, I agreed to introduce.

On the day of his reading, I picked Dick up for lunch, at which time I hoped to discuss with him some details of his life. But he spent most of the afternoon discussing his new lover, a boy named Roger, who, he almost proudly declared, he had met through his daughter. "She came home with this boy," he chuckled, "and I took him to bed. It seems amazing that he found me attractive."

Yes, it did, I thought to myself when I encountered the willowy kid. Soon after, I began to realize that one of the enticements that Dick had provided him was a constant source of marijuana.

Roger, evidently, was a drummer, and Dick intended to employ him in the performance. Higgins gave me a large hardback publication which he had recently published containing numerous photos of their "performances to the sun," Dick looking up at the skies, Roger, stark-naked, beating upon something that looked to me more like a can than a drum.

I had a sinking feeling that Dick's infatuation might not be so easily assimilated by the Folger Shakespeare crowd.

I introduced him as best I could, noting his remarkable career and pointing to his evident achievements. Dick stood and began to read. So far everything was fine. But then he announced that several of his works featured an accompanist, and Roger, dressed in white T-shirt and blue jeans, was called out to pound the drums. Several of the audience members' faces turned pale, others had frozen in rigid smiles.

A short while later, Roger was called out again. "Roger, Roger," Dick called. But no Roger appeared.

"Roger, Roger," he repeated. Still no drummer in sight. Finally, the boy stumbled out from backstage ready again to thump upon his instrument.

After a brief intermission, the remaining audience members returned to their seats to encounter yet another piece featuring the duo. "Roger, Roger," Dick screamed out. Once again, Roger did not appear. "Douglas," Dick called over, "will you go back and bring Roger out?" I found the boy huddled in a corner puffing away. "You're wanted," I told him. He stood and shuffled off.

I returned to my seat, somewhat red-faced, but still delighted that Dick had dared to confront this obviously puzzled room of people with something different from their previous experiences.

Later that year, I was asked to return to the Folger, this time to introduce my dear friend David Antin. Things were apparently changing, and a few years later my friend and former student, Joe Ross, joined the Folger Shakespeare committee for performances.

LOS ANGELES, OCTOBER 6, 2008

On the Other Side of the Page

ASCHER/STRAUS **ABC STREET** (LOS ANGELES: GREEN INTEGER, 2002)

IN APRIL 1992 Sheila Ascher and Dennis Straus wrote me to ask if I'd be willing to read a manuscript of theirs, *ABC Street*. I suspect the manuscript arrived soon thereafter, but in my files the next serious correspondence was dated five years later, July 1997, at which time they sent me the dedication to the book. Only this year (2001) did they send photographs for the cover of the book, now scheduled for 2002. My only reaction is that Ascher/Straus must be the most patient couple in the universe, having now waited nearly 10 years for their book to appear—combined with the fact that another manuscript of theirs, to have been issued as an early side-stapled book on the nascent Sun & Moon Press in 1978, was never published!

These incidents are made even more ironic by the fact that, although Dennis and I have kept in fairly close touch by telephone over the years, I have never met Sheila or Dennis, but simply followed their migrations from Rockaway Park and Canaan, New York to Captiva Island, Florida through phone conversations and occasional correspondence.

Given their immense patience, I thought it might be appropriate to at least indicate through this short essay what I found so interesting about their writing, particularly since a history has developed around this work that makes it very appropriate to this year's thematic stitching of *My Year*.

For despite the rather long relationship I have now had with Ascher/Straus, like the writing itself, it is a narrative without a coherent story. *ABC Street* is part of an ongoing project on which the two have been working since 1977, titled *Monica's Chronicle*, a day-by-day journal penned by the seemingly observant, but determinedly passive narrator, Monica. This chronicle alternates between intense depictions of the daily weather—evocative descriptions of the rain, snow, and sun Monica observes through her window and on her occasional walks—and the often gossipy comments of a large cast of characters Monica describes as "A Constellation," mostly lesbian women friends, and the various neighbors of what is obviously a location similar to Rockaway Park.

There are also silences ("Days intervene, unwritten"), undated entries, and sporadic ruminations on the nature of her writing activities. There is a strong sense that in writing Monica is forgetting or, at least, replacing the act of memory with the writing itself. If, as Lyn Hejinian argued early in her career, "Writing Is an Aid to Memory," in *ABC Street* "Writing isn't an aid to memory, but a replacement for it." History, accordingly, is eaten up by the narrator's acts, and as quickly becomes part of the ongoing snowfall of words that pour from Monica's pen. Individuals and their statements just as quickly are swallowed up into a kind of nonjudgmental commentary.

Just as the landscape Monica describes, the numerous human figures she portrays often collide in the reader's mind as a jumble of abstract flesh. Some families are so extended with sons and daughters, their best friends, various lovers and boarders that, although on the "Monica's Chronicle Website," created by the authors, all characters are listed, the reader loses sight of the individual, and ultimately can hear only the chorus of communal voices, which is perhaps appropriate, since all the choristers are themselves singing of one another. Accordingly, although Monica can see Manhattan's Empire State Tower from her window, *ABC Street* is a tale of small-town living, a world in which everybody is somehow interrelated and involved in each other's lives.

Yet unlike, say, *Winesburg, Ohio* or any of Sinclair Lewis' tales, *ABC Street* does not comment on or evaluate—and only seldom satirizes—its characters. Rather, they become somewhat flattened reporters of their own destinies without an audience to coherently receive their messages. As Monica describes her own conversation with one of the most memorable figures of the book, Nancy St. Cloud:

> It was windy and Nancy's navy blue wraparound skirt kept blowing open in the middle of sentences. Every time she reached down words got irretrievably whisked away across the flat, dazzling surface littered all the way to the horizon with sparkling bits of green, blue and amber bottle glass, so Monica remembered the story as incoherent, though it may not have been.

Unlike the utter falsity of normalized fictions, accordingly, Ascher/Straus' collaborative work is not just a collaboration between authors, but a collaboration between characters and readers. As in our everyday experiences, what we receive from one another is not always what has been communicated—or even what each of us attempted to communicate. People make their own conclusions and impact one another, much as in the old game of "Telephone," through incredibly garbled readings of one another's lives by people they have never met.

Although the members of the "constellation" have all had regular encounters with Dr. DaVinci, a psychiatrist influenced by Wilhelm Reich, their psychological interpretations of one another are most often mistaken and motives are regularly confused or, as in Monica's encounter with Nancy's handsome and charming husband, Andre, are represented in multiple possibilities:

> (1) Real, husbandly concern. (2) Enlisting the aid of a trustworthy friend who happens to be intruding in any case. (3) Aligning himself with Monica's involuntary look of distress… (4) Distancing himself (*and not only in the eyes of others*) from any accusation of complicity.

In short, in Monica's chronicles of the world around her, there are no answers, and relationships between people and events are at best tentative.

While normative fiction carefully constructs a set of interrelated histories that ultimately work together to present a vision of an individual or community,

Ascher/Straus' work, like the characters and events of real life, keeps their histories secret—even while attempting to reveal them. Like the streets and lawns of this primarily wintertime landscape, history is buried under an avalanche of information: readings and misreadings, interpretations and interventions. As Monica writes: "Our lost history is a daily panorama though not necessarily a panorama of the everyday."

Despite the enormous joy of encountering this canvas of colorful characters, accordingly, the reader realizes that in Monica's chronicles there is no way to imaginatively reach out and touch these figures, nor any way to interweave their actions into a coherent or even consistent pattern. Writing is ink on paper, and any narrative, as much as it may seek mimesis, is as absolutely flat as unprimed canvas. At the end of Ascher/Straus' book, Monica closes her winter night's tale with the words:

> February turns its sharp edge, black winter on the other side of the page.

Not only is the tale over, but the human beings it has mentioned have yet to appear, as they stand in wait on the "other side of the page."

LOS ANGELES, DECEMBER 22, 2001
Reprinted from *Green Integer Blog* (December 2001).

THREE FILMS BY ANDRZEJ WAJDA

A Stuporous Dance of Death

JERZY ANDRZEJEWSKI AND ANDRZEJ WAJDA
(SCREENPLAY, BASED ON ANDRZEJEWSKI'S NOVEL), AN-
DRZEJ WAJDA (DIRECTOR) **POPIÓL I DIAMENT (ASHES
AND DIAMONDS)** / 1958

WAJDA'S MASTERWORK, *Ashes and Diamonds*, begins
in a seemingly bucolic world, with two men, Maciek
Chelmicki (performed by the gifted actor Zbigniew
Cybulski) and Andrzej (Adam Pawlikowski), lying on
the ground near a small country chapel. A young girl is
attempting to open the chapel door, and asks their help.
Slowly the men, clearly exhausted, are roused, Maciek,
in dark glasses, taking a long while to awaken. Suddenly
another man signals them, a car is coming, and we recognize that we have misread the peaceful scene. The girl
is sent off, and, as the car comes into view, Maciek and
Andrzej ready their guns, brutally murdering driver

and rider.

It is, as we discover later, a botched murder; the two killed were factory workers, not the Communist party leader Szczuka, whom the assassins were ordered to kill. Entering the nearby provincial city on the last day of World War II, the two meet up with a local contact, the secretary to the city's mayor, who gives information, but refuses to participate in their activities. While reporting on their success, Maciek overhears of the arrival of Szczuka in a small hotel, and realizes their mistake. There is no choice now but to finish the assignment, Maciek checking into a room next to Szczuka's.

Szczuka is in town to celebrate his return from the Russian front and his appointment from the mayor to a ministry position. The banquet is to be held in the hotel itself. Maciek and Andrzej seek out the hotel bar, where Maciek discovers a beautiful barmaid, Krystna (Ewa Krzyzewska), and proceeds with a kind a crazed flirtation with her that in his behavior reminds one of a mix between the American actors James Dean (Cybulski was later described as the "Polish James Dean") and Marlon Brando. He is clearly toying with danger, daring the world about him, a world where he has daily had to face death.

Both men have been part of the Polish underground, and now hope to defeat the rising Communist influence. Yet neither Andrzejewski's original novel, nor Wajda's film, sides with the partisans or the Communists. Although a formidable and bureaucratic-like figure (no match for the appealing Maciek), Szczuka has fought against Franco in the Spanish Civil War, and later warns of the dangers of "having power."

Andrzej is called away for further instructions, while Maciek determines the best moment to kill Szczuka is late at night, when the man has fallen asleep. In the meantime, he continues to woo Krystna, eventually seducing her into his room, where the couple celebrate their youth and sexuality at the very same moment that the banqueters celebrate their political futures, and the townspeople the end of the war.

Throughout the long night, we begin to see

that nothing in this celebratory world is quite right. Through Wajda's brilliantly surreal imagery, we witness a wooden image of Christ hanging upside down in a bombed-out church, a white horse loosed upon the streets. While Maciek and Krystna discover love, the banqueters grow drunker and drunker, ultimately throwing over any remnants of respectability and civility.

In this whirlwind of change, bringing both a corrupt new leadership and hopeful love, the young assassin is confused. He has never before disobeyed an order, but is now seemingly ready to give up his previous ways for the new possibilities of life—a life of young idealism he has never had the opportunity to experience.

Yet the system in which he has been living will not permit escape. Andrzej returns to remind Maciek of his duty.

As Szczuka awaits a car to take him to his son, arrested with a group of failed partisan rebels, Maciek shoots, killing Szczuka; the body falls forward into his own arms so that the two appear to be embracing death together, symbolizing the pact that the Polish people will ultimately make with the Communist forces.

Inside the banquet hall, the participants, worn out and drunk, demand the orchestra play Chopin's *Polonaise in A flat*: while the tired musicians perform a rendition that is hardly recognizable, the celebrants enact what appears more like a stuporous dance of death rather than a spirited polka.

Attempting to escape the city, Maciek, spotted by troops, is shot. Stumbling forward he finally reaches the dump at the town's edge, collapsing and convulsing, little by little, into death. Krystna, the diamond of his world, is forced to join in the devil's dance.

Wajda's great film may not openly take sides, but by comparing the death of the beautiful Maciek with the surreal Polonaise, we know that Poland's future will not be a thing of beauty, that the ashes of World War II will fall over anything that shines.

LOS ANGELES, MARCH 21, 2009
Reprinted from *World Cinema Review* (May 2009).
Reprinted from *Reading Films: My International Cinema* (2012).

The Paragon

ALEKSANDER SCIBOR-TYISKI (SCREENPLAY),
ANDRZEJ WAJDA (DIRECTOR) **CZLOWIEK Z MARMURU**
(**MAN OF MARBLE**) / 1977

WAJDA'S DOCUMENTARY-LIKE FILM, *Man of Marble*,
centers around a young film student, Agnieszka (a
character based, in part, on the real-life film director
Agnieszka Holland), who has chosen as her subject a
national hero of the 1950s, a bricklayer, Mateusz Birkut
(played by Jerzy Radziwiłowicz). Her faculty advisor
strongly discourages her from tackling this subject, trying to steer her on to something about steel and industry, as opposed to the now obscure figure who helped
build the Polish city for 100,000 people, Nowa Huta.

> No one has yet touched on the '50s. Why don't you
> deal with a subject that has no risk of ambiguity? A
> better project would be facts—facts are steelworks
> and their output.

Exactly why Agnieszka has chosen her subject is unclear; apparently she is simply interested in finding out more about her father's generation. But once she has begun her research she (and the audience) becomes more and more spellbound by the mysterious story surrounding Birkut. At first, even the head researcher is skeptical about the young director, and is disinterested in the forgotten documentaries she has uncovered for Agnieszka: obvious propagandist pieces of the day with titles such as "Birth of a City" (an uncompleted film, where the second director, so the credits list, was Wajda himself) and "Architects of our Happiness." But as she grows to know the younger woman, it is clear she becomes more and more fascinated by her behavior and obsessions.

Indeed the lanky Krystyna Janda plays Agnieszka in a manner attuned to the blaring, jazz-inspired score of composer Andrzej Korzynski. Her every move is a rush forward, her body itself a dare to anyone who might stand in her way. Awake, she is in near-constant motion, edgy, nervous. The rest of the time she collapses into sleep. With the help of three camera men, one an old-timer who admits this may be his last film, and who has a somewhat difficult time adjusting to her insistence on the use of a hand-held camera, she barges into a national museum and slips into a back room where no one is allowed to enter, clandestinely shooting a large marble image of Birkut. When the assistant queries her about her interest in the back room, insisting, "We've got better sculptors here now," Agnieszka's response is an ironic, "I daresay."

Through these forays into the past, interviews, and the documentaries, the filmmaker comes to play the role of detective, gradually revealing the story of a simple believer, a true "paragon." Like thousands of other such workers, Birkut, lured from a small village to work on the vast construction project, was, as he is later described, a real country bumpkin. His handsome good looks and his obvious innocence and belief in the system—despite the deplorable working conditions and the insufficient food served the workers—make Mateusz the perfect victim for the up-and-coming filmmaker Jerzy Burski, who in order to promote Stakhanovite principles (ideas based on the theories of Aleksei Grigorevich Stakhanov, who encouraged workers to engage in competitive battles, resulting in contests in which miners, for example, mined 607 tons of coal in one shift, etc.) challenges the young bricklayer to participate in an event where he and others will lay 30,000 bricks in just a few hours. To Agnieszka, Burski boasts, "He was my greatest discovery, my biggest coup!"

Birkut wins the challenge, laying 30,509 bricks before he nearly falls over in exhaustion. That film and

his youthful, handsome demeanor make him a national hero, and for a short while, the young country bumpkin rises in the party ranks, touring the country with his friend Wincenty Witek, in an attempt to explain his techniques and stimulate the workers.

At one such event, however, Birkut is handed a heated brick and badly burns both hands. Instead of recognizing the dissention of workers against the Stakhanovite methods, authorities prefer to describe the event as a traitorous act emanating from outside the country, focusing on Witek (who was wearing gloves when he handed his friend the burning brick). Birkut's attempts to defend Witek end in Kafka-like episodes. At one point when Birkut accompanies Witek to the criminal offices, he watches his friend enter a small room with one door, only to soon after discover within an official sitting alone at his desk, who insists he has not seen Witek. Traveling to Warsaw in Witek's defense, Birkut is told to leave the case alone; if there is an error, it will be corrected.

Having displeased the authorities, Birkut and his

wife are forced to leave their Nowa Huta apartment; in one documentary Agnieszka observes authorities removing a banner of Birkut and replacing it with another. The man of the people, the "paragon," has fallen into disgrace. Clearly now disillusioned, Birkut hires a gypsy band and travels with them to the office of Internal Security, where he throws a brick through the front door.

In yet another documentary discovered by the film school's researcher, we see Birkut at the trial of Witek. Hearing that Witek has confessed to delivering the burning brick, Birkut astonishingly admits that he has been a co-conspirator, that he knew about the event beforehand. Birkut is found guilty, along with the so-called Gypsy Band of conspirators, and is himself imprisoned.

Later in the film the young director discovers that Witek has been rehabilitated and is now head of the Katowice steel mills. Flying over the mills in a helicopter, we witness a Witek who has sold out to the system, ironically running a company that Agnieszka has been encouraged to focus on for her diploma film.

Birkut is also released, but he returns to Nowa Huta as a stranger, discovering that his wife Hanka has left after having denounced him. Tracking her down in a bourgeois apartment where Hanka has indentured herself to a local restaurant owner, Agnieszka is told the story of how Birkut came to Hanka, pleading for her return. Her answer is a painful admission of her moral decline. Now an alcoholic, she is beaten by her restaurant-owning lover.

Certainly by this time in Wajda's powerful film, we have witnessed enough to know that Agnieszka's film within a film is a significant one, a work of utter honesty about a world where everything is lied about or hidden. In such a world it seems inevitable that the school refuses to accept the reels she shows them and demands that she return the camera.

Dispirited for the first time, we now witness her at her father's home, lying upon a couch in a near stupor. Her father argues that it is ridiculous that they have turned down a project to which they had previously committed. If I were making such a film, he argues, I would want to talk to the subject. As he leaves the house, he slips his daughter some money.

Previously Agnieszka has been unable to find either Birkut or his son. But she now suspects that the son is working, not under the name Birkut, but with his mother's name, Tomczyk, in Gdansk. There, armed with a camera she has obviously purchased with her father's gift, she finds a man that looks amazingly like Birkut (the role is also played by Radziwiłowicz) who admits he is Maciej Tomczyk and explains that his father has died. That death is unexplained in *Man of Marble*,

but in Wajda's later film, *Man of Iron*, we discover that Birkut has been killed along with other striking workers in Gdansk. (That Wajda has brought us to this place three years before the Gdansk Solidarity Movement is no accident; the leader of the 1980 strike, Lech Wałęsa, lost his job there in 1976, and appears as a character in Wajda's 1981 film.)

Tomczyk enters the shipyards, while Agnieszka waits. Upon finishing his day, Maciej finds her where he left her, admitting that he knew she would not give up. In the last scene we see them quickly striding forward down the hall of the film school, apparently convinced that her picture will now be made.

It is a hopeful ending to a rather ambiguous reality. In truth, Wajda was forced to cut his original ending, which showed the 1970 events in which Birkut was supposedly killed. Although the film was released in Poland in 1976, it was withdrawn from distribution two months later, with Wajda being accused of "falsifying history." Perhaps the image of one of Agnieszka's instructors about to enter the hall as the young director and Birkut's son move purposefully forward is more telling; that man quickly returns to his office, closing the door. Truth is always a difficult thing to face.

LOS ANGELES, FEBRUARY 27, 2009
Reprinted from *Green Integer Blog* (March 2009).
Reprinted from *Reading Films: My International Cinema* (2012).

Where Sheep Eat Wolves

ZBIGNIEW KAMINSKI (SCREENPLAY, BASED ON A
STORY BY JAROSLAW IWASZKIEWICZ), ANDRZEJ WAJDA
(DIRECTOR) **PANNY Z WILKA (THE GIRLS OF WILKO)** /
1979

WIKTOR RUBEN, who manages a farm connected to a
school for blind girls, has just lost his "friend," Jurek.
Standing over the gravesite of a man whom Wiktor describes as "ordinary" (but whom the priest later reveals
as a poet), he falls to the ground, temporarily fainting.
The doctor suggests Wiktor take a few weeks off by returning to a popular summer spot where he has, before
the war, regularly visited, and where Wiktor's aunt and
uncle have a farm.

Wiktor arrives at the neighboring farm, Wilko, a
peacock running ahead of him which he seems to be
prodding with a horse crop. Indeed, what he discovers
at Wilko will demand that he control his pride (which
the peacocks symbolize) as much as possible; for inside
the house sit five sisters, Julcia, Jola, Zosia, Kazia, and

Tunia, four of whom he has known—along with another now-dead sister Fela—from his childhood visits to this spot. The women have all grown a bit older, and what one can imagine as their lithe, youthful bodies have rounded out a little, but they are all still quite glorious beings, the first four now married with children. They are astounded to see Wiktor after a 15-year absence, but it is obvious that they are also delighted by his return; he is still fit and handsome, and they, it quickly becomes apparent, were, at one time, all in love with him.

"Where is Fela?" Wiktor wonders. Slowly it dawns on the viewer that her death has been connected to his departure so many years ago.

Wajda's quiet and sumptuously beautiful film appears, accordingly, to be headed in the direction of a meditation on past and present, focusing on these beautiful women, none of whom, apparently, won his heart. Tunia, not of age on Wiktor's previous visits, is now solicitous of his love. Certainly his aunt and uncle encourage him in that direction, but as his aunt mentions, divorce is always a possibility in the Wilko house; for the women of Wilko are all unhappy in their marriages, particularly the eldest, Julcia, whose husband now penuriously controls the estate. While it is clear that she was once beautiful, in her hairstyle and dress she now looks quite spinsterish, having long ago retreated into her intellect—and kitchen, where she cans hundreds of jars of jam.

Accordingly, while Tunia, who fondly reminds Wiktor of the dead Fela, devotedly watches over his comings and goings, each of the daughters attempts to rekindle her past love and perhaps win him over to her cause. Clearly Wiktor is attracted to and amused by all of these appealing—and sometimes, emotionally, not-so-appealing—beauties. And Jola, specifically, seems quite ready to fall into bed with him. Yet, as Dan Schneider has noted in an online review of the work in 2007, instead of greeting these attentions with joy, Wiktor (Daniel Olbrychski) "deftly conveys the sense that the character is not in conscious control of his reactions, with seemingly involuntary twitches and facial expressions" that, I would further argue, reveal his discomfort in the various situations. Asked why he never chose any of them for marriage, he admits he was a "coward."

That has, in turn, led many critics to see the film as a portrait of a failed man, a man unable to accept the joys of life; Wiktor seems more comfortable, as he mentions earlier in the film, working; life's pleasures seem as elusive now as they evidently were in his youth.

As Schneider also astutely points out, however, the "lambs" of Wilko—who seem so willingly led to sexual slaughter—live in a world, as one of the sisters describes it, where "wolves are eaten by the sheep." If the sisters work as a kind of sexual unit, they also cleverly manipulate the men around them, and as each secretly vies for Wiktor's love, they employ everything from military-like maneuvers to various kinds of passive aggression.

In Wiktor, however, unlike their equally unhappy husbands, these "maidens" have met their match. Despite all their ploys and gestures, their suicidal threats, he remains aloof, as if, he suggests, he were "a strange soul from another planet." Accordingly, the past repeats itself, as Wiktor once more leaves these lovely "girls" of Wilko in the lurch in order to return to a world of the blind.

Perhaps Kaminski and Wajda were attempting to create just such a shadowy figure, a man trapped in his own indecision, a being unable to truly engage in love. But I believe, if one carefully focuses on the earliest scenes of this film, it becomes quite apparent why Wiktor has chosen none of these manipulative women for his wife.

The only truly emotional response he demonstrates in this work, one must remember, is his collapse at the grave of his friend, Jurek, the man he describes not simply as his *best*, but his *only* friend. Without pinning Wajda's subtle film to one reading, I would venture to suggest that Wiktor is gay*, and that the cowardice to which he admits, has little to do his inability to fall in love with one of the Wilko women, but with his refusal to admit his love of men. He is, indeed, from another planet, a world outside of the orbit of these provincial beauties. His world is not so much a world of the blind—even though he is surrounded by the blind—but of the hidden, faced as he is by an unnamable love, now forever lost.

---

*I should note that nothing in Iwaszkiewicz's original story, nor in Kaminski's script, for that matter, says anything specific about Wiktor's sexuality. Jurek is simply described as his "only close friend." The key passage in Iwaszkiewicz's story begins with Wiktor telling the local doctor of his relationship with Jurek: "He couldn't sleep at night, he felt very nervous and he couldn't work at all. And he couldn't stop thinking about his friend who had died of consumption two months earlier. He told his story casually, but he couldn't talk about Jurek without emotion. Jurek was the only close friend he ever had. He was a seminarist, the nephew of the camp's Mother

Superior, not an unusual person, but Christian, quiet and good." The key words here, that Wiktor "couldn't sleep at night," that he "felt very nervous," that "he couldn't stop thinking about his friend," and that Jurek was his "only friend," might, obviously, also suggest that Wiktor had simply been moved by Jurek's death to ponder his own fate, particularly since he is an extremely isolated individual. But the combination of these statements suggests something else lying just below the surface, particularly the description of Jurek being his "only close friend," code for a friend with whom one did not simply have a causal relationship.

LOS ANGELES, VALENTINE'S DAY, 2009
Reprinted from *Green Integer Blog* (February 2009).
Reprinted from *Reading Films: My International Cinema* (2012).

Shortly after writing the piece above, I sent it to the author of the script, Zbigniew Kaminski, who, coincidentally, lives in my condominium building. Zbigniew wrote that "Your main argument is absolutely true. Nobody before you discovered it."

We later met to discuss my publishing the work in the Green Integer book series, and he explained that Iwaszkiewicz was gay, although evidently closeted by Polish society.

In relation to my Wajda essays, Zbigniew inquired whether I had seen Roman Polanski's early film, Knife in the Water. *I replied that years earlier I had watched it on TV, but remembered very little of it. He suggested that I view it again.*

By chance, a few months later that film was announced for a two-day revival at the Laemelle Theatre's Music Hall in Beverly Hills "Essential Art House" series, which on July 19 Howard and I attended. My comments on the film were paired with the arrest in 2009 of Roman Polanski in Switzerland for his 1977 rape of an American 13-year old girl in the 2009 volume of My Year: Facing the Heat.

In late May of 2013, Wajda, after Kaminski had given him a copy of my first film volume, which included the three Wajda reviews, wrote me personally, thanking me for the essays: "It's very important to me that you have become interested in my three movies, and more importantly, that you were generous enough to include them in the first chapter of you book, which contains an analysis of the most important works of European cinema. It is a great honour for me." He went on to describe that he was currently working on a film about Wałęsa, which he described as "one of the most difficult movies in my long life, not only because the character on the screen is alive and has been so thoroughly described in my books, but also because the selection of events in his life was not easy." I was, obviously, quite delighted by Wajda's response.

LOS ANGELES, FEBRUARY 27, 2009 AND JULY 26, 2009
Reprinted from Reading Films: My International Cinema *(2012).*

Reading Films

ZBIGNIEW KAMINSKI'S COMMENTS on what he described as my "astute" reading of his *The Girls of Wilko*, and his near-astonishment that I had noticed such details as the peacocks in the yard upon Wiktor's re-entry to the Wilko house, suggested that perhaps my encounters with films were different, in some respects, from many other film commentators. Having no close friendships with film reviewers and critics, I can't be sure that my way of working with films is any different from theirs. And, accordingly, my comments below may seem painfully unoriginal. But I feel, nonetheless, that it is perhaps useful, if nothing else, to explain my approach to viewing and writing about the cinema.

Obviously, the most important aspect of any film is its images. Film, unlike other fictions and narratives, is made up of visual images, a fact that some English department-based teachers seem to have forgotten in their teaching of the art. On the other hand, other such professors argue against any narrative discussion.

As a graduate assistant, I taught film for a couple of semesters at the University of Maryland. The professor of that course, Joe Miller, a likeable enough fellow, seemed to me a bit like a recent convert to some new religion. Miller would speak only of the images in his lectures, insisting the students recognize every camera movement: "You see that rack-focus?" "Look how he uses the montage," "Watch this low shot," etc., etc.

Certainly students should be made aware of the cinematographer's methods—Bresson's *Notes on the Cinematographer,* a book published by my Green Integer press, is perhaps one of the very best books in helping students perceive that fact. I was a good teacher, moreover, in the discussion sessions of Miller's course; I recall one class in which (today I still marvel at my youthful enthusiasm) I aptly described from memory every image and camera position of a long scene from Orson Welles' *The Magnificent Ambersons.* The best way to see those images is in a large theater with an excellent sound system and up-to-date equipment, such as those we have in Los Angeles—the nearest one to me being at the Grove Theatres on Fairfax Avenue.

But we also cannot forget that most films, other than highly experimental ones, tell stories, and work as narratives much in the way that novels and other forms of fiction do. To ignore that entirely would be to miss the very purpose of the marvelous cinematographic decisions. The camera generally is trying to tell a story, not simply moving in an isolated space. Accordingly, I find it necessary not just to *see* movies, but to *read* them. If possible, I try to see them first at a regular theater, although the kinds of films in which I am most interested are generally not available in the larger houses, and many of them must be viewed on the flat-screen of my television. In that case, I demand complete immersion in the film; while I'm watching a movie I want to totally enter its time and space. I find it best to watch serious films alone.

Moreover, if at all possible, I try to see any movie about which I intend to write numerous times. The more often I can see a film, the better. As I have suggested in the pages of *My Year* before, this can amount to 50 or more viewings of a particular film. I have seen Alfred Hitchcock's *Vertigo* in theaters and at home more than 100 times! And I have not yet attempted to write about that motion picture. Pauline Kael, on the contrary, was proud to claim she saw each movie only once.

This kind of obsession with the images and story, rather than disinteresting me in the work, brings me closer to it, until finally I began to see all anew. What first may have seemed a simple narrative grows more and more complex until I begin to rediscover the images and recreate what I originally thought of as a more obvious fiction. It is as if I suddenly have found a way to get behind the screen, as if I have found my way to the other side of the curtain of a play.

If I cannot see the film several times before writing about it, I have no compunction in replaying certain sections of the tape, and writing down parts of the dialogue and images I might have missed on first viewing.

In short, I both *see* a movie, let the images and story wash over me in a kind of passive appreciation, and study it, *read* it, going backward and forward in it the way one is able to do in the pleasurable process of reading a book.

Obviously, there are times that simply do not permit this kind of close observation. Indeed, I saw Kaminski's film only twice before writing about it. And many movies I feature in the volumes of *My Year* I have seen only once in the theater. Yet by so carefully studying so many films, I find that I have become more attentive to all films, even the weakest of those I encounter. That, in turn, has helped to make my own experience with movies a far richer one.

Given the obvious factual errors I encounter in so many newspaper movie reviews, I have the feeling that most critics have not been able to find the time to fully attend to the films on which they write.

LOS ANGELES, MARCH 2, 2009
Reprinted from *Reading Films: My International Cinema* (2012).

Finding It Hard to Navigate

ROBERT CROSSON **THE DAY SAM GOLDWYN STEPPED OFF THE TRAIN** (NEW YORK: AGINCOURT, 2004)

SIGNS / & SIGNALS: THE DAYBOOKS OF ROBERT CROSSON, EDITED BY GUY BENNETT AND PAUL VANGELISTI (LOS ANGELES: OTIS BOOKS/SEISMICITY EDITIONS, 2008)

ON THE MORNING of December 10, 2001, Paul Vangelisti's wife, Małgosia, found our mutual friend Robert Crosson on the floor of the small studio he inhabited behind Paul's house. He had collapsed, evidently after having delivered the daily newspaper to Paul's door. As Paul left the house on his way to work, he yelled out to Bob, not realizing that Bob had fallen inside to the floor, dead.

Crosson's last journal entry, published in *Signs / & Signals: The Daybooks of Robert Crosson*, is a painful reminder of how everything around him became fodder for writing: dated Sunday, December 9, Bob describes

the comings and goings of those near to him before,
between two slanted lines at the center of the page, reporting the ominous news:

"very-
    <u>still</u>"
       (out):

      all I can hear is
      "my heart-beat"
           —in my left ear
              : ((a passing "plane"
                in the distance.))

At 6:45 p.m. he eats macaroni salad and "Angels-De-
light," purchased from the Pioneer Market. At 6:50
Małgosia returns.

These are the major facts of his life, as I reported them in *The PIP Anthology of World Poetry of the 20th Century, Volume 5 / Intersections: Innovative Poetry in Southern California*:

Born in Canonsburg, Pennsylvania in 1929, Robert Crosson remained in the East until his family moved to Pomona, California in 1944. He attended the University of California, Los Angeles, and received his B.A. in English in 1951, briefly joining the Communist Party during his college years. After college he began working as an actor in television and film, in 1954 landing a small role in *White Christmas*. The following year he appeared as the character Danny Marlowe in *I Cover the Underworld*, and acted on television in series such as "Dragnet," "The Millionaire," and—through the help of his friend Jack Larson, who for years played Jimmy Olsen—"Superman." During those years Crosson encountered the several celebrities he describes in his later book of poetry *The Day Sam Goldwyn Stepped off the Train*. But Crosson grew increasingly dissatisfied with the Hollywood scene, which, combined with his brief political activities, dimmed his prospects for further Hollywood employment. In 1959 he traveled to Europe, working his way through various countries as—so he reported—a piano player, a black-marketer, and pimp.

In 1960 he returned to the United States, enrolling in Library Science at the graduate level at the University of California, Los Angeles. Eventually he dropped out, taking night jobs and attempting by day to write his first novel, *Midland*. Jobs as a painter and carpenter, another movie role in *Mike's Murder* (1984), and a 1989 Poetry Fellowship from the California Arts Council allowed him to survive during these lean years; however, as he grew older, Crosson grew increasingly dependent on "the kindness of strangers" and friends, particularly Los Angeles poet Paul Vangelisti, who—when Crosson was evicted from the Laurel Canyon house where he was caretaker—took him in. Crosson lived with Vangelisti from 1993 until his death in 2001.

I knew Crosson, however, not as a has-been actor, but as an incredible storyteller and wonderful poet. I first heard Crosson's name and read some of his work on the 1989 California Arts Council panel which awarded him a small fellowship. I had never met Crosson, but Vangelisti, who was also on that panel, assured me that we would instinctually like one another. And when I met Bob a few months later, Paul's prediction became fact. Like many others, I loved Bob, primarily, because of his complete disregard of cant and doctrine, against which he would rail in brief asides in the manner of W. C. Fields or Mae West, but also because of his gentle friendship.

True, Bob was both an alcoholic and a heavy smoker. Although his death was listed as a heart attack, he was told by a doctor previously that his smoking would soon result in his death. In 1991, Bob appeared in my performative work, *The Walls Come True*, picking me up in his truck at least two times so that we could travel to Diana Daves' home in the Valley to rehearse. The trip on both occasions was excruciatingly frightful, as Bob drove at a snail's pace so that we might not hit anything along the way, while nonetheless nearly clipping any car parked *en route*. When Bob was later arrested for drunken driving in 1996, he described his ordeal as a 67-year-old man who could hardly keep up with the other prisoners:

> I find it hard to navigate (I cannot navigate steps). Outside officers order to come out *fast*. I can't. (I pull at the chains). Black gentleman in front of me, in face of the order, retorts: "We're coming—but *this old man is holding us up*."

In response to the charges, Crosson pleads "No contest," and is released. Bob continues in his *Daybook*, "Paul picks me up... Find truck (yet) parked at curb." A footnote explains that they "celebrate with a drink at Rustic," one of Bob's favorite watering holes.

The following year, 1997, Bob joined numerous other poets and artists at the conference on Catalina Island I describe below in the essay titled "History." The trip over by ferry had frightened and exhausted Bob, so when most of the conference participants decided to walk down the hill into town for dinner, Bob and I stayed behind. It gave us several long hours to renew our friendship, to discuss gay issues, and, for me, to hear more of Bob's salacious tales. He retold one of his favorites: how when he and his brother where young, they had had sex, his brother afterwards responding, "How could anything that feels so good be bad?"

At Bob's memorial service (where I also met Bob's friend Jack Larson) Crosson's brother—from whom he had been separated most of his life, the boys having been sent to different families—reported that several of Bob's stories were simply not based on fact. "I love Bob dearly," he said, "but...well, he loved to make up stories." For example, Crosson's long insistence that his mother died upon his birth, we were told, was simply not the case. She died a few years after his birth.

As far as I was concerned, the veracity of Crosson's tales about himself and others was of no matter. I could have listened, and did listen, for hours at a time.

Perhaps more importantly, as I grew to discover, Crosson's own poetic work, although clearly eccentric, was fascinating. He published, during his lifetime, only a few books—*Geographies* (1981), *Wet Check* (1983), *Calliope* (1988), and *The Blue Soprano* (1994)—but he continued to write until his health began to seriously deteriorate the year of my dinner with him. In 1997 Guy Bennett published a short chapbook, *In the Aethers of the Amazon: Poems 1984-1997*; and in 2004, Agincourt printed a collection I once had hoped to publish, *The Day Sam Goldwyn Stepped off the Train*. Like the man, Crosson's work in this volume was irreverent, witty and yet, at times, heart-wrenchingly beautiful. His poems always surprised, never fitting into easy patterns or reader expectations, which, I suspect, often put some readers in the position of the poet himself, finding it "hard to navigate." A few lines from the last poem of that latter book will have to suffice as example:

Of Course

Whilst I still can.
Whilst. I do.
Whilst the otter to the edge of the pond
Whilst

(I have never seen an otter)

Whilst the midnight of morning
holds me close
Whilst the dogs are quiet

(especially the birds)
Whilst the hush of a new day
allows no helicopters
and prayer is silent.

Whilst memories yet hold me prisoner
of my hulk, whilst Whitman yet holds
such daring of his & lord of his affection.
When silence pervades

and any punctuation is unnecessary.

(as a child I was told "you think too much."
Parentheses rarely apply.

Beginning with a Beckett-like "I can go on, I do," Crosson both mocks Romantic conventions (with the repeated "Whilst" and his pretended devotion to nature) and yet embraces them, like his beloved poet-friend Whitman. The work is both a commentary on itself, is itself *about* the language which he uses, and an old-fashioned ode to the surrounding world of early morning. Bob was like that, an irreverent postmodern Romantic, who as he bent down to pet a cat might spew some dark comic quip out the side of his mouth. And in that respect, Crosson was an antidote for all seemingly passionate fakers one faces every day. The other morning, Paul Vangelisti admitted to me: "I miss Bob.

Our world needs him even more now." I agreed.

LOS ANGELES, MARCH 6, 2009
Reprinted from *Green Integer Blog* (March 2009).

In 1997, in conjunction with a conference by the same title held on Catalina Island near Los Angeles on the weekend of May 2-4, Paul Vangelisti asked me and several others to write on the concept of "History"—poems, essays, and artworks he published in Ribot 5 *that same year. My contribution was attributed to my pseudonym Claude Ricochet (translated from the French by another of my pseudonyms, Peter Fahrni). Ultimately, it was included in my fiction (written under the name of Joshua Haigh)* Letters from Hanusse. *Given the focus of* My Year 2001, *it appears appropriate to reprint it here.*

History: Maquette No. 33

HISTORY DOES NOT EXIST. Like a great, great grandfather, it lies rotten in its crypt. Only through bits and pieces of memory, storytelling, exaggeration, lies, and forgetfulness, do we the living create it, make it up. And in this we know, instinctively, history has nothing at all to do with facts, with the truth of our existence. It is a pile of rubbish each of us sorts through to figure out what might be saved.

This fact saddens us. It would be easier to have learned from the past, to discover how not to repeat the

terrible stupidities, atrocities, the general foolishness of the human race. If history could exist, how we might learn from it! But we know, inwardly we know, the moment it becomes history, it becomes something no longer connected with the truth we seek within each moment of our day. We are left with threads, old remnants that we try to weave together without success.

Imagine if history did exist, if it could live along with us, as a breathing force. How heavy it would weigh! So many dead heaping up reality upon so few living left. We would only suffocate.

All the more important that, ineffectual as we are, we attempt to resew the pattern over and over again. Like Penelope, we must weave to unwind and weave once more, each time ever so slightly varying the design—until, as we are about to fall into our own burial plots, we have created something completely different from what we thought at the beginning we might create. As in the child's game of telephone, we have repeated the words so many times that we, each of us alone and each of us as a part of generation, have utterly transformed the message. What might have once been feared is now revered, the sacred is at last profane.

LOS ANGELES, 1997
Reprinted from *Ribot*, No. 5 (1997).

Anatomy of Self

BERNADETTE MAYER **ERUDITIO EX MEMORIA** (NEW YORK: ANGEL HAIR BOOKS, 1977)

MEMORY, HISTORY, personal history, autobiography, metaphysical autobiography, *Eruditio ex Memoria* is all of these. Yet this book projects a memory not of self, but of the self as defined by the knowledge which makes up the self, which perceives the world in which the self lives. And in this sense Bernadette Mayer's new work is a cosmology, an encyclopedic anatomy, which as a genre is related to Menippean or Varronian verse satire, from the Greek cynic Menippus and the Roman satirist Varro, both of whose works are now lost. The anatomy has continued in Lucian, Petronius, Apuleius, Rabelais, Voltaire, Swift, Rousseau, Peacock, and, in our own century, Aldous Huxley, Wyndham Lewis, Djuna Barnes, and, most recently, in *Seeking Air* by Barbara Guest. Unlike the picaresque—which is a satire of society and of its structures—the anatomy is a satire

built up through a presentation of a vision "of the world in terms of a single intellectual pattern." Northrup Frye continues (in *Anatomy of Criticism*), "The intellectual structure built up from the story makes for violent dislocations in the customary logic of narrative, though the appearance of carelessness that reflects only the carelessness of the reader or his tendency to judge by a novel-centered conception of fiction." The shortest form of the anatomy is the dialogue, but there is a strong tendency toward a display of erudition, of encyclopedic knowledge, of complications, catalogues and lists (see Burton's *Anatomy of Melancholy, Tristam Shandy,* Flaubert's *Bouvard et Pecuchet,* Norman Douglas' *South Wind,* and portions of *Moby Dick*).

Does Mayer know anatomies? Perhaps not. The impulse here seems to come as much from her obsession with memory, from a compulsion for autobiography that is related to the confession such as Saint Augustine's. But for Mayer memory is never an end in itself. It is not memory past that most interests her, but memory continuing, repeating, memory in the present made new through language in Pound's sense of that concept. Mayer's art is not a seeking for what was but what *is*, and how what *is* was made by that past. Mayer's memory is not nostalgic—as in Proust—but is a past that makes the new, makes possible the new: an ending that is a beginning ("Each end is a beginning"). She seeks not for old structures, not for a *re*creation but for a *de*creation: "I put these words on paper because they were once written by me, no, I too yearn for a world without meaning." As she previously wrote in her fiction *Memory*, "A whole new language is a temptation."

But Mayer's world, the world she discovers, is not without meaning. The past *de*created gives rise to a new created or *re*created world. As with Adam, Mayer calls things into meaning by naming. Through memory's order "Hemispheres become loose in the country, there are new forms."

Is this different from a Surrealist allowing the subconscious to create new structures, using dream images as the basis for a new reality? Yes. Mayer's past is not a dream, not archetypal, not mythical, but a socially lived experience. These are school notes, a pre-existent text rewritten (?) or almost intact, a life wrenched out of chronological context not by chance but by fact, a life perhaps not *experienced* as discontinuous but which was (and because was can only be *is* in memory), *is* in fact.

No coy discontinuity is this, no clever dissociations. Actually there is an attempt in *Eruditio* at lucidness, to see through the veil of *experience* to a reality of flux, of life, of duration. And in this there is a basic recognition of the ineffectuality, of the destructiveness of the written word as opposed to spoken language. "There's no use writing down Greek words if no one is going to know what I'm saying." Mayer is always after language, then, after the reality that is language. *Eruditio* is a search for that reality not as written word but as language, which as a thought process *is* the thing itself. Saying is thinking is perceiving is knowing. In fact, although this work may often seem ineffable, there is throughout a drive for an absolute clarity of language: "Add up a column of numbers, it comes to William Carlos Williams."

All of which brings us back to the genre of the anatomy, which comes from the Greek *anatomé*, a cutting up, an analysis or minute examination, to show or examine the position, structure, and relation of the parts. That is what this book is to me; it is an attempt to explain, to demonstrate, to show how Mayer has come to know whatever it is she has come to know. And in that sense, this book is a sharing, a removal of the veil, an admission, an apology, a true confession.

In doing so, moreover, it is itself a sign, an image, an emblem of language which stands for Mayer and the world she has *re*created, an emblem like the red letter

Hester Prynne wears. *Eruditio ex Memoria* ends with such an image: "In a painting I am a Chinese woman turning away from a bowl of fruit." Is this an Eve with a second chance, this time redeeming by giving up the knowledge, by releasing it? To pin the image down that way is to miss the point, is to turn back to the fruit and eat it. It is nothing more than itself, a Chinese woman turning away from a bowl of fruit, "its own sure image."

Reprinted from *L=A=N=G=U=A=G=E*, no. 7 (March 1979). Collected in *The L=A=N=G=U=A=G=E Book*, edited by Bruce Andrews and Charles Bernstein (Carbondale: Southern Illinois University Press, 1984).

It seems strange in hindsight that, despite my close friendships with editors Bruce Andrews and Charles Bernstein, I published only this short essay above and an inconsequential experimental diagram in the legendary L=A=N=G=U=A=G=E magazine. While I was obviously concentrating on more academically-oriented writings in those days, I do recall that at the time of writing about Mayer's work, I was quite exhausted by critical writing, and looked forward to the opportunity to pen a more loosely structured and poetically conceived piece. It is obvious that in many of the sentences above I was imitating some of Mayer's own catalogues and listings, writing a piece itself affected by the work it was describing.

I had discovered Mayer's poetry at about the same time I was researching the writing of John Wieners in 1975 and 1976 (see My Year 2002*). Also in 1976 I purchased a copy of the newly published book by Mayer,* Poetry, *from the Kulcher Foundation, Lita Hornick's press, which later invited me to submit a manuscript for publication—however the book on which I was then working was not near enough to completion.*

Mayer's book, although somewhat inconsistent in quality, was brilliant, I felt, when it was at its best in poems such as "Corn," "Three Men," "Anthology," "The Aeschyleans," "The People Who Like Aeschylus," "The Port," "House Cap," and numerous others.

I shared my enthusiasm for Mayer's (and other poets' writing) with Marjorie Perloff, who, while embracing several of the poets I admired—Charles and Bruce among them—never came to a full understanding of my love of Mayer's writing. A couple of years later, Angel Hair Press published Mayer's The Golden Book of Words, *another book I highly admired, particularly the poems "The End of Human Reign on Bashan Hill," "Lookin Like Areas of Kansas," "Carlton Fisk Is My Ideal," and "Who Wants to Go Out into the Bitter Wind." These two books remain my favorites of Mayer's extensive output, and, except for particular poems in her later books, represent to me the apogee of her poetic contributions—although I am sure* there are many who would disagree.

I also wrote to Mayer during this period, requesting work and publishing some of her poems in my Sun & Moon: A Journal of Literature & Art. *Later I published*  *a selection of her poetry in my anthology* From the Other Side of the Century: A New American Poetry 1960-1990 *and wrote a poem to which she responded in my collaborative work,* Between.

After my 1980 reading with Susan Howe at the Poetry Project at St. Mark's, I met Mayer for the first time, and we spoke at length about poetry at a nearby bar. As I wrote in My Year 2005, *I encountered Mayer again at a party and dinner afterwards for the publication of Russell Banks'* The Relation of My Imprisonment, *an occasion in which Mayer, having just broken up with her husband Lewis Warsh, was extremely vulnerable—and I was very ill. A while later Mayer had a very serious heart attack.*

Years after, at the University of California, San Diego, I once again encountered Mayer at the 1998 Page Mother's Conference, organized by Fanny Howe and Rae Armantrout. On this occasion, however, our meeting was very brief, with no chance for discussion. However, I did snap her photograph with poet Quincy Troupe.

In May 2006 Charles Bernstein and I attended a birthday celebration for and reading by Mayer at the Bowery Poetry Club in New York. Although all of her children and Lewis were in attendance, Mayer herself arrived late, and showed no signs of preparing to read. I spoke with her for a short while before Charles and I left the event.

LOS ANGELES, JULY 19, 2008

At Point Zero

ANNE PORTUGAL **NUDE**, TRANSLATED FROM THE
FRENCH BY NORMA COLE (BERKELEY, CALIFORNIA:
KELSEY STREET PRESS, 2001)

WITH OVER FOUR BOOKS of poetry published in
France—all on the list of the distinguished publisher
P.O.L—Anne Portugal is fast becoming recognized as
one of the major French poets. Her book *Le plus simple
appareil* has been translated in a beautiful edition as
Nude. Before I go any further with this review, however, I must admit that it was originally to have been published by my own Sun & Moon, but given the financial
duress of the last few years, it was taken on by Kelsey St.
Press. So I am prejudiced to like it. However, in reread-
ing the work—years after my original encounter—I do
feel I have some observations to make.

The work, divided into seven parts—"the bath,"
"the exhibition," "the garden," "the elders," "the visitors," "Susanna's letters," and "the painting"—is really

 one long work thematically based on the Biblical tale of *Susanna and the Elders*. That story, canonical in Catholicism and apocryphal in Protestantism, added sometime in 100 B.C. to the Hebrew-Armaic version of Daniel, tells the story of Susanna, a beautiful woman married to Joakim, whose house is the site of the local court. Two of the elders of that court desire Susanna and plot her rape. As she takes a bath in the garden, they hide themselves, observing, and then offer her the choice of sexually submitting to them or being accused of adultery. When Susanna refuses to give in to their demands, they denounce her, trying her in the court and sentencing her to death. Enter Daniel, who interrogates the two elders, proving their guilt and Susanna's innocence. Praised by her parents, Daniel becomes a hero among the people.

Portugal's work, however—although containing the bath, garden, nudity, elders, and sexual encounters—is hardly a literal retelling of the Bible tale. Rather, this author's work is an interweaving of what it means to be a woman in contemporary France and a study in formal structures, a kind of verbal painting, which she lays out early in the book with a series of panoramas. Indeed, the work is addressed to an unknown who "knows painting" ("You really know painting"), presumably the individual to whom the book is dedicated, Marc Silvain. But the author could be addressing anyone else, even possibly the poet Guillaume Apollinaire, to whose poems Portugal makes reference throughout *Nude*, and, who, as the author of *The Cubist Painters*, certainly did also *know* painting. Already in the second section, "the exhibition," Portugal alludes to Apollinaire's poem "Annie," which describes a Mennonite living on the shores of Texas between Mobile and Galveston, passing a garden filled with roses by a villa "Which is one huge rose." And in "the garden" she connects that poem with images from Apollinaire's "White Snow" and "Palais." The last section reverberates with Portugal's references to Apollinaire's "Rosemonde" ("the rose of the world"), and again to "Palais," as Susanna turns back to Rosemonde's palace.

To focus on these echoing patterns, however, would be to mislead the reader. Portugal's work, far from being a sort of academic compilation of literary references, is lyrically dense and complex in its structure. And for that reason, if for no other, I long for a bilingual edition, where I could compare the complexity of the original—its multiple puns and enjambments—with Cole's translation. For, if the poem begins with the simple image of Susanna at the bath, a plump and blonde Swede, as the author sees her, "limned" by "the two elders' heads," it soon swirls into a series of multiple images, of numerous Susannas, a woman naked in a field in Normandy while at the same time a passionate girl in a sateen nighty. The poem becomes a "vessel borne upon multiple waves," just as Susanna comes to represent opposing visions of women, both Venus and "a plump woman who's put on weight she's put on weight." Portugal's work, in fact, is like a cubist painting, a series of images overlapping each other which together portray not an instant in time, a symbolic flash of womanhood, but all women through time, being both preyed upon by the opposite sex and sensually aroused by its attentions, a woman moving forward in history while turning back to the romance of Rosemonde's palace—which leaves man eternally starting out again "at point zero."

LOS ANGELES, FEBRUARY 3, 2004
Reprinted from *The New Review of Literature*, I, no. 2 (April 2004), in slightly different form.

I met Anne Portugal briefly at a party held for me by P.O.L publisher Paul Otchakovsky-Laurens and his wife of the time in the mid-1990s after a reading I gave at The Village Voice bookshop. Both Henri Deluy and Jacques

Roubaud, as well as other French poets, attended the reading, after which we were invited to Paul's apartment.

Anne and I spoke very little, but I immediately felt at home with her, and liked her enormously. But many of P.O.L's writers had been invited to the event, and I had little time, accordingly, to talk with any one person.

I recall being served various wines and, in the kitchen, being faced with a sumptuous spread of French cheeses upon the table, which, in their variety, overwhelmed me. As I paused in my wonderment, Paul must have sensed a slight discomfort, but misunderstood it as a problem of the American palette. "Perhaps, like many Americans, you don't have an appetite for these kinds of cheeses." I assured him I did very much love cheese, but was unsure of which to try first!

LOS ANGELES, NOVEMBER 20, 2009

Remembering What Everyone Might Like to Forget

DURING THE SEVEN YEARS since the horrific events of what is generally referred to these days as simply "9/11," I have resisted writing about the subject, in part because it seemed to me that nearly everyone in the United States had experienced the destruction of the World Trade Towers, the attack upon the Pentagon, and the crash of United Airlines Flight 93—which was to have been crashed into the US Capitol building—near Shanksville, Pennsylvania, and there could not possibly be anything new I might say.

I still believe that to be so. Any of us might write about our experiences on that morning and throughout that September day—and many have. Moreover, with the confirmed deaths of 2,974 individuals, and the subsequent illnesses of firemen, police, and other workers who tried to help individuals to safety and later worked in cleaning up the disastrous collapse of both towers, there are hundreds of individuals who have much deep-er experiences than my distant witnessing of events.

What we all generally forget, however, is precisely that—our general forgetfulness. Howard reminded me last night that most of his students at SCI-Arc (the Southern California Institute of Archi-tecture), where he is teaching this semester, were only 11 years of age when these events took place, and, ac-cordingly, their memories of it were those of children rather than adults. Millions of grade-school children today could not possibly comprehend how far-reaching those events, occurring before their births, have been upon their lives: that the war we continue to fight in Iraq was an indirect result of that terrible day in 2001 and that some of their individual freedoms have been permanently curtailed because of those events in the years since.

Perhaps we owe it to our future generations, even to ourselves, to once again share our experiences of that day. And in a series of books such as my cultural mem-oirs, I now perceive it is absolutely necessary to remember my own experiences of the day—even if they might vary little from millions of other folks and I, like most others, might like to forget.

Howard and I arise quite early, he at 5:00 each morning, I at 6:00. Accordingly, when a short time after 5:46 Pacific Time on September 11th Howard heard the news report and saw the image on television of American Airlines Flight 11 embedded in the North Tower of the World Trade Center, he quickly woke me to tell me what had happened. I ran to the television set to see the same image.

Although we now know that many people working on the 95th to the 103rd floors and dining in the Windows on the World restaurant were killed immediately, it looked eerily quiet from the camera's vantage point. I commented to Howard that obviously the crash had killed people, but we were uncertain even how large the plane was. It looked almost like a small-engine plane on our TV set.

"How could such an accident happen?" asked Howard in a tone that sounded more like a lament.

"People don't just accidentally fly into The World Trade Center," I answered, with suitable bluff. "No planes are allowed in that air path." And immediately we both contemplated the possibility of a terrorist attack.

For a few minutes we sat spellbound by the scene

before us. We were nearly speechless. "I have to go to the bathroom," I reported, as if somehow seeking Howard's permission.

As I began my walk down the hall, Howard screamed out: "Come quickly, come quickly. Another plane has just crashed into the other tower!"

I hurried back to watch the scene replayed, a clearly full-sized jet crashing into the South Tower. Now we and everyone knew: these were terrorist acts.

Our eyes were cemented to the television, when a few minutes later an ABC newscaster announced that they were temporarily switching to a developing story in Washington, D.C., where it appeared that the Executive Office Building, near the White House, was on fire.

The D.C. newscaster, however, soon reported that from a distance it appeared that it was the Executive Office Building, but it was believed to be coming from the area of The Pentagon, across the Potomac in Virginia. And soon we saw a fire billowing from the Pentagon itself, where, we now know, American Airlines Flight 77 crashed, killing another 189 individuals.

Sep. 12, 2001, 17:37:22   #3 impact

"What's happening?" I asked in utter disbelief.

And a few minutes later, as if in answer, it was reported that yet another plane apparently had been hijacked.

In Los Angeles, September 11th was a voting date, and the front of my Sun & Moon Press offices was a polling place. I was forced to abandon the television to shave, shower, and dress. By 6:45 Pacific Time, I was opening up my office for the voting registrars.

I greeted them and briefly helped to set up the voting booths. We all expressed the hope that the local election would be called off. But, by the time we were to open, we had still received no word of cancellation.

I was almost angered by all the noise of the gossipy women behind the voter sign-in desk, and retreated to my back office to watch my office television set. Although it was illegal to bring a television into the voting area, one of the women working there called to ask her daughter to bring in her TV.

At almost the moment they opened the doors to voters, I witnessed the South Tower of the World Trade Center collapse, people running in absolute horror in all directions. I was incredulous. Peter Jennings, the

ABC newscaster, was nearly in tears. He would continue to report all day and into the night, for 17 hours straight, and I watched almost every moment.

About 11 minutes after the collapse of the South Tower, it was reported that the missing hijacked flight, United Airlines Flight 93, had crashed into a hillside in Somerset County, Pennsylvania.

When the North Tower collapsed at 7:28, I finally began to cry. I was now worried for friends. Playwright Jeffrey Jones worked in the Towers; I had met with him there on one trip to New York to discuss theater.

Poet Tan Lin (brother of Vietnam Memorial sculptor Mya Lin), whose book *Lotion Bullwhip Giraffe* I published, lived nearby. Artist Susan Bee's studio was within view of the Towers. Fortunately, these friends all survived.

As I report in "Death of the Father" [*My Year 2002*], I called my parents, who at the time had still not heard what was happening. How could anyone not know what was going on? I wondered.

Yet the television showed even President George Bush peacefully sitting in a classroom at Emily E. Booker Elementary School in Sarasota at a time when one imagined he might instead be rushing back to Washington. Evidently the President did not know what millions of others in his country did, and when his advisors heard the news of the first crash several of them, including his Chief of Staff Andrew Card, presumed it was simply an accident. Card is quoted saying, "It was first reported to me...that it looked like it was a twin-engine prop plane, and so the natural reaction was—'What a horrible accident. The pilot must have had a heart at-

tack.'" After being taken aside in the school corridor by Karl Rove, where Bush was told of the crash, Bush himself reportedly replied: "What a horrible accident!"

While Bush was on route to the school photo opportunity, Condoleeza Rice made an urgent call to the President; but even upon hearing of that call, he took time out to talk with Florida Congressmen and the Teacher of the Year before returning Rice's call; and once he had heard from her, he continued to the classroom, remaining there to hear the story of a pet goat even after the second jet had completed its mission, despite the fact that the newest information was relayed to the President in front of the classroom students and millions of watching Americans.

For a number of reasons, including arguments

between Bush and Cheney and the indecision of his staff concerning where Air Force One should travel, Bush's flight was diverted to the Louisiana Air Force Base before flying on to the Strategic Air Command at Nebraska's Offutt Air Force Base. As the press attempted to follow the various maneuvers of Air Force One and the President, rumors grew, at one point some reporters even suggesting that his plane had crashed near Camp David. It was clear to nearly anyone who could read the signs that neither Bush nor his administration knew how to proceed.

Moreover, as the details of deaths and destruction became more and more apparent over that horrific day, there was a continued feeling, registered even on the faces and voices of news commentators like Jennings, of being caught up in a nightmare from which one couldn't awaken.

In the weeks following, it was gradually revealed that not only were the Twin Towers of the World Trade Center destroyed, but 7 World Trade Center, 6 World Trade Center, 5 World Trade Center, 4 World Trade Center, the Marriott World Trade Center and St. Nicholas Greek Orthodox Church were also destroyed or severely damaged. The Deutsche Bank Building and Fiterman Hall of the Borough of Manhattan Community College were condemned and torn down.

In short, a whole section of the US's most populous city was devastated; and one only can wonder what might have happened in Washington, D.C. had Flight 93 been successful in its attack. It still today seems nearly impossible to imagine that four American airplanes could have been utilized to bring about such widespread destruction, resulting in so many deaths.

LOS ANGELES, SEPTEMBER 11, 2008
Reprinted from *Green Integer Blog* (September 2008).

Discovering What Everyone Never Remembered

LAWRENCE WRIGHT **THE LOOMING TOWER: AL-QAEDA AND THE ROAD TO 9/11** (NEW YORK: ALFRED A. KNOPF, 2006)

PERHAPS NO BOOK more clearly details the US's determination to keep history a secret than *The Looming Tower*, Lawrence Wright's brilliant post-9/11 study of the Muslim terrorist world and its interactions with the American FBI, CIA, and other government organizations.

Wright begins by lucidly outlining the various terrorist organizations and the individuals who led them, starting with a young Egyptian student studying in the US at what is now the University of Northern Colorado in Greeley. Sayyid Qutb had mixed feelings in this community, originally planned as a temperance colony by Nathan Meeker. Greeley was a planned community

that "would serve as a model for the cities of the future," drawing from the virtues of "industry, moral rectitude, and temperance." Accordingly, Qutb, a devout young Muslim, had, as Wright describes it, "stumbled into a community that exalted the same pursuits that he held dear: education, music, art, literature, and religion." But just as Qutb had found New York life frantic and unfamiliar, he found disturbing forces at work in this small Western Eden as well. Although the community had been founded on Prohibition, students in the summer of 1949 could easily procure alcohol for their weekly parties, and Qutb perceived the fall of Prohibition as an American failure. As a man of color, Qutb witnessed a black man beaten by a white mob. And although in the summers students from many different racial backgrounds attended, in the regular season there were only a couple of black students, one of whom, Qutb noted, could not get a haircut in the local community. At one point, Qutb and a friend were turned away from a local theater because the owner saw them as being black. Although the theater owner ultimately apologized, Qutb refused to return.

Even the sport of football "confirmed Qutb's ideas of American primitiveness," since he felt it less a team sport, like soccer, than a game in which one player attempts to run with the ball, while others try "kicking him in the stomach, or violently breaking his arms and legs...." Women teachers outraged him. Accordingly he returned to Egypt more radicalized in relation to his religion than he left it. Qutb went on to establish the Muslim Brothers, the first of a series of radical reactionary groups against what they felt was Egypt's failure to keep the tenants of the Muslim faith.

The pattern was to become a quite typical one, with many of the well-educated and often wealthy young radicals receiving their educations in the West, opening them to experiences that only hardened them in their beliefs. The fascinating story of Ayman Al-Zawahiri, who grew up in a planned community, Maadi, Egypt—that in its conception, at least, was not so very different from Greeley, Colorado—is a high point of the book. With his father working as a doctor and his mother a professor of pharmacology at Ain Shams University, Al-Zawahiri was raised in one of the most liberal and prominent families in Egypt. But as he grew older, Al-Zawahiri, influenced, in part, by Sayyid Qutb's writings, became more and more dissatisfied with the

Egyptian government, ultimately creating, along with others, the Al-Jihad movement, and involving himself, if only through his friendships, with the assassination of Egyptian President Anwar Al-Sadat. Through his friendship with Abdullah Azzam, Al-Zawahiri was ultimately drawn to Afghanistan, there befriending the charismatic Osama bin Laden.

Wright outlines these and numerous other relationships, introducing us, one by one, to most of the major figures and their families of the Muslim Brothers, Al-Jihad, the Taliban,  Al-Qaeda, and other terrorist groups, including the numerous young, violent, and dissatisfied youths that eventually would make up the growing worldwide attempt to destroy anything American. It is Osama bin Laden, obviously, who through his early financing of terrorist activities and his gathering of many of these forces in Sudan to train them, is the most fascinating— and puzzling—of figures. Even Wright's extensive presentation of bin Laden's family history and other major Saudi figures reads like an account by T. E. Lawrence.

Through bin Laden's machinations, what began as fairly local attempts in the Muslim world to rid individual countries of Western influences, became a general call to destroy what they came to see as the common enemy: the United States.

Through hundreds of interviews gathered over a five-year period, Wright brilliantly puts all the pieces of the puzzle together, so that the reader can discover that what seems to be a myriad of terrifyingly unrelated events grew, as the millennium approached, into an interwoven skein with the aim of strangling what Muslim radicals began to see as the cause of all their misfortunes.

Of course, hindsight is always a superior position than that of suffering blindly through history. But how one wishes that minds like Wright's might have been employed in the very organizations whose function it was to piece these threats together! Instead, we are shown that American fact-gathering organizations such as the CIA, the FBI, and the White House itself began by doubting any real threat, and later, when it was almost too late to change course, deliberately withheld information from each other. Given a directory intended to protect them from later court hearings, the various organizations perceived the so-called "wall" as a barrier to any shared knowledge. FBI Chief of Counterterrorism John O'Neill was perhaps the one man who had the tenacity and intelligence to bring the data together that might have saved the nation from the events of September 11, 2001. However, his own often dictatorial methods, his far-flung affairs with various women, and even his dashing way of dressing made for many enemies, including coworkers in the FBI and, in particular, the director, Michael Scheuer, of the so-called Alec Station in the CIA, which was also attempting to track the activities of Osama bin Laden and Al-Qaeda.

In the rivalry between the two, O'Neill ultimately won, with Scheuer suffering a psychological breakdown. But O'Neill's breaches of security—at one point he had brought one of his mistresses into FBI headquarters and, at another event, his computer, filled with sensitive information, was temporarily stolen—also brought reprimands and the threatened termination of his job. Yet, even in those difficult days, had the CIA reported to other organizations that Nawaf al-Hazmi and Khaled al-Mihdhar, both Al-Qaeda operatives, had entered the US on January 2001, and lived for a while in San Diego, O'Neill likely could have acted, spoiling bin Laden's plans.

O'Neill's abilities are outlined throughout Wright's book, epitomized, perhaps, in his clever extraction of

information from figures involved with the bombing of the USS *Cole* without any torture—tracing, with the help of his Yemeni specialist Ali Soufan, the first real connection between the *Cole* and Al-Qaeda. But even in Yemen, O'Neill was dogged by personality differences, in this case with US ambassador to Yemen, Barbara Bodine, who forced him to exit the country.

Even as O'Neill was scheduled to leave the FBI to become—in one of the most ironic situations in American history—head of security for the World Trade Center, he sensed something very large was in the air. "We're overdue," O'Neill told friends.

Only a week before O'Neill's retirement, a report from a flight school in Minnesota to the FBI noted that one of their students, Zacarias Moussaoui, was asking suspicious questions about flight patterns and locked cockpit doors. When the agent in Minnesota asked permission to search Moussaoui's computer, he was told he was "trying to get people 'spun up.'" His answer: "I am trying to keep someone from taking a plane and crashing into the World Trade Center."

Wright asks several of his interviewees why the CIA had been so determined to keep the crucial information that two Al-Qaeda operatives had been in the country secretly, particularly since the men had been discovered on US soil, where the CIA had no jurisdiction. The answers range from the belief in CIA plans to use them as potential informants to the often stated argument that for legal reasons they simply could not share that knowledge. But the truth, perhaps, is what Wright describes simply as the radically different make-up of the two major information-gathering organizations, the CIA consisting of internationally-seasoned individuals who often gathered information as a kind of protective act, using it only behind-the-scenes, so to speak, to influence the actions of other countries. That is not say that the CIA has not been involved in the deaths of others or has not stood behind many covert coups. But the FBI persona had long been symbolized by their direct and, often, public response. The agency, Wright suggests, was made up primarily of Italo-American and Irish-American men, who, much like the immigrant communities out of which they came, believed in information as a justification to act; from the earliest Hoover days, as Michael Mann's recent film, *Public Enemies,* reiterates, they were men of action. Each organization highly suspected (and perhaps still does suspect) the other as being ineffectual. Their failures to work together, however, along with a weak grasp of the situations by the Bush administration—which clearly led to thousands of deaths—should be repeatedly retold and remembered by all.

O'Neill survived the original attack, running, as bodies fell from the towers into the plaza below, to assess the damage. He reentered the South Tower, which, a short while later, collapsed, entombing him within.

LOS ANGELES, JULY 4, 2009
Reprinted from *Green Integer Blog* (July 2009).

Rehearsals for Abandoning Love

WONG KAR-WAI (WRITER AND DIRECTOR) 花樣年華 (IN THE MOOD FOR LOVE) / 2000, USA 2001

SUPERFICIALLY, HONG KONG director Wong Kar-wai's 2000 film, *In the Mood for Love*, might appear to be a thwarted love story. Two neighboring couples, the Chows and the Chans, renting adjoining rooms in an apartment building owned my Mrs. Suen, coincidentally move in on the very same day, many of their possessions becoming temporarily intermixed—a forecast of events to come. Both Chan and Chow's wife are business people who often travel, leaving their spouses alone for long periods at a time. Lonely, the two, Chow Mo-wan (Tony Leung), a journalist, and Su Li-zhen (Maggie Cheung), a secretary, individually visit the local rice kitchen to take home food to eat alone in their rooms.

Early on in this film, Wong portrays their comings

 and goings—accompanied by the senuous music of composers Michael Galasso and Shigeru Umebayashi, and songs sung by Zhou Xuan and Nat "King" Cole—as the central characters enter into a series of something like slow-motion dances, a bit like flamenco and passo double movements, as the attractive loners pass each other on the streets and in their apartment halls. Not only are they forced to take stock of one another's comings and goings, but, as the days pass without the return of either of their spouses, they begin to notice other things, Chow that his wife has a purse she has purchased in her travels very similar to one Su Li-zhen carries, Mrs. Chan that Chow wears a tie, purchased by his wife, very similar to the one which her husband claims was given to him by his boss. Sadly, they must face the fact that their spouses are seeing one another.

Before long, the beautiful Su Li-zhen (wearing absolutely stunning slinky Chinese dresses popular in the Hong Kong of the 1960s) and the well-groomed Chow begin meeting.

At first, determined not to behave like their spouses, the two create an intense platonic relationship, discovering that they share a great many interests, including an enjoyment of martial-arts serials, which Chow soon begins to write, Su Li-zhen  reading them and making suggestions. The two also share a love of certain foods and music; both like films.

But, as the director himself has noted, they are not as innocent as they might first seem. Like the characters of Alfred Hitchcock's *Vertigo*, Scottie and Madeline, they circle round one another, dangerously toying with various dramatic possibilities in their own lives. At first, they simply try to comprehend how their spouses originally fell in love with one another, as Chow and Mrs. Chan play out, almost like school children, various versions of a first meeting.

Those dramatic scenarios soon turn to more serious ones, wherein Su Li-zhen acts out her demand that her husband (played by Chow) admit that he has a mistress. If it begins as a kind of playful acting-out of anger and suffering, it quickly grows more serious as the couple discovers that, despite their best intentions, they too are falling in love. The fact that they continue to resist their own attraction and wrap their meetings in a series of secretive encounters, aiming at protecting them-

 selves from suspicion by the other boarders in their building and from their office mates, only creates further tensions that increase their frustration and would-be lust.

In a sense, while their spouses have been more open and honest about their relationship, Chow and Su Li-zhen rehearse again and again their abandonment of love. Given that their spouses seem to have left forever, one might have thought that this almost perfectly matched pair would find joy and take pleasure in one another. Instead they torture one another until not only is Chow forced to take a hotel room, but he becomes determined to leave Hong Kong for Singapore to escape the emotions he now deeply feels.

Su Li-zhen equally suffers from the secrecy of their romance, and when, finally, Chow makes a call asking if he were to have two tickets might she join him, after a period of resistance, she suddenly runs to his room, arriving too late.

In any normal "love" story she would have quickly followed him to Singapore, and they might have been joyfully reunited. But in Wong's tale, the two merely continue to punish one another and themselves through their abandonment of love.

A year after Chow has left, he discovers in his Singapore apartment a cigarette in an ashtray with lipstick on it, and realizes that his room has been visited in his absence by Su Li-zhen. Dining with office mates, Chow has the following discussion:

CHOW MO-WAN: In the old days, if someone had a secret they didn't want to share...you know what they did?
AH PING: Have no idea.
CHOW MO-WAN: They went up a mountain, found a tree, carved a hole in it, and whispered the secret into the hole. Then they covered it with mud. And leave the secret there forever.
AH PING: What a pain! I'd just go to get laid.
CHOW MO-WAN: Not everyone's like you.

Later that evening Chow receives a telephone call, clearly made by Su Li-zhen, but she never speaks and hangs up soon after.

Years later, at Angkor Wat, where he is visiting, Chow stares into a hole in the ancient edifice, whispering for several moments into the gap before filling it with mud. Clearly he has now buried the secret and his own now empty past.

Returning to his old abode in Hong Kong at a later time, he finds his friends, who were living in his

 old apartment, have now moved away. As he turns to go, he asks who lives next door and is told that the apartment is now owned by a woman and her son.

He leaves without realizing that it is Su Li-zhen. Whether the son she now has is Chow's from their one night together or from her former husband after a temporary return home we never discover. But it is clear that she continues to lead a life without a lover. If the couple's refusal to give in to their passions might be perceived by some as representing a moral high ground, it surely can be seen by most of us as a lack of courage to live life to its full—which also, just maybe, explains why their spouses have left them in the first place.

LOS ANGELES, AUGUST 19, 2001
Reprinted from *World Cinema Review* (August 2001).

Index

498

GREEN INTEGER

SELECTED NEW TITLES

2011

±**Julien Gracq** *The Peninsula* [978-1-933382-39-5] $12.95
Richard Kalich *Penthouse F* [978-1-55713-413-4] $15.95
Joe Ross *wordlick* [978-1-55713-415-8] $11.95
†**Nelly Sachs** *Collected Poems 1944-1949* [978-1-933382-57-9]
    $13.95
Ko Un *Himalaya Poems* [978-1-55713-412-7] $13.95

2012

Blaise Cendrars *Films without Images* [978-1-933392-55-5] $14.95
Jean Frémon *The Botanical Garden* [978-1-55713-411-0] $13.95
Peter Glassgold *Hwæt!* [978-1-933382-41-8] $12.95
Douglas Messerli *Dark* [978-1-933382-14-2] $12.95
    Reading Films: My International Cinema [978-1-55713-427-1]
    $29.95
Jules Michelet *The Sea* [1-933382-11-2] $15.95
±**Ivo Michiels** *Book Alpha and Orchis Militaris* [9978-1-933382-15-9] $12.95
Yuri Olyesha *Envy* [978-1-931243-12-4] $13.95

2013

Eleanor Antin *Conversations with Stalin* [978-1-55713-420-2] $14.50
Ascher/Straus *Hank Forest's Party* [978-193338-247-0] $12.95
±**Reiner Kunze** *Rich Catch in the Empty Creel* [978-1-933382-24-1]
    $15.95
Lucebert *The Collected Poems: Volume 1* [978-1-55713-407-3]
    $15.95
Douglas Messerli *My Year 2003: Voice Without a Voice* [978-1-933382-35-X] $15.95
Xue Di *Across Borders* [978-1-55713-423-3] $12.95

2014

Lee Si-young *Patterns* [978-1-55713-422-6] $11.95
Robert Musil *Three Women* [978-1-55713-419-6] $12.95

2015

Ece Ayhan *A Blind Cat Black* and *Orthodoxies* [978-1-933382-36-4]
$11.95
Kim Soo-Bok *Beating on Iron* [978-1-55713-430-1] $12.95
Sigmund Freud / Wilhelm Jensen *Gradiva* and *Delusion and Dream
in Wilhelm Jensen's Gradiva* [1-892295-89-X] $13.95 [REPRINT]
Douglas Messerli *My Year 2002: Love, Death, and Transfiguration*
[978-1-55713-425-7] $15.95
　My Year 2007: To the Dogs [978-1-55713-424-0] $15.95
　My Year 2008: In the Gap [978-1-55713-462-4] $15.95
Paul van Ostaijen *The First Book of Schmoll* [978-1933382-21-0]
$12.95

2016

Douglas Messerli *My Year 2009: Facing the Heat* [978-1-55713-429-
5], U.S. $15.95
F. T. Marinetti *The Untameables* [978-1-933382-23-4], U.S. $12.95
Régis Bonvicino *Beyond the Wall: New Selected Poems* [978-1-
55713-431-8] $12.95
Douglas Messerli *My Year 2010: Shadows* [978-1-55713-432-5]
$15.95
Lucebert *The Collected Poems: Volume 2* [978-1-55713-434-9]
$17.95
August Stramm *26 Poems* [978-1-55713-435-6] $12.95

† Author winner of the Nobel Prize for Literature
± Author winner of the America Award for Literature

THE AMERICA AWARDS
*for a lifetime contribution
to international writing*

The 2016 Award winner is:

CÉSAR AIRA
[Argentina] 1949

Awarded by the Contemporary
Arts Educational Project, Inc.
in loving memory of Anna Fahrni

PREVIOUS WINNERS:

1994 Aimé Cesaire
[Martinique] 1913–2008

1995 Harold Pinter
[England] 1930–2008

1996 José Donoso [Chile] 1924-1996
(*awarded prior to his death*)

1997 Friederike Mayröcker
[Austria] 1924

1998 Rafael Alberti
[Spain] 1902-1999

1999 Jacques Roubaud
[France] 1932

2000 Eudora Welty
[USA] 1909-2001

2001 Inger Christensen
[Denmark] 1935–2009

2002 Peter Handke
[Austria] 1942

2003 Adonis (Ali Ahmad Said)
[Syria/Lebanon] 1930

2004 José Saramago
[Portugal] 1922-2010

2005 Andrea Zanzotto
[Italy] 1921-2011

2006 Julien Gracq (Louis Poirier)
[France] 1910-2007

2007 Paavo Haavikko
[Finland] 1931

2008 John Ashbery
[USA] 1927

2009 Günter Kunert
[GDR/Germany] 1929

2010 Javier Marías
[Spain] 1951

2011 Ko Un
[South Korea] 1933

2012 Ivo Michiels
[Belgium] 1923

2013 Reiner Kunze
[GDR/Germany] 1933

2014 László Krasznahorkai
[Hungary] 1954

2015 Edward Albee
[USA] 1928